HOW
I MADE
$1,000,000
IN
MAIL ORDER

E. Joseph Cossman

A FIRESIDE BOOK
Published by Simon & Schuster, Inc.
NEW YORK

Library of Congress Cataloging in Publication Data

Cossman, E. Joseph.
  How I made $1,000,000 in mail order.

  "A Fireside book."
  1. Mail-order business. I. Title. II. Title: How
I made one million dollars in mail order.
[HF5466.C6 1985]   658.8'72   85-22091
ISBN 0-671-61822-9

DEDICATED TO MY WIFE, PEARL

Who helped me lick hundreds of postage stamps
Type countless letters
Stuff thousands of envelopes—
All because she had faith!

Do you want to contact the author? From time to time, there may be new developments in mail order about which you would like information. If you wish to be placed on the author's mailing list (without charge or obligation), send your name and address to E. Joseph Cossman, P.O. Box 4480, Palm Springs, California 92263

(*Note:* Throughout this book, I refer to these and other products. But remember, it's not the products themselves that are important; it's the techniques and formulas I use to sell them that are important. These same techniques and formulas can be used to sell almost any kind of product or service in the United States.)

FACT SHEET ON E. JOSEPH COSSMAN, M.B.A.

1. Founder and President of E. Joseph Cossman & Company, marketing his own products, ideas, and services throughout the world. Sales volume over $30 million.
2. Retired from the business world and began giving business seminars in most of the major cities of the U.S.A. Over thirty thousand people have attended.
3. Won "Sales Promotion Man of the Year" by Los Angeles Chapter of Sales Promotion Executive Association.
4. Wrote two best sellers, *How I Made a Million Dollars in Mail Order*, and *How to Get $100,000 Worth of Business Services Free Each Year from the U.S. Government*.
5. Conducted seminars for prisoners at Cook County Prison, Chicago, Illinois.
6. Conducted seminars for the National Business League, an Association of black businessmen.
7. Conducted seminars for the State of California, through their CAL JOB Program. Had over one thousand minority men and women in attendance.
8. Conducted overseas marketing seminars for small businessmen and women under sponsorship of Chapman College in Hong Kong, Korea, Taiwan, Japan, Europe, Africa, and Russia.
9. Was special guest speaker at ISEED, International Symposium on Entrepreneurship and Enterprise Development, an international workshop held in Ohio.
10. Appeared on most of the major TV talk shows in America, including the Johnny Carson, Merv Griffin, and Mike Douglas shows.
11. Initiated entrepreneurship courses at Chapman College, Pepperdine University, and College of the Desert.
12. Keynote speaker on entrepreneurship to over two hundred organizations in America.
13. Introduced American marketing methods to businessmen throughout the major cities in Europe.
14. Created, developed, and produced a complete video-cassette course on entrepreneurship.
15. At present developing a complete video-cassette course on foreign trade.
16. Conducted overseas marketing seminars for small businessmen and women throughout the major cities of South America.

"One good product or service can support you in style for the rest of your life!"

E. Joseph Cossman

 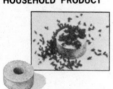

A Personal Introduction from E. Joseph Cossman

If you are on salary and want to be your own boss . . . if you want to make additional income in your spare time . . . if your have a product, or an idea for a product and want to know how to market it . . . if you are in your own business and want to increase your sales . . . then you should read this book with great care.

My name is E. Joseph Cossman. I have earned more than $25 million in the past twenty years, not just by dreaming or wishing for wealth, but through hard work, long hours, trying this and that technique—making mistakes along the way, but learning hundreds of little-known secrets in the process.

In the beginning I purchased almost every book available that promised me great wealth through plans or schemes that required no work, but I discovered most of the information was worthless! I have also learned that most people selling plans that promise to show how to make money using little or no effort make their money on the books and plans themselves, rather than on the formulas outlined in those books!

It has taken thousands of dollars and many, many years to gain this knowledge, and also to learn what I know today . . . priceless, little-known secrets for making money!

In the past few years, I have been retired from active participation in business. I consult with people from all over the Western Hemisphere as a business consultant for $500 per hour. I also have been holding seminars across the country that over thirty-five thousand people have attended. I am proud to say that my seminars have changed the lives of many who follow my teachings.

I guarantee that if you take the little-known secrets in this book and apply them using your own talents, you **will succeed** in making a new life for yourself. You will no longer be dependent on an employer or a job; you will no longer suffer from "salaryitis." And if you apply these little-known secrets successfully, you will not be at the mercy of recessions, depressions, inflations, or any of the other monetary ills that beset most people.

It is no fairy tale. My first business started at a time when I was earning only $35 a week as a correspondence clerk. I made $30,000 on my first transaction (equal to nineteen years of my salary at that time). From that day on, I have never called another person "boss" and have made all my money by being an enterprising entrepreneur. This book can teach you how to free yourself from the bondage of working from paycheck to paycheck; it can show you how to become a successful entrepreneur. An entrepreneur is a person who works at his or her own venture. He or she is his or her own boss! He or she is a person who takes orders from no one else—and that is the foundation on which this country was built.

Entrepreneurs are survivors! They prosper in any economic climate, even in depression years. They are never without work; they are never without income—because they know how to survive. They are the guerrilla fighters of capitalism. In the 1930s, 40 percent of the work force in America was unemployed. Imagine! Four out of every ten people in America were looking for jobs, but the entrepreneur did not hurt! He started chain letters; he started plastic factories; he started jukebox routes; he started comic books. All of these things took place during the Depression years. When you learn the techniques discussed in this book, you will also be able to swing with the times whether they are good or bad!

Now to survive as an entrepreneur, you need three things. The first thing you need is knowledge, and that's what you'll get in this book! The second thing you need is self-confidence. How do you get self-confidence? With proper knowledge! When you know how to do something, you have self-confidence. The third thing you need, the most important of the three, is perseverance. Do not quit! Hundreds of times I have watched people throw in the towel at the one-yard line while someone else comes along and makes a fortune by just going that extra yard.

For those of you who are now employed, this book will show you dozens of ways to create a second income in your spare time. It will also show you how to be a much more valuable employee so that you can guarantee yourself a sizable promotion and increase in salary, because this book will start you thinking like an entrepreneur, not just an employee.

For those of you in your own business, this book will show you how to increase your business without increasing your overhead.

If you are retired, handicapped, or unemployed, this book will show you how to take your skills, your desires, your dreams, and your God-given talents and develop them into a product or service.

Just one more important issue: The little-known secrets in this book are not geared for the lazy person—they are designed for the intelligent, diligent individual who is already motivated and has a strong desire to succeed.

The world is filled with "get-rich-quick" schemes. Most of them do not work. What I am offering you is not a get-rich-quick scheme, but a sound opportunity like the one that enabled me to retire early in life while I still receive a continuous income from products and services.

This book has been inspired by the knowledge that I have made it and can help others achieve this masterful goal. To me, the world's greatest gift is to show a person how to make a living. That is why I have a slogan on all of my stationery that speaks from my heart, simply describing my philosophy:

If you give a man a fish, you can feed him for a day.
If you teach a man to fish, you feed him for life!

Yours for success,

E. Joseph Cossman

What This Book Can Do for You

If you want to break out of the old rut—start your own business, with little or no capital necessary, and be your own boss at last—mail order is the greatest business opportunity that can do this for you.

In this book, I will show you how to think up a mail order product and test it inexpensively (following the advertising system given in these pages), produce it, and market it. Starting with just one product and working in your spare time or just on weekends, it is actually possible to bring in several thousand dollars a day in cash-in-advance orders!

That is what makes mail order the fastest growing and most profit-making business in the world today. This book will show you how to go about it, from getting the first idea right on through to establishing an entire line of successful merchandise for your own mail order business.

I started out using the kitchen table as a desk, working on weekends while keeping my regular nine-to-five job. Today I own the office building in which I work and sit behind a $5,000 desk.

In these pages you'll discover how with common sense, imagination, and perseverance you can do the same, building a business with unlimited potential and adventure.

Contents

4 | How to Test Your Products   66

5 | How to Develop and Produce Your Products   76

6 | Selling Your Products   84

7 | Promoting Your Products   101

8 | Ten Secret Rules of Mail Order Success   115

9 | How to Get the Most from Trade Shows   124

10 | The Spud Gun: A Case History   134

11 | Our 35 Best Mail Order Letters   144

12 | 22 Trade Secrets and Ideas   177

13 | How to Sell Your Products Overseas 202

14 | How to Sell a Service 213

18 | New Techniques in Mail Order and What Is to Come   258

HOW I MADE $1,000,000
IN MAIL ORDER

1 | How I Started in Business

*"What you can do, or dream you can . . .
begin it. Boldness has genius, power, and
magic in it!"*

WHY YOU SHOULD GO INTO THE MAIL ORDER BUSINESS

I know of no business in the world that requires such a small investment to start, yet holds promise of such tremendous financial gains as mail order. There are literally hundreds of people today who went into the mail order business a few years ago with extremely small sums of money, yet today the annual volume of each of them runs into a million dollars or more.

Do not be concerned if you think you're undercapitalized. The mail order business is one business where money is secondary to original ideas, perseverance, and ambition. You can start a mail order business in your spare time and hold on to your present employment until your own business is strong enough to support you.

One tremendous advantage in mail order is that you have the greatest partner in the world working with you . . . the United States Government. Uncle Sam's postage stamp gets you into places that would be impossible to contact otherwise, and the first-class letter is one of the best bargains existing in the world today.

I could have entitled this book *How I Made $1,000,000 in Business* instead of *How I Made $1,000,000 in Mail Order*, since most of the details included are about business in general. However, because we applied mail order principles to general business practices, we reached our goal much sooner than the average business beginner. And it is due to these mail order procedures that I was able to start my business on a kitchen table measuring two feet by three feet and costing $8.00 . . . and now find myself doing business from a desk measuring twelve feet across and costing almost five thousand dollars.

Also, the very nature of mail order made it possible for me to conduct most of my business without leaving my office. In fact, I have never seen 99 percent of my customers! A postage stamp was my salesman, and an envelope was my briefcase.

THE BEST TIME TO START IN THE MAIL ORDER BUSINESS

The best time to start in the mail order business is *now*. Right now! Starting in business is like getting married . . . there is really no good time and no bad time. The time is now.

When I returned to the United States after three years of World War II service, my total assets consisted of one wife, one small daughter, $276 in the bank, and an idea. The idea was for an export business to supply items badly needed everywhere in Europe.

The year was 1946 and our country was flooded with returning G.I.'s, all looking for the same thing I was looking for—a job. The situation forced me into my first mail order activity . . . I used the mailman to help me find the kind of job I wanted—a job whereby I could gain experience in the import-export field.

Twenty-five copies of the following reprint of my home-made brochure were sent to companies in the Pittsburgh area engaged in world trade:

DO YOU WANT 180 LBS. OF RAW MATERIAL?
now ready for civilian service
RELEASED BY ARMY ONLY TWO WEEKS AGO
Ambitious—Able—Adaptable
THIS ITEM COMES IN ONE SIX-FOOT LENGTH
and has been
SEASONED FOR TWENTY-EIGHT YEARS!
Operating expenses shared by
G.I. BILL OF RIGHTS
No Strings Attached
NO OBLIGATION TO YOU!
You can get immediate delivery
MAIL ENCLOSED FOR FREE INSPECTION!
Thank You!

Within one week I landed a job as correspondence clerk with a well-known import-export firm. My starting salary was only $35 a week, but the work gave me a valuable opportunity to learn the fine points of letter writing, merchandising, and the inner workings of the export trade.

With my first paycheck, I made a down payment on a $50 portable typewriter and opened my office on our kitchen table. I would put in eight hours' work each day at the export company and come home to peck away on my typewriter for another eight hours, writing to people I had met in Europe during the war.

My thinking was as follows: The war had upset all recognized channels of trade in Europe. Consequently, I was starting on an even keel with other United States companies, even though they were bigger, stronger, and richer than I was. But here's where the United States Government came in. I subscribed to *Business America*, a Government publication listing all kinds of import-export opportunities. Before long, I had built up a sizable correspondence file with people all over the world. Actually, it made no difference if my office was on a kitchen table in my home or in a magnificent suite in some large building . . . my letterhead proclaimed I was in business, and no one in Europe, Africa, or Asia doubted it when they received my correspondence.

But the going was rough. It took fancy juggling to support my wife, my daughter, and myself—plus correspondence expenses—on $35 a week. Many a night we would skip a cheap movie so I would have money to buy stationery. And many a day I skipped lunch to buy postage stamps or pay for overseas telephone calls.

I'll never forget the times I would leave my desk at work on the pretext of going to the wash room, then run to a pay station telephone at the neighborhood drugstore to call London, Paris, or Johannesburg on some important matter. In those days, I carried a pocket full of quarters, dimes, and nickels for calls to my agents overseas, and carrying your business in your pocket can sometimes assume aspects of high comedy. My home telephone number and address were printed on my "business" stationery and quite often a call would come to my home from overseas while I was at work. Sometimes my small daughter would answer the telephone prattling about her dollies, her school, and other subjects while the amazed party at the other end mentally pulled his hair as he paid $4 a minute for the privilege of hearing her talk!

Then, after one year of stretching pennies, skipping meals, and working from hand to mouth, my first big break came from a small classified ad in the *New York Times*. The ad offered large quantities of exportable laundry soap—a commodity in short supply throughout Europe and Asia. I answered the ad, requested samples, and airmailed them to six of my overseas correspondents. Back across the ocean flew an order from my South African correspondent for the complete stock. And best of all, the order was accompanied by a letter of credit for $180,000!

My mail order business story really begins here. The year of work, of study, and of hope had culminated in one big stroke of luck—but the effort to make that luck pay off was just beginning. And during this, my first encounter with "big business," I was to learn that success.requires more than work, study, imagination, and faith . . . it requires other people. Yes, other people. I could never have accomplished what I did in the next sixty days without the help of other people.

But frankly, that letter of credit frightened me. It represented more money than I had seen in my entire lifetime. The letter of credit was a document issued by a South African bank and sent through my American bank. This document stated that the American bank would pay me $180,000 as soon as I presented to them bills of lading showing the laundry soap on board a ship bound for South Africa. It also stipulated a deadline date . . . the bills of lading had to be presented to my bank within sixty days, or the letter of credit would be worthless.

I didn't know what to do. I was afraid to quit my $35 a week job and at the same time, I was afraid of losing this order. Since a trip to New York had to be made to close the transaction, I approached almost everyone I knew in my hometown promising them half of the profits if they would go to New York for me. Incredible as it may seem, my offer didn't find one taker!

In desperation, I went to my boss and told him I needed a thirty-day leave of absence. Fortunately for me, that good man granted my request without question, and I made preparations to go to New York. At that time, my total life savings were $254, which I immediately withdrew from the bank.

Upon my arrival in New York, I telephoned the man who ran the ad in the *New York Times* and told him I was ready to buy his complete stock of soap. Imagine my shock and disbelief when he said he didn't own a single bar of soap! He had put the ad in the paper on speculation, and although he suspected that the soap existed somewhere in the United States, he didn't know where to get it. He happened to be one of those "Five Percenters" who were so prevalent after World War II. They would offer critical, "hard to get" merchandise for sale and then look for the merchandise after they found an interested buyer.

I was frantic! I had a letter of credit for $180,000 in my pocket and didn't have the merchandise to fill the order. I had to find that soap, and my only clue was its trade name. Wasting no time, I went to the New York Public Library and spent the entire day listing names and addresses of every soap manufacturer in the United States. The next day I locked myself in my hotel room with the telephone. My first call took fifteen minutes to get through because of a telephone strike. I had page after page of telephone numbers to call and the situation began to look hopeless, but luck—in the person of a friendly telephone operator—promised to stay with me! He pushed call after call through for me, but after fifty completed calls, I found no one who had even heard the name of my soap! Exhausted and hoarse, I fell into bed for a few hours and got up with the sun to begin again. At noon, I hit the jackpot! With a wave of relief, I heard the voice at the other end say, "Yes, our company manufactures that soap. Yes, that's our brand name. Yes, we have thirty thousand cases sitting in our Alabama warehouse waiting to be sold."

I later discovered I had run up a telephone bill of $810 before I found the soap company, but I didn't care. I was riding on a $180,000 cushion! My spirits soared, for it looked like the deal would go through, and I would be able to meet the letter of credit deadline.

I told the party I would fly to Alabama that afternoon. Laughing, he said, "You'd better stay in New York City as it's useless to come to our factory. Our offices are only a few blocks away from your hotel, and negotiations will have to be made there!"

Hurrying from my hotel, I ran all the way to their offices. I must have made a strange impression as I rushed into the building, took the elevator to the twenty-eighth floor, and broke my way into a suite of offices demanding in an almost hysterical voice, "Take me to your president!" Following a brief moment during which my sanity was silently questioned, I was ushered into a large office and introduced to the president of the soap company. Explaining the situation to him, I stated I was ready to buy his entire stock. Showing him the letter of credit and the actual order, we completed negotiations right then and there. I still faced one big hurdle. The soap was in Alabama, and it was my responsibility to get it on board ship to Africa. To do that, I had to bring it to New York. I didn't know how I was going to do it, but I was so relieved and happy at the time that I readily agreed to the conditions.

Armed with a letter from the president stating that I was to get delivery of the soap in Alabama, I began pounding the pavements of New York City looking for a trucking outfit who would loan me thirty trucks on credit. Since I had agreed to buy the soap F.O.B. Alabama, this was the only way I knew how to bring it to New York. I had no money to pay freight charges and prayed I could find someone who'd speculate with me. After two days of searching, pleading, begging, and more searching, I finally located a truck operator who was willing to gamble with me on the trip.

A few hours later we were ready for the long haul to Alabama. I got into the front truck with the driver and our caravan began to move. At this time, I didn't have a cent to my name. In fact, during the trip I had to borrow money for food from the truck drivers, and many times I wanted to quit and return home to the security of my $35 a week job.

We finally arrived in Alabama and went directly to the soap factory. I showed them my letter of purchase and they directed us to a warehouse containing 30,000 cases of soap. We loaded 1,000 cases in each truck, and as the loading progressed, I stood by marking each case with export symbols and the destination address in South Africa.

Then we began our trip back to New York and arrived in the big city on the evening of June eleventh. I'll never forget that date, because my letter of credit was due to expire on June twelfth! All night long we loaded soap on "lighters"—the little boats that carry cargo to freighters in the harbor. I worked with the stevedores and was so busy loading soap I wasn't aware of the time until the following afternoon. As the last case of soap was loaded, I looked at my watch. It was two o'clock on the afternoon of June twelfth. In one hour the banks would close, and my letter of credit would be worthless. I still didn't have "on board" bills of lading, and I got that frantic feeling in my stomach again.

Fortunately, the offices of the steam-ship line were near the docks, and I ran into the office barging my way into the president's suite. I must have been a sorry sight, for I hadn't shaved or changed clothes in two weeks. But without preamble, I told the president the whole story . . . how I had left my $35 a week job to come to New York . . . how I found no soap on my arrival . . . how I finally located the soap factory . . . how I had to beg for thirty trucks . . . and, now, with victory almost within my grasp, I did not have the "on board" bills of lading and could not get them until the following day.

All during my story, the president had listened in silence. When I had finished, he replied, "If you've gone through this much to put over a business deal, you're not going to lose it now. I'll get you your 'on board' bills of lading!" He rang a half-dozen buzzers on his desk, and people appeared from everywhere. Within ten minutes I had my documents, and one minute later I was in the back seat of his limousine being chauffeured to the bank in Wall Street.

We got to the bank about fifteen minutes before closing time. I rushed in and presented all my documents to the teller and in return was given a check for $180,000. I left the bank with my head in the clouds but suddenly realized I didn't have cab fare to get back to my hotel. Going back into the bank, I asked for a breakdown of the $180,000 and had a check made out to the soap company for $150,000, a check made out to myself for $25,000, and took $5,000 in cash.

I went back to my hotel, paid my bills, and immediately telephoned my wife. I told her the good news and she began crying. It seemed she had written a check for a grocery bill for $8.25, and the check had bounced. Talk about playing it close!

The next day I flew home and the following day reported back to work on my $35 a week job. Somehow or other, the company had heard about my success with the soap deal, and my personal stock with them went up, up, up. They gave me a $25 a week raise; I was now making $60 a week . . . which was pretty good money right after the war.

About a week later, I got a call from the soap company executive in New York asking if I wanted to travel around the world selling the raw materials that go into the manufacture of soap. I told him I didn't know anything about soap manufacturing, but he countered this argument by offering to send a technician from the factory with me. The company was willing to pay my expenses and the expenses of the technician, in addition to giving me ten percent of any business I did during the trip.

This proposition created one of the biggest decisions in my life . . . whether to stay on the job with a secure $60 a week or to give it up and go into business for myself. I found myself faced with a common ailment among married men everywhere—I call this ailment "salaryitis"—the fearful dependence on that weekly salary. "Salaryitis" is when you become so accustomed to that salary that you no longer have the gumption to pull out of the rut and strike out on your own. It destroys the nerve of ambitious, imaginative men, and bowing to it has meant sure defeat for more people than any other sickness, mental or physical.

I didn't know what to do, but the decision was made for me when I returned to my job the next day. I noticed the absence of one employee who had been with the company for over eighteen years. Asking for his whereabouts, I was told that he had exchanged several heated words with his superior and had been discharged the previous afternoon.

That made up my mind. If eighteen years of a man's life could be washed down the drain with a few heated words, then a job and "salaryitis" were not for me. I called the soap people in New York and accepted their proposition. As it turned out, it was one of the best decisions I've ever made.

And what has all this to do with the mail order business? Well, I took that trip around the world and sold soap in a dozen countries or more. On my return to the States, I continued frequent, personal correspondence with people I had met in every country. One man in particular, living in Sweden, had become a good friend. By a simple gesture of friendship on my part, he also became my first real mail order customer. He asked to receive a soap quotation, and I sent it to him along with half a dozen toy balloons for his four small children. One week later, via long-distance telephone from Sweden, I had an order for $10,000 worth of toy balloons! This "out of the blue" mail order started a train of thought that led me to the idea of "balloons for American kids." Why not? Because of the war, most American children had never seen a toy balloon. I found a local balloon company and got into the balloon business.

This chain of events leading around the world and home to a toy balloon as my first real mail order item may seem devious and may smack of fiction—but it is true. And I think a balloon, as my first item, was rather prophetic. I had no place to go but up!

Making $30,000 on my first business deal was exciting, but not as exciting as the sudden knowledge that I did not have to work for anyone again. Here I was, a person with nothing but a high school education—no business connections, no business knowledge, no money to speak of, less than $300. I had a wife and baby to care for, and I was making $35 a week at a job. Yet back in 1947, I was able to put a package together that netted me $30,000. How much money would that be today? Probably $300,000 or more in today's dollars. That is why I am constantly encouraging people to clear off their kitchen tables and start an enterprise that they can control, not one that controls them. Lack of education, lack of money, lack of business connections, lack of business knowledge are not important. What is important is that you live in the only country in the world where you can put together a package like this. You live in a country where over 200 million people speak the same language, 200 million people use the same currency, and you can ship a package from Los Angeles to New York without going through one foreign border and without paying any duty on that package. This country is conducive to making money. Once you learn this lesson and make your first deal, you will really appreciate the tools available to you in the United States, the tools that will help you "boot-strap" yourself into a large income. Your goals should be to have the system work for you, instead of your working for the system! Be the hammer—not the nail!

2 | How You Can Go into the Mail Order Business

"All things are difficult before they become easy!"

MAIL ORDER DEFINED

Just what is the mail order business and how does one get into it? What are the opportunities and what are the hazards involved in getting it started?

First, let's define mail order. Mail order—as described in this book—is any business activity done through the mails, whether it is buying, selling, promoting, advertising, or merchandising. It is, in fact, any action where the mails are used, either directly or indirectly, to obtain a variety of objectives which ultimately lead to the sale of merchandise or services.

So that we will be talking about the same thing, let's give a definition to mail order as it is covered in this book. Mail order, as practiced today, can be divided into three categories:

1. *The catalog way.* This form of mail order is conducted by companies like Montgomery Ward, Spiegel, Sears Roebuck, and Alden's, who sell by mail. They publish large catalogs and send out tremendous quantities of them. Their reputations and their lower prices bring them their business. It takes years and years and money and brains to build such a business.

2. *Advertising in magazines and newspapers.* Many companies, both large and small, carry on a mail order business by inserting advertisements of their products in magazines and newspapers. Suc-

cess depends primarily on the value of the product or service being offered, plus the skill of the originator of the ads. *This is a rough business and you can lose your shirt if you do not know the ropes.*

3. *Direct mail.* Here is the kind of mail order business that you hear about most often. Usually an offer is made by mail to a selected mailing list; the order is obtained by mail; the shipment of the merchandise is usually made by mail; collections and payments are handled by mail. Most of the mail order described in this book is covered by this third method.

THE MAIL ORDER BUSINESS IS UNIQUE

There are a number of peculiar problems in the mail order business which do not exist in any other trade. In the mail order business, there is no local competition—your market is the United States. Location is not a significant factor, nor is it important to have elaborate facilities. Some of today's large mail order houses started from scratch. Since your customers never appear in person, your office may be a corner of a room.

HOW MUCH MONEY IS NEEDED?

The mail order business is unique in that it can be started with a minimum of capital and without any specified set of experiences. Anyone with imagination, determination, and a willingness to study and experiment has a likely chance of getting started and succeeding in the business. To learn it, do it. There are very few businesses today where one can start an enterprise of one's own that requires as little capital as does a small specialized mail order business. In mail order, organizing skill and merchandising ability can replace much of the investment required for conducting a typical local business. The largest mail order businesses in the United States started with practically nothing—often as side lines. On the other hand, a number of spurts into the mail order business have been made in this country by wealthy persons. These people poured large sums of money into the planning, launching, and operating of the business yet failed miserably.

These two extremes show that the amount of capital required is not the only ingredient for success in starting a mail order business. As I mentioned in the previous chapter, initiative, originality, and perseverance are many times more important than money. I know of a young man in Miami who went into the mail order business with a total investment of $200. His product was a pair of live mated seahorses, and his $200 bought a mail order ad in a small magazine. The ad was so successful that his $200 expenditure snowballed into a national advertising campaign on this unique product. He did well over $100,000 in his very first year. However, for every person successful in the mail order business, there are dozens and dozens of others who never quite make the grade. But for most people who fail in the mail order business, lack of capital is not the major reason for their failures. Most failures I've seen were because of a lack of personal requirements—not a lack of money.

PERSONAL REQUIREMENTS

With a little determination and common sense, the average person can master the principles of selling by mail. You have within you the potential of success if you have:

1. *The ability to visualize a proposition, stay with it, and make it develop.* What one man casually passes by may prove to be another man's treasure. A successful mail order deal often consists of giving a new twist to, or revamping, what otherwise would just be an ordinary product.

2. *The ability to write.* This is essential, for it is necessary that you express your personality and ideas in your advertising copy and correspondence. Of course, if you do not have writing ability, you can always hire an advertising agency or free-lance writer to do this work for you.

3. *A "sixth sense" to interpret trends.* The ability to observe what is happening and what people want is a necessary talent in the mail order business.

4. *Perseverance.* You must be able to hold on to your plans despite many frustrating delays and unexpected complications. Unfortunately, the spirit of the "quitter" often pervades the mail order ranks because there is no supervisor or boss present to supply the motive power. You are your own boss; it is up to you and no one else.

LEGAL FACTORS

If you are starting in the mail order business for the first time, you need a company name. If you use a fictitious name or any title other than your own personal name, you must record this fact at your local post office so it will know to deliver the mail to you. Also, if you do use a name other than your own, contact your county clerk to learn what limitations are imposed by your state on the use of a fictitious name. Some states require a fictitious name to be registered; others require that the name be advertised in the local paper for a set number of days. It certainly is poor business to invest in letterheads, advertising, etcetera, using a fictitious name only to be stopped from using it because you failed to register it. Remember, if your company name is a fictitious name, be sure to get it cleared with the proper authorities first.

YOUR POST OFFICE

Every person engaged in the business of selling by mail should have a working knowledge of the rules and regulations pertaining to the use of the mails. The postal service welcomes new mail order businesses, and you'll find the postal employees quite cooperative and helpful. So call on them when you need any postal information. The postage stamp is perhaps your greatest sales tool in mail order, but bear in mind that it carries a heavy obligation to be scrupulously honest at all times. It's a good idea to get a copy of the postal guide from the Superintendent of Documents, Government Printing Office, Washington, DC 20402, so that you may get acquainted with the laws and regulations pertaining to mailing.

Many times you will be well within every postal requirement and yet run afoul of two other government agencies, the Federal Trade Commission and the Food and Drug Administration. The FTC, through its Bureau of Anti-Deceptive Practices, constantly checks all advertising media for unfair or deceptive advertising practices. When the bureau considers an advertisement doubtful, or if a customer complains about the product, it will open an investigation leading to regulatory action. Examples of what it looks for include misrepresentation of the benefits derived from drugs and cosmetics; failure to warn against poisonous ingredients; claiming foreign products are manufactured in the United States. More information concerning the FTC and its advertising standards can be obtained from any of its regional offices, or by writing the Bureau of Anti-Deceptive Practices in Washington, DC.

The Food and Drug Administration concerns itself only with food, drugs, and cosmetics. Pitfalls with this agency occur when these products include fantastic, unproven claims: advertisements for a cosmetic cannot *banish wrinkles forever* nor a drug product *cure,* if they only give temporary relief. The FDA is also concerned with proper labeling and the purity of a product's ingredients. For more information, you may contact the FDA.

Since the powers of the FTC and the FDA, along with the post office, often overlap, you must be certain that your mail order advertising satisfies the requirements of all three of these agencies. Generally, if you're conducting your business honestly, you will have nothing to worry about. There's the possibility, however, that you may innocently go against these regulations if someone has given you erroneous information about your product or its advertising claims. You can avoid this happening:

1. Know your product thoroughly.
2. Check out any possibility of misleading claims.
3. Know where you can get first-rate legal advice.

THE MECHANICS OF GETTING STARTED

Since a mail order business is at best a gamble, risk as little capital as possible to test out your ideas. Spend no money except for essentials, and limit your purchases to bare necessities. Above all, however, do not skimp on your sales literature. Ways of cutting corners during the exploratory stages include items like these: rent a typewriter instead of buying one, type your own letters, learn to set up and maintain a simple record system using improvised files. If you need copying or addressing done, contract it out to firms specializing in these things. In the beginning, your "office" can be any quiet corner in your home; about the only supplies you'll need will be letterheads, envelopes, mailing labels, a typewriter, a small filing cabinet, and an inexpensive set of books for your records. I have often seen beginners in the mail order business invest a major part of their starting capital in expensive office equipment, which later had to be sold in order to pay their bills. Keep in mind that you very rarely see the customer to whom you are selling your merchandise; therefore, it is not necessary to put up a "front" or invest in expensive furniture or equipment in order to impress anyone. I started business on our kitchen table and several months passed before I indulged in the luxury of buying a second-hand desk. This is what makes mail order so attractive . . . a beginning is possible on very little capital and even less equipment. Furthermore, you can start it in your spare time and hold on to your present job.

STARTING YOUR OWN MAIL ORDER BUSINESS

To get an idea of the scope of mail order selling, look carefully through the advertising sections of any general magazine and also through the mail order pages of the large metropolitan newspapers. You will find mail order ads for almost any kind of product, as well as mail order ads for an unlimited number of services. In fact, you'll see so many dozens of items offered for sale that you'll probably become confused as to just what product you yourself should start with. However, if you will carefully study the different items and services offered by mail, you'll soon develop a feeling for what sells best through this medium. Remember that the various and sundry needs of the consumers who make up the American market present many opportunities to start your own mail order business. Ours is the largest country in the world in which almost all of the people not only speak but also read and write the same language. Our country also has one of the best postal systems in the world. In addition, we have magazines and newspapers that cover this country like a blanket. With all of these advantages on the side of the mail order operator, it's little wonder that large sums of money are made each year by people who have found the way to sell successfully through mail order. Just remember that every successful mail order operator started in the business with no more experience than you now have. The one big difference is that he started . . . why don't you?

TOP MAIL ORDER PUBLICATIONS IN 23 CATEGORIES

For addresses, advertising rates, special shopping sections, and so forth, please check with *Standard Rate & Data* at your local library.

AUTOMOTIVE/
  MOTORCYCLES

Hot Rod Magazine
Motor Trend
Car and Driver
Road & Track
Cycle

Easyriders
Car Craft
Cycle World
Popular Hot Rodding Magazine
Pickup Van & 4WD

BUSINESS/FINANCIAL/ ENTERPRISE

Wall Street Journal
Nation's Business
Management Leisure Time
Money
Business Week
Moneysworth
Forbes
Fortune
Inc.
Washington Report

CRAFTS/GARDENING

Organic Gardening
Decorating & Craft Ideas
Workbench
Flower and Garden
Family Food Garden
Crafts 'N Things
Fine Woodworking
Plants Alive
House Plants and Porch Gardens
Crafts Magazine

ESCAPISM

Official Detective Group
Ellery Queen's Mystery Magazine
Heavy Metal
True West
Real West
Frontier Times
Fate
Firehouse
Magazine of Fantasy/Science
    Fiction

FAMILY RECREATION

Crossroads
Michigan Living Motor News
New York Motorist
Woodmen of the World
Trailer Life
Camping Journal
Home & Away Minnesota
Woodall's RV Travel
National Motorist
Ohio Motorist

FARM/RURAL

Farm Journal
Progressive Farmer
Successful Farming
Farm Industry News
National Future Farmer
Harvest Farm Unit
Farmland News
Texas Co-op Power
Carolina Country
Hoosier Farmer

FASHION/YOUNG MODERNS

Woman's Day
McCall's
Cosmopolitan
Glamour
Young Once
New Woman
Vogue
Mademoiselle
Apartment Life
Self

GENERAL AUDIENCE

Parade
TV Guide
Reader's Digest
Family Weekly
Time
Newsweek
People
U.S. News & World Report
Changing Times
Life

HEALTH

Prevention
Weight Watchers
Family Health Magazine
Better Nutrition
Today's Living
Bestways
Let's Live Magazine
Nutrition Health Review
Healthways
Life and Health

HOBBIES
Popular Photography
Games
Flying
Early American Life
Photographic Magazine
AOPA Pilot
Lens
Model Railroader
American Photographer
Western Horseman

INTELLECTUALS
New York Times Magazine
Psychology Today
Forum
National Lampoon
American Teacher
Saturday Review
The New Yorker
Atlantic
Spotlight

LEISURE/TRAVEL/
GOURMET/ART
National Geographic
Playboy
Penthouse
Smithsonian
Bon Appetit
New York Playbill
Pace
Where Magazine
Travel & Leisure
Cuisine

MECHANICS/SCIENCE/
ELECTRONICS
Popular Science
Mechanix Illustrated
Popular Mechanics
Omni
Scientific American
Stereo Review
Popular Electronics
Science Digest

Science 80
High Fidelity

MILITARY/FRATERNAL/
RETIREES
Modern Maturity
American Legion Magazine
VFW Magazine
Elks Magazine
Moose Magazine
Columbia
Eagle Magazine
Rotarian
Ladycom
Family

OUTDOORSMEN/SPORTSMEN
Field & Stream
Outdoor Life
American Rifleman
Sports Afield
Guns & Ammo
Ducks Unlimited
Bassmaster Magazine
American World
Fishing World
Hunting

REGIONALS
Southern Living
Sunset
Yankee
Metronet
Midwest Roto
Westways
New York
Chicago Tribune VIP Section
Texas Monthly
Chicago

RELIGIOUS
Jacob's Religious List
Lutheran
Lutheran Standard
Catholic Digest
Hadassah Magazine
Our Sunday Visitor

Saint Anthony Messenger
Moody Monthly
Episcopalian
Christian Herald

ROMANCE/SENSATIONALISM

National Enquirer
Star
MacFadden Women's Group
True Story
Midnight Globe/National Examiner
Sterling Women's Group
Rona Barrett Publications
Soap Opera Digest
Ideal Women's Group
Ideal Romance

SHELTER/FOOD

Better Homes and Gardens
Good Housekeeping
One Thousand & One Decorating
    Ideas
House and Garden
Family Handyman
House Beautiful
How To
Colonial Homes
New Shelter
Cookbook Digest

SPORTS

Touchdown Illustrated
Sports Illustrated
Sport
Golf Digest
Golf Magazine
World Tennis
Tennis
Skiing
Sporting News
Runner's World

WATER ACTIVITIES

Poolife
Skin Diver
Sail
Boating
Yachting
Motor Boating & Sailing
Salt Water Sportsman
Surfer
Cruising World
Trailer Boats

WOMEN'S SPECIAL INTEREST

Family Circle
Ladies' Home Journal
Redbook
Parents
Workbasket
Expecting
American Baby
Mothers' Manual
Baby Talk
Girl Scout Leader

YOUTH/MUSIC

Marvel Comics Group
DC Comics
Harvey Comics
Scholastic Magazine Group
Archie Comic Group
Charlton Comics Group
Boy's Life
Seventeen
Teen
Junior Scholastic Magazine

3 | How We Find Our Products

"Ideas come from exposure. If you're in the rain long enough, you're bound to get good and wet!"

New products are the life blood of any business. This particularly holds true in mail order, and our company is constantly looking for fresh ideas. Over the years, we have created a source list we periodically investigate for new ideas. Here it is:

1. USE YOUR PUBLIC LIBRARY

Visit your library and study the material available to you. Tell the librarian you're interested in reviewing business books and magazines as a source of new ideas; she'll quickly put before you an amazing variety of information.

I make it a point to spend at least one day out of every month in our library, and every time I do, I discover new idea sources. For instance, on my last visit I learned that most libraries have on file classified telephone directories for many major cities in the world. I was looking for good sales representation in such areas as Paris and Calcutta and found a wealth of leads in the directories as well as stimulating ideas on products and services offered in those faraway cities.

As for services and sales tools, I have listed below just a few of the many services available to anyone visiting the Los Angeles Public Library; many of these services are probably available at your library as well.

(a) The periodical room provides duplicate copies of over 200 popular magazines for home use and about 60 magazines to be used only in the library. Circulating back files of many of these magazines are maintained for four years.

(b) The newspaper room contains current issues of newspapers from many cities throughout the world as well as back issues of selected titles, either bound or on microfilm. In addition, indexes to the *New York Times*, the *Wall Street Journal*, the *Christian Science Monitor*, and the *London Times* are available here.

(c) The audiovisual service circulates 16-mm films on a variety of subjects for use by groups and individual patrons. In addition, it also maintains and circulates a large collection of mounted pictures and clippings for study and research.

(d) The science and technology department has about a thousand current trade, technical, and scientific journals, with back files retained on many of them.

(e) United States Government publications in many subject are available.

(f) The patents room provides a complete file of United States patent drawings and specifications and indexes.

In addition to the above, there are so many other services available at no charge that it constantly surprises me how few people take advantage of this treasure house of information.

Incidentally, the Los Angeles Library has over 2.5 million books and employs over 900 people on a full-time basis . . . and it's all at one's disposal, free of charge. Get into the habit of visiting your library at least once a month, and you'll soon have more ideas available than you ever thought possible.

2. SUBSCRIBE TO TRADE PUBLICATIONS

Part of the problem in the constant search for new product ideas is knowing where to turn for free or low-cost information. Trade journals can be one of your best outlets, since there is a trade journal for almost every kind of business in the country, covering subjects from agriculture to zoo maintenance, toys, and novelties, from farm equipment and astrology to medicine. And you may find most of them in your public library.

A complete directory of all the trade publications is *Standard Rate & Data*, available in your library or from most advertising agencies. A majority of the trade publications listed in the *Data* are devoted entirely to new products and ideas, and many have classified sections offering new products for sale.

Compile your own list of trade magazines peculiar to your business, and contact their editorial offices. Many have other services to offer you besides subscription to their publication. As an example, the trade magazine *Playthings* prints a listing of toy buyers, which is given free to those who request it. This small but valuable pamphlet gives the toy buyer's name, his company, the company's address and telephone number, and the buying days of each buyer. If you place your name on mailing lists of trade magazines, you will receive those additional pieces of information not necessarily published in the magazine itself.

3. TRADE AND SERVICE DIRECTORIES

In addition to being a good mailing source, trade and service directories are also a fertile field in which to locate new products. These directories are usually the first to hear of new products or improvements in their field.

Many directories other than *Standard Rate & Data* are published in our country covering every field of business. An excellent source of directory material is B. Klein & Company, P.O. Box 8503, Coral Springs, FL 33065. We have used their *Guide to American Directories* for many years, and it tells where to locate more than 2,300 directories and rosters. The *Guide* lists some 250 categories of associations such as retailers, wholesalers, manufacturers, government agencies, scientific societies. Each listing gives the directory publisher's name and address, the quantity and specific kind of name in each directory, and the price of the directory. In many cases, the directories listed in the *Guide* are the same sources from which mailing list houses compile their expensive lists. Many of the listed directories are free.

The Thomas Register of American Manufacturers is published in three volumes annually by the Thomas Publishing Company, One Penn Plaza, New York, NY 10001, and may be found in most public libraries. Volumes I and II contain lists of American manufacturers classified by products with detailed descriptions of the product, plus address and capital rating of each manufacturer. Volume III provides an alphabetical listing of American manufacturers describing each manufacturer's business function, principal office location, branch addresses, factory location, and names of top executives. Volume III also provides alphabetical listings of trade names, showing the manufacturer of each.

MacRae's Blue Book, published annually by MacRae's Blue Book Company, 100 Shore Drive, Hinsdale, IL 60521, contains an alphabetical listing of names and addresses of more than 40,000 manufacturers classified by type of product and trade names. You can find a copy of this directory in most public libraries.

Most of the trade and service directories listed on pages 49–50 are basic to business, particularly the mail order business, and may be found in your public library; however, you will wish to use some of them daily, and we have found the best three for office use to be: *Standard Rate & Data, Guide to American Directories,* and *The Thomas Register of American Manufacturers.* You will save time and money by owning these three important publications.

4. READ YOUR LOCAL PAPER FOR NEWS OF BANKRUPT COMPANIES OR FIRMS GOING OUT OF BUSINESS

For products with revision possibilities, there is no better source available than a company going out of business! A few years ago, a toy company in Los Angeles went bankrupt, and we contacted them after reading the news item in the paper. They had tooling for sale which made plastic military figurines. They had tried to sell the item as a toy package containing 50 figurines for $1 but failed. We bought the tooling outright for $2,000, created a hard-selling ad offering 100 (instead of 50) toy figurines for $1 and pulled more orders than we had believed possible in our wildest speculation. To date we have sold close to 2 million sets. Revising this "dead" product proved very profitable for us. We are still moving thousands of units each month—all from a $2,000 set of tooling!

5. STUDY THE BUSINESS OPPORTUNITY COLUMNS IN YOUR NEWSPAPER

I believe the Classified section of a newspaper—especially the "Business Opportunities" column—can tell you more about your city "business-wise" than any other publication. It reports who's going into business, who's going out of business, who's looking for business, and what businesses are available. It's the pulse of a city, and when you learn to read it, you'll recognize trends and economic signs that can mean much to your business.

Some time ago we saw an ad in "Business Opportunities" offering a new type of fly killer. We contacted the company and realized that they had something new and different. The product was a solid insecticide shaped like a small doughnut and had two distinct advantages over the other fly killers: (1) It killed flies within seconds after they alighted on it, and (2) each cake lasted for an entire season or more.

We offered to promote the product on a worldwide basis in return for exclusive sales rights to it. The company readily agreed to this, for it was not too familiar with merchandising and didn't know what to do with this incredible product. We immediately packaged the insecticide in a dramatic-looking box and christened the product Cossman's Fly Cake. The first year we sold over 2 million Fly Cakes, even though we started late in the summer season. And we found this wonderful product by reading the "Business Opportunities" column in the *Los Angeles Times*!

6. ATTEND TRADE SHOWS

We deal fully with the importance of trade shows in another chapter, but mention of this source for new-product ideas must also be incorporated here.

Almost every large city in the United States sponsors trade shows. Visit them at every opportunity, even though they cover a field foreign to your business. It's the old "exposure" rule all over again.

A few years ago, we visited a book and stationery show in Los Angeles and noticed that many of the new products being exhibited carried a circus theme. There's always room for one more, so we jumped on the bandwagon and put out a set of plastic circus figurines. Offering 41 circus toys for $1, the item became our top mail order seller for that year and developed into a standard. Although our circus toys had no relationship with books and stationery, we got the idea by visiting that particular trade show.

Expose yourself to the products and promotions of other manufacturers, and your own field of new ideas will greatly increase.

7. USE YOUR OWN LOCALITY AS A SOURCE OF IDEAS

My son, Howard, cashed in on the worldwide reputation of Hollywood by selling book covers with old-time movie stars printed on them.

A mail order house in New England built up a fantastic business selling live lobsters through the mails! A company in New Mexico offers Indian wares by mail.

Look at your city from a national viewpoint, and you'll discover dozens of products or services that distinctly characterize your own locality and would be welcomed by mail order customers in other parts of the country.

8. BROWSE THROUGH OLD BOOKS AND MAGAZINES

I recently visited a used-books store and found complete sets of back issues covering many years of *Popular Science* and *Popular Mechanics* magazines. I find them to be excellent idea starters for new products. Many past products advertised in old publications can be profitably promoted all over again. Sometimes, just by giving them a new twist or modern application, you'll hit a real winner.

9. COLLEGES AND UNIVERSITIES

Most colleges delegate funds for the purpose of developing new products and improving old ones. Some universities even maintain complete research departments for this specific purpose. Use this prolific source for stimulating ideas for new products in your business.

If you contact a college or university in this respect, ask for the Public Relations Department and tell them what you are specifically interested in. They in turn will connect you with the proper department.

However, when you contact the college or university, do not expect to pick up information regarding fully developed products. As a general rule, they work on advanced theories which can be applied to practical purposes.

Several years ago the University of Wisconsin discovered a new formula for a rat poison that made a fortune for two enterprising young men. Each rat colony has one or two "tasters" and it is the rat taster's duty to eat any new food exposed to the colony. The other rats in the colony watch the tasters for days before they themselves will eat the new food. If nothing happens to the tasters, then the entire colony will eat the new food source.

This shrewd animal instinct presented a difficult problem to manufacturers of rat poisons, for it was almost impossible to fool the rat colony. Then the University of Wisconsin developed a poison which in effect was a blood thinner. The taster could eat this poison and nothing would happen to him for days. However, continual eating of the poison would thin out the blood of the rat to the point where he would die of internal hemorrhages, but by this time the complete rat colony would be eating the same poison, as they had seen no ill effects displayed by the taster during the first week or ten days of eating the poison.

Nothing spectacular was done with this particular rat poison until a company got the formula from the University of Wisconsin, began manufacturing it and promoting it among farmers. The rest is merchandising history, for they sold their entire company a few years later on a capital gains of several million dollars!

Incidentally, here is an interesting note. When the company first began marketing the rat poison, their sales were practically nil. They were down to almost their last dollar when they discovered the reason why the product was not selling to farmers. It seems that they were packaging the product in a colorful box with the words *Rat Poison* prominently displayed on the top lid. Since farmers do not wish to admit to anyone, not even the mailman, that they are troubled with rats, they stayed away from the product in droves! It wasn't until the company ran out of the colorful boxes, and for the sake of economy packaged the product in plain boxes, that they stumbled across the successful way to promote and sell the product!

10. USE THE UNITED STATES GOVERNMENT PUBLICATION SERVICES

No other single source can give as vast, as consistent, and as reliable information on business and new-product development in our country and in foreign markets as Uncle Sam . . . and most of it is free or costs but a few pennies. A thorough study of this one source could fill many books, but we will try to list here those booklets, pamphlets, and services that we ourselves use in searching out new products and ideas.

One of the best sources of new-product ideas is the United States government "R & D Reports." These reports are the result of United States government research and development in defense, space, nuclear energy, and other national programs.

With these programs requiring over two-thirds of the nation's total research effort, it's the policy of the government to make the unclassified scientific and technical knowledge developed through this tax-supported research rapidly and easily available to the public. For this purpose, the National Technical Information Service (NTIS) has been established.

While many of these reports are devoted to the development of the most sophisticated hardware and systems of which man is capable, all of the developments call for new or better metals, chemicals, plastics, electronic devices, fuels and lubricants, and other materials and components. Also included are new, improved, or more economical production processes. It is the reports of new products and process research, developments that may have commercial application, that the NTIS collects from other agencies for distribution to you. When you realize that more than 30,000 new documents are available from the NTIS each year, you get an idea of the tremendous scope of this program. You can get full information on these "R & D Reports" by writing to National Technical Information Service (NTIS), United States Department of Commerce, Springfield, VA 22151, or by contacting your local United States Department of Commerce Field Office.

11. CONTACT PATENT ATTORNEYS

You will find your local patent attorneys to be prime sources of new-product ideas. They can put you in touch with inventors in your own area, since they are usually the first to hear of new products. Due to the very nature of their business, they're glad to share this information with potentially interested manufacturers.

You can usually get the name and address of a patent attorney by consulting the Yellow Pages of your local telephone book. Since fees for different legal services vary from state to state, it is advisable to check with the attorney and arrive at a price for his services before you employ him.

You may also use a competent patent attorney for a specific patent search on products. He will write to the Patent Office and outline your particular interest, manufacturing facilities, and other details. The Patent Office will furnish a special list of patents in the field in which you are interested, which will include patent registration number, name of patent, date patent was issued, brief description of patent, and name and address of patent owner. This list will be tailored to fit your requirements and interests. Such special lists are made up from unexpired patents on the Register that have been offered for license or sale as well as government-owned and dedicated patents. Also, you or your patent attorney may request the Patent Office to place your name on the mailing list to receive future announcements of additional patents as they are placed on the Register.

12. YOUR LOCAL BANK AND CHAMBER OF COMMERCE

Make yourself and your business interest known to these two organizations. They are usually the first to hear of new-product development and will soon begin channeling new ideas and new products your way.

Many banks and chambers of commerce publish a monthly newsletter listing new businesses that are started, new products being developed, etcetera. Contact your local bank or chamber of commerce and ask to be put on the mailing list, if they have such a service. Also find out the extent of their interest in new-product development.

13. CONTACT PLASTICS FACTORIES IN YOUR CITY

Plastics factories are good sources of supply, particularly for old tooling or products no longer on the market. At least twice each year, we send the following letter to plastics firms in our city and are always amazed at the tremendous response. Some of our top mail order items originated from this little-known source.

Gentlemen:

Do you have any tooling around your shop that you would like to sell? We are continually looking for obsolete dies or finished products that never have made the grade.

If you have any old tooling, prototypes, or even an inventory of "dead" merchandise, will you please call us at 327-0550? If you have nothing at the present time, will you please keep this letter on file?

Sincerely,

E. JOSEPH COSSMAN & COMPANY

EJC:sh

14. HOW 29 MANUFACTURERS LOCATED IDEAS FOR NEW PRODUCTS

The Small Business Administration of the United States Department of Commerce recently published a guidebook entitled *Developing and Selling New Products*. The following list from that book shows 29 companies and where they got their ideas for their new products:

Company	New Product	Source of Idea
Meat packer	Chicken soup	Executive's wife
Meat packer	Canned chicken product	Salesman
Manufacturer of industrial equipment	Steam-producing unit	Advertised sale of manufacturing rights
Tinplate converter	Breadbox	Market research agency assigned to study new product possibilities
Electric appliance manufacturer	Food warmer	Customer inquiries
Manufacturer of golf equipment	Golf bag "toter"	President of company
Manufacturer of service equipment for garages	Hoist for garage	Garage mechanic contacted during survey of product users
Chemical company	Deodorant for garbage	Advertising agency which learned of local use
Chemical and film company	Detergent	Laboratory
Die casting company	Line of dejuicers	Company executives
Manufacturer of plastic product	Film viewing device	Inventor
Manufacturer of kitchen utensils and gadgets	Kitchen gadget	Register of patents available for licensing or sale (U.S. Patent Office)
Chemical products company	Insecticide	List of government-owned patents available for licensing
Manufacturer of office equipment and machinery	Index device, envelope opening device, pencil gripper	Office managers. Also jobber and wholesale catalogs
Canner	Apple juice	Food broker
Appliance manufacturer	Electric bottle-warmer	Customers

Company	New Product	Source of Idea
Film company	Film	Engineer
Landscape supply and equipment company	Fiber glass blanket to place around tree to keep down weeds and retain moisture in soil	Register of patents available for licensing or sale
Container manufacturer	Re-use container	President of company (noticed waste of materials)
Plumbing equipment and supply manufacturer	New washer	Sales report
Manufacturer of hardware	Bedroom door knockers (also miniature jewelry door knockers)	Executive in considering idea of reducing size of regular door knockers
Pottery manufacturer	New vase	Museum exhibit
Plastic products company	Plastic shield for wall light switch	Inventor
Plastic products company	Film slide viewer	List of needed inventions published by bank
Chemicals manufacturer	New type detergent for automatic washing machine	Market observations showed need for sudsless detergent
Engineering consultant	New type air regulator valve	Observation of industry need not previously satisfied
Legal firm	Canned fresh water for storage in lifeboats	Ship's captain asked lawyer specializing in marine claims to try canning drinking water. Idea succeeded and new firm was started. Some canning companies previously considered such storage in the cans impossible
Marine engineering	Toy	Accidental dropping of coiled spring at head of stairs. Engineer's children enjoyed watching it "walk down." He decided it would make a satisfactory toy and started new company

Company	New Product	Source of Idea
Machine tool builder	Machine for textile industry	Examination of machinery needs of non-customer industries. The company knew that the textile industry didn't use lathes but reasoned it might use machines which could be produced by a machine-tools manufacturer. After a thorough study of the textile industry, the company selected 4 textile machines for manufacturers.

15. USE YOUR OWN IDEAS

Last, but far from least, your own ideas may be your best source. Harvey Firestone, the great industrialist, said, "Capital isn't so important in business. Experience isn't so important. You can get both those things. What is important is ideas. If you have ideas, you have the main asset you need, and there isn't any limit to what you can do with your business and your life. They are any man's greatest asset—ideas."

Most of our products are the result of our own ideas. In the long run, you're on your own, so let your judgment be your guide. But keep this in mind . . . a new idea is a delicate thing. It can be killed by a sneer or worried to death with a frown. Treat your own ideas like children—coddle them, keep them away from the chill of adverse criticism, have faith in them—and they'll grow up into strong, mature products to support you in your old age!

SOURCES OF INFORMATION AND DIRECTORIES ON AMERICAN FIRMS

Manufacturers' Agents' Guide. Manufacturers Agent Publishing Co., Inc., 663 Fifth Avenue, New York, NY 10022.
Covers more than 12,700 manufacturers who distribute through agents. Includes manufacturer's name, address, principal products, and credit rating, name and title of sales executive.

Mail Order Business Directory. Bernard Klein Publications, Box 8503, Coral Springs, FL 33065,
Covers 5900 firms in the United States doing business by mail order and catalogs. Includes name, address, list of products or services, and name of owner or contact, arranged geographically.

Direct Selling World Directory. Direct Selling Association, 1730 "M" Street, N.W., Suite 610, Washington, DC 20036.
Covers 25 direct selling associations, associated member companies, the World Federation of Direct Selling Associations, and the European Federation of Direct Selling Associations. These associations and firms are concerned with selling of consumer products door to door and through party plans. Includes organization name, address, and phone number.

Amusement Rides and Games Buyers' Guide. Billboard Publications Inc., Box 24970, Nashville, TN 37202.
Covers manufacturers, importers, and suppliers of amusement rides and games. Includes company name, address, phone number, list of products or services, and name of principal executive.

Apparel Trades Book. Dunn and Bradstreet Inc., 99 Church Street, New York, NY 10007.
Covers approximately 125,000 apparel retailers and wholesalers in the United States that are rated by Dunn and Bradstreet and included in its national reference book. A separate apparel trades book is published for each state. Includes company name and principal lines of merchandise, listed in order of importance.

Specialty Advertiser. Lakewood Publications Inc., 731 Hennepin Avenue, Minneapolis, MN 55403.
A quarterly magazine featuring information about the specialty advertising industry.

The Directory of Directories. Gale Research Company, Book Tower, Detroit, MI 48226.
A guide to business and industrial directories, professional and scientific rosters, and other lists and guides of all kinds.

Directory of Incentive Sources. Bill Communications, Inc. 633 Third Avenue, New York, NY 10017.

A directory of give-away products and services. Includes trading stamp services and specialists in various forms of promotion, such as contests, sweepstakes, close-outs, bank and financial promotions. Also includes manufacturers' reps.

MacRae's Blue Book. MacRae's Blue Book Company, 100 Shore Drive, Hinsdale, IL 60521.
Covers 60,000 manufacturing firms in the United States. Volume I is an alphabetical list of the companies. Volume II, III, IV are product indexes. Volume V is catalog pages. Includes company name, address, products, phone number, and cities and phone numbers of branches and sales outlets.

Manufacturers' Agents' National Association Directory of Members. Manufacturers' Agents' National Association, 2021 Business Center Drive, Irvine, CA 92713.
Covers 6,000 independent agents and firms representing manufacturers of all types in specified territories on a commission basis, as well as manufacturers' consultants and others interested in the agency-principle method of marketing.

Salesmen's Opportunity Magazine. Opportunity Publishing Company, John Hancock Center, Suite 1460, 875 Michigan Avenue, Chicago, IL 60611.
Monthly magazine emphasizes direct sales and individually owned business opportunities. Notes new products and sales tips.

Modern Packaging Encyclopedia and Buyers' Guide. Morgan-Grampian Publishing Company, 2 Park Avenue, New York, NY 10016.
Covers 3,500 manufacturers' consultants, associations, and service organizations that supply packaging products or services. Includes company name, address, and phone number.

Specialty Salesmen and Business Opportunities. Specialty Salesmen Magazine Inc., 307 North Michigan Avenue, Chicago, IL 60601.
A monthly magazine containing articles about business opportunities in direct selling.

Standard Rate & Data Service. Standard Rate & Data Service, Inc., 5201 Old Orchard Road, Skokie, IL 60076.

Six directories containing information on radio, television, consumer magazines, trade magazines, direct mail, and newspapers. Includes rates, representatives.

Standard Directory of Advertisers. National Register Publishing Co., Inc., 5201 Old Orchard Road, Skokie, IL 60076.
Annual directory offers a register of 17,000 corporations responsible for 95 percent of United States advertising. Notes sales volume, advertising budget, and agencies.

Standard Directory of Advertising Agencies. National Register Publishing Co., Inc., 5201 Old Orchard Road, Skokie, IL 60076.
Covers 4,400 advertising agencies, their gross billings by media, annual billings, and clients.

Standard Industrial Classification Manual. United States Department of Commerce, Bureau of the Census, Washington, DC 20233.
Defines industries in accordance with the composition and structure of the United States economy. Includes conversion tables for the standard industrial classification codes.

New Product—New Business Digest. General Electric Company, Business Growth Services, Building 5-311, No. 1 River Road, Schenectady, NY 12345.
Monthly digest describing over 500 new product and business programs available by purchase or license.

Newsletter on Newsletters. Hudson Associates, 44 West Market Street, Rhinebeck, NY 12572.
A monthly newsletter that discusses new developments in the newsletter field. Gives case histories and tips on promotion, graphics, and editorial content. Also published is the *Newsletter Yearbook-Directory,* an annual directory to 1,500 newsletters, arranged by subject.

Modern Plastics Encyclopedia. McGraw-Hill Inc., 1221 Avenue of the Americas, New York, NY 10020.
Covers 4,500 plastics processors and converters and suppliers of products and services to the plastics industry in the United States and Canada. Includes company name, address, phone number, list of products or services.

Direct Marketing Marketplace. Hilary House Publishers Inc., 1033 Channel Drive, Hewlett Harbor, NY 11557.

Covers several thousand direct marketing companies, service firms and suppliers, and creative and consulting services concerned with direct marketing, including mail, radio, and television broadcasting. Includes company name, address, phone number, description of products and services, names and titles of key personnel.

National Association of Chain Drug Stores Membership Directory. National Association of Chain Drug Stores, 1911 Jefferson Davis Highway, Arlington, VA 22202.

Covers approximately 200 chain drug retailers and their 15,000 individual pharmacies, 400 supplier companies, state boards of pharmacy, and retail associations. Includes firm name, headquarters, address, and phone number, number of owned and leased pharmacies, names and titles of key personnel.

Shopping Center Directory. National Research Bureau, 424 North Third Street, Burlington, IA 52601.

Covers 19,000 shopping centers in four volumes. Includes shopping center name, address, mailing address, phone number, names of executives, merchants' association secretary, and gross sales.

Working Press of the Nation. National Research Bureau, 424 North Third Street, Burlington, IA 52601.

Covers over 6,100 daily and weekly newspapers; 13,600 radio and television stations; 4,800 magazines; 2,500 syndicates, feature writers, and photographers; and 3,500 internal house organs. Listings include name of publication or station, address, phone number, names of executives, talk-show hosts, etcetera.

International Trade Newsletter. International Trade Newsletter, 160 Broadway, New York, NY 10038.

A monthly newsletter reporting on international trade developments including export controls, freight rates, exchange rates, and dumping regulation.

Billboard International Recording Equipment and Studio Directory. Billboard Publications Inc., 9000 Sunset Boulevard, Los Angeles, CA 90069.

Covers recording studios, equipment manufacturers and importers, independent record producers, and blank-loaded cassette manufacturers in the United States and 25 other countries. Includes company name, address, phone number, names of principal executives, trade names or list of products or services.

Resident Buying Offices. Salesmen's Guide Inc., 1140 Broadway, New York, NY 10001.
Lists paid and commission resident buying offices servicing 11,000 accounts connected with sporting goods and men's, women's, and children's wear.

California Manufacturers' Register. Times Mirror Press, 1115 South Boyle Avenue, Los Angeles, CA 90023.
Covers 19,000 manufacturing plants in California having 4 or more employees. Includes company name, address, phone number, names of executives, numbers of employees, sales volume, products, SIC numbers, and date established.

Consultants' and Consulting Organizations' Directory. Gale Research Company, Book Tower, Detroit, MI 48226.
Covers over 6,000 firms, individuals, and organizations active in the consulting field. Includes individual or organization name, address, phone number, and specialties.

Decor—Sources Issue. Commerce Publishing Co., 408 Olive Street, St. Louis, MO 63102.
Covers more than 500 wholesale suppliers of pictures, picture frames, interior accessories, sculpture, mirrors, and so forth, to art galleries, picture framers, and home accessory retailers. Supplies name, address, and phone number.

Dial Free: Dial 800. J.M.O. Publishing Inc., Box 995, Radio City Station, New York, NY 10019.
Includes approximately 4,000 companies, organizations, hotels, and airlines with toll-free (800) telephone numbers.

Directory of Conventions. Bill Communications Inc., 1422 Chestnut Street, Philadelphia, PA 19102.
Covers over 18,000 meetings of North American, national, regional, state, and local organizations. Includes name of organiza-

tion, title and address of executive in charge of event, dates, sites, expected attendance, and scope of event.

Directory of Corporate Affiliations. National Register Publishing Co., Standard Rate & Data Service Inc., 5201 Old Orchard Road, Skokie, IL 60076.
Covers 3,750 United States parent companies and about 46,000 domestic and foreign divisions, subsidaries and/or affiliates. Includes company name, address, phone number, annual sales, number of employees, name and address of corporate counsel.

Annual Directory of Trade and Industrial Shows. Bill Comunications, Inc., 1422 Chestnut Street, Philadelphia, PA 19102.
Covers trade, industrial, and public shows worldwide. Gives show name, name and address of contact, number of booths, dates, locations, expected attendance, headquarters, and show frequency.

Gift and Decorative Accessory Buyers' Directory. Geyer-McAllister Publications Inc., 51 Madison Avenue, New York, NY 10010.
Covers manufacturers, importers, jobbers, and manufacturers' representatives for gifts, china, glass, lamps, and home accessories, stationery, greeting cards, and related products. Gives company name, address, product lines, trade and brand names.

Directory of Hardware Distributors. Chilton Company, Chilton Way, Radnor, PA 19089.
Covers over 4,200 hardware wholesalers, specialty distributors, manufacturers' reps, and retail chains in the hardware, general retail, home and auto supply, and specialty stores. Includes firm name, address, phone number, date established, sales volume, area served, lines handled.

World Convention Dates. Hendrickson Publishing Company Inc., 79 Washington Street, Hempstead, NY 11550.
Covers 13,300 meetings of international, national, regional, state, and district organizations up to ten years in advance of meeting dates. Includes names of sponsoring organizations, name, title, and address of person in charge of the event, date, site, expected attendance, etcetera.

Japan External Trade Organization Business Information Series.

Japan Trade Center, 1221 Avenue of the Americas, New York, NY 10020.
A series of booklets giving information for foreign businessmen who want to do business in Japan. Also, Japan marketing series of reports covering Japanese trade, import regulations, consumers, and distribution businessmen.

World Wide Chamber of Commerce Directory. Johnson Publishing Company, Inc., Eighth and VanBuren Streets, Loveland, CO 80537.
Covers Chambers of Commerce in about 7,750 localities in the United States and 275 localities abroad, foreign diplomatic offices in the United States and American offices overseas. Includes organization name, name of executive, address, phone number, and population of area covered.

Direct Marketing. Hoke Communications, Inc., 224 Seventh Street, Garden City, NY 11535.
A monthly magazine emphasizing direct mail advertising and other direct marketing techniques.

Most of these directories can be found in your local library. Prices have not been included since they change so quickly. If you are interested in buying any of these directories, please contact the publisher directly and ask for the current price.

4 | How to Test Your Products

"Rules are for when brains run out."

Test, test, and test again before spending money on production. I can't stress this point too strongly. The number of people willing to sink thousands of dollars into a product before they know its sales value is incredible. The axiom, "Look before you leap," is truer in new-product development than in any other field of business. The most foolish business practice in the world is starting production before sales-testing the item. Time after time we are offered products by manufacturers who tooled up, packaged, and tried to merchandise a finished product—only to find no market for the item.

Sometimes it's difficult to test before you have the finished product. But with a little ingenuity you can get a good idea of the over-all possibilities before you're involved dollar-wise in tooling and production. We have developed several foolproof ways of pre-testing a new product:

1. ASK FOR BUYERS' OPINIONS

Department store buyers are very good judges of product possibilities. Their job depends on guessing right most of the time. Take your idea or a prototype of your product to these people and ask for their comments. Will they place an order after you're in production? Is the price too high? Do they like the packaging? What constructive criticism can they offer? Conducting a poll with a few friendly buyers will give you an invaluable test for your product.

Since each department in the department store has its own buyer, it is advisable to call the store first and find out the name of the buyer of the department you are interested in. Then call that particular buyer and find out the most convenient time you can contact him personally. Each department store also has its own buying hours, and in many cases the specific departments in the same store may have different buying hours. If you don't call for a specific appointment, you may find yourself cooling your heels for hours in the waiting rooms of the buying offices.

2. MAKE UP A FEW SAMPLES AND DISPLAY THEM AT TRADE SHOWS

No other medium will give you quicker answers as to a product's sales possibilities than the trade show. These shows are attended by hard-headed buyers who are not influenced by sentiment, personal favoritism, or emotion. If they like your product, they'll buy; if they don't like it, they won't buy—it's as simple as that. And in most cases, they are correct in their judgment. In fact, we attach so much importance to trade shows that we have devoted a full chapter to the subject.

Some time ago, we tried to cash in on the mosaic craze then sweeping the country. We developed a kit made up of plastic, varicolored fabric materials, and the idea was to make cutouts and paste them on a diagrammed background. The completed item could be framed, and we developed eight different subjects and made a finished sample of each of the eight kits. We took these samples to the National Hobby Show in Chicago, and displayed them in our booth. It took only a few hours to discover we did not have a hot item. Based on the lukewarm reception our product received at this trade show, going into production was not practical. The sample kits had cost us $4,000 in time and materials, but we considered this very cheap money and never put the product on the market.

Of course, $4,000 is a lot of money, but considering the stakes we were shooting for, we considered it a wise investment. In some cases, it is not necessary for you to actually take a booth in a show. Many times you can make arrangements with a company that intends to exhibit anyway, and for a consideration (to be decided between you and the company) let them exhibit your new product along with products they manufacture.

Only recently we had a novelty item that looked as if it would make a good premium. The National Premium Show is held in Chicago each year, but our novelty item wasn't big enough in potential business to warrant a trip to Chicago and the expense of a booth at the show. Instead, we contacted a company that intended to exhibit their products and worked out an arrangement whereby they would exhibit our product along with their own line. In this way we learned the truth about our product's salability at practically no cost to us.

3. GET THE OPINIONS OF YOUR FRIENDS

This is not a reversal of our rule, "Do not rely on the opinions of others," but can be useful in a certain sense. Your friends' comments—if carefully evaluated by you—may sometimes bring out new improvements and uses for your product.

4. COMPARE YOUR PRODUCT WITH SIMILAR ITEMS ON THE MARKET

Are they selling? Is your product better? Cheaper? More practical? For example, there were many ant farms on the market prior to ours, but most of them were made of glass . . . cumbersome, bulky, and very expensive. Our product, which was made of plastic, was better because it was cheaper to produce, therefore cheaper to sell. It could be cleaned easily, re-used, and was practically unbreakable. Furthermore, the novelty of mailing live ants free to each ant-farm customer lifted our product above the ordinary and made it a dramatic, exciting, and educational item.

If you have an idea for a new product or even manufacture the new product yourself, you're sure to find something similar in the average department store in your neighborhood. Today, the department store is a treasure trove of products that will give you a basis for comparison with your own new products.

Get a copy of a trade magazine in the field covering your project. These publications will give you a great deal of information that will help you determine whether your idea or product has a place in that field. If you live in a big city, most trade magazines have local representatives who will be glad to send you a free copy of their publication. And almost any large library subscribes to most of the trade magazines on a monthly basis. I know that the library in Los Angeles gets between 500 and 600 different trade magazines every month, and of course anyone is free to browse through these publications at his leisure. This is a great opportunity for you to become acquainted with the national and regional magazines serving your special trade, profession, or interest before you buy a subscription to any one publication. Also, when you see the hundreds of different fields covered by these publications, you're almost certain to find several magazines covering the particular area in which you are interested.

5. MAKE UP A SAMPLE RUN OF YOUR ITEM AND ADVERTISE

Regardless of the material your finished product will be made from, there are many inexpensive ways of making up a few samples. If the item is to be injection molded, for example, you can make temporary tooling good for a production of two to three hundred pieces. After you have made up a few hundred samples, run an ad and study the results. No test in the world can beat the returns of a good mail order ad. Your product must stand by itself, and the results of your ads will tell you whether or not you have a real winner. It isn't necessary for you to run a big ad in an expensive magazine. Many newspapers today have shopper's columns which are, in effect, a mail order page offering mail order merchandise to their readers.

6. OFFER YOUR PRODUCT TO MAIL ORDER HOUSES

Although it is possible to buy a list of mail order houses from many commercial concerns, we do not advise that you do so. Many names and addresses of mail order houses become obsolete within a year and many new concerns come on the scene that would not be in the list you purchase.

We get our lists of names and addresses for top mail order houses from current ads run in magazines such as *House Beautiful, Better Homes and Gardens, Redbook*, and many others. We make it a point to buy the October and November issues of these publications each year. In this way we are able to compile a fresh list of 500 or more good mail order companies yearly.

If you're unable to submit samples, try to show first-class artwork or professional photographs of the product, accompanied by a good description. Mail order houses buy merchandise on the same emotional and visual basis that their mail order customers buy from them. A good visual presentation of the product made up of excellent copy, photographs, or drawings is more important than actual samples. You will know by the reception your presentation receives whether or not the product warrants full-scale production.

The original tooling cost on our Ant Farm was $18,000. We were reluctant to spend this much money on an untested product, so we had our artist make up a wash drawing which looked like an actual photograph of the item. We sent a copy of the drawing, along with the following letter, to every large mail order house in the country.

> Dear ....:
>
> You know our company . . . you know our reputation for coming up with real winners . . . you know that many mail order houses, including yours, have made thousands of dollars on our products.
>
> Well, now we have a winner to end all winners! It's our *new* **Ant Farm** and it is fully described on the enclosed drawing.
>
> We will soon be starting production on the tooling to make this Ant Farm, and we are giving you first choice to schedule your ads on the product. The Ant Farm will be all plastic, will come complete with soil and a coupon good for a free supply of live ants, and the complete package will come to you in a corrugated mailer ready for your postage and label.
>
> We suggest a $2.98 retail—and your cost will be $1.35.
>
> Let us know where and when you want to advertise this product (it will be ready in about 60 days), and we will give you "protection" on your space commitments.
>
> > Best regards,
> >
> > E. JOSEPH COSSMAN & COMPANY

Within a few days, enthusiastic replies came pouring in, and we knew we had a real winner. But only after the major mail order houses had committed themselves to more than $100,000 in ads, did we go into the tooling investment.

7. USE YOUR OWN JUDGMENT

Sometimes, all the advice in the world cannot equal your own hunch or your own idea. In a later chapter, I will discuss a product which was a good example of this test . . . our Spud Gun. Buyers didn't like it; representatives didn't like it; nobody liked it. And yet we sold over 2 million Spud Guns because we played our hunch in spite of the opinions of others.

8. OFFER YOUR NEW PRODUCT WITH A TESTED PRODUCT

If you have another product in the same category as the new one, and you already know its tested mail order pull—run the untested item along with the tested product. Compared returns will truly evaluate the new item.

Some newspapers and magazines offer this service and it is called a split run. They will take two ads from you and run ad "A" in half of their circulation and ad "B" in the other half of their circulation. If ad "A" is a tested mail order product and ad "B" is the untested product, your returns from both ads will quickly indicate if the new product has as much pull as the tested one.

9. RUN A ONE-STORE TEST

This is one sure way of testing your product's acceptability. Leave a few samples with a retail store. Does it sell off the counter? What comments, if any, did the customer make? Does it hold its own against competitive items? There are times when you can learn more from a one-store test than you can learn from costly ads

Many stores in your neighborhood will be willing to let you leave a few samples of your merchandise in return for giving them an additional discount on the product, or even giving them some extra merchandise being left there on a test. It should be treated in the same manner that he would treat any item he buys for resale.

Some time ago, we ran a one-store test on a new product and we were amazed at the wonderful results. Upon investigating, however, we discovered that the storekeeper, wishing to be helpful, had put our test merchandise alongside the cash register and had even taken it upon himself to print a large sign calling the product to the attention of his customers. This, of course, completely invalidated our test, for we knew we wouldn't get such favorable treatment from other stores once the product was put on the market.

10. CONSUMER-TEST YOUR PRODUCT

Sometimes, faults in a product are not apparent until it is on the market, as the following true story will illustrate. A friend came into

2 *Fascinating* ANT FARMS

F23

GIANT SIZE ANT FARM
10" HIGH · 15" WIDE

Includes: year's supply of ant food, liquid feed-er, supply of California sand, ant watchers hand-book, stock certificate for generous supply of ants. Packed ½ dozen to car-ton. Weight 25 lbs.

No. H33

6⁹⁵ RETAIL

HERE'S AN ANT'S ENTIRE WORLD!

Watch them dig tunnels — see them build rooms — marvel as they erect bridges and move moun-tains before your very eyes. Ants are the world's tiniest engineers . . . and seeing them plan and construct their intricate highways and subways is fascinating. But they do much more than that! Through the clear plastic walls of your ANT FARM you can see the ant soldiers guarding the roads . . . the laborers carrying their loads . . . the supply corps storing away food for the rest of the colony. Yes, the ANT FARM is actually a LIVING TV SCREEN that will keep you interested for hours.

REGULAR SIZE ANT FARM
6" HIGH · 9" WIDE

Includes: ant watchers handbook, stock certificate for generous supply of ants, supply of California sand. Packed 3 dozen to carton. Weight 35 lbs.

No. H15B

2⁹⁸ RETAIL

A STOCK CERTIFICATE
with each Ant Farm. Customer mails certificate to us for free supply of ants.

FOR PRODUCTS OF QUALITY
E. JOSEPH COSSMAN CO.

my office wearing a long face and mumbling about trouble with his new cat food item. I was surprised, as I'd heard he was doing great with the product. He shrugged and said, "I thought so, too. When I first came out with this new cat food, I didn't miss a trick. I used a top agency and told them to spare nothing. I wanted the best package they could make, and they did a terrific job. Turned out a label that almost jumped off the shelf. They designed window streamers and counter cards that were works of art . . . really the best point-of-sale pieces I've ever seen. I had it all printed by a first-class house and then showed the finished product to some key jobbers. They practically begged me to take their orders! I sold over 2,000 cases of cat food the first week and then put my men in the field to presell dealers. It was too easy! With those point-of-sale pieces and that prizewinning can, it was a cinch to get dealer cooperation. Even the press got behind the item and wrote up several terrific editorial stories about it."

"I don't understand," I broke in, "the agency did a prizewinning job, jobbers liked the can, dealers went for the product—even the press cooperated. What are you grumbling about? What's wrong?"

"Just one thing," he replied sadly, "cats hate it! They won't touch that cat food with a ten-foot pole!"

The moral to this story is test, test, and test again—especially with the consumer in mind!

5 | How to Develop and Produce Your Products

"Working with the same material, one man may build a work of art, while the other whittles a pile of shavings."

After you have found your product and tested it, you are now ready to produce it. If you have unlimited funds and don't care how much you spend, you have no problem—but if you're out to cut corners and want production with the smallest outlay of dollars, then follow our procedure.

Many times we've asked experienced production people to guess the manufacturing cost of our product. Invariably, they will give a higher figure and are amazed when we tell them our *actual* cost of production. Here are some of the tricks we've learned:

1. GET AS MANY BIDS AS POSSIBLE

This may sound simple, but it is surprising how many companies give a job to the first bidder. We have records on file from reputable organizations showing as much as 200 percent variance in bids for the same job. When we were planning the Ant Farm tooling, we received bids from $14,000 to $32,000 for the same type of die. On the Spud Gun tooling, the range was even wider, and these were bids from experienced companies.

The same holds true for manufacturing and production. One highly respected company gave us a production price for the Ant

Farm which was more than three times the final bid. This wide difference in price production is not because one company is more honest than another—it's just that one operates more efficiently than another, or may have equipment capable of more economical production than another. Remember . . . never begin tooling or production until you have at least five company bids.

Of course, price alone is not the only factor when giving out a job to a manufacturer. You should always look into the reputation of the company and if the job is important enough, even go to the extent of interviewing other people who are at present doing business with that particular company.

2. FARM OUT AS MUCH WORK AS YOU CAN

Emulate our government by subcontracting. Government contracts are given to one major company, which, in turn, subcontracts various components of a specific product to other organizations. However, the major company, receiving the contract from the government, is wholly responsible for the entire job.

When our Spud Gun hit the market, we were so swamped with orders we had to have mass production quickly and efficiently. Based on this demand, we subcontracted orders to four separate die-casting factories; together, they turned out sufficient quantities of guns to meet our daily requirements.

Each Spud Gun operation consisted of six individual manufacturing steps:
   (a) A metal die-casting . . . which was then,
   (b) Plated . . . then,
   (c) Assembled with a metal spring and neoprene washer. The completed unit was then,
   (d) Packed into an individual display box . . .
   (e) The display box was packed into a three-dozen container carton . . .
   (f) The container carton was packed in master shipping cartons holding twelve dozen units, ready for delivery.

As the metal die-casting was the major part of the unit, we asked several die-casting plants to submit bids for this one operation. From bids received, we selected four of the best and gave these four factories our orders.

Now, here's where we copied the government method of subcontracting. Although our four factories produced only the metal die-casting of the Spud Gun, we contracted for each factory to be responsible for parts, labor, assembly, and packaging; that is, all of the other parts and operations which went into the finished, boxed product.

We then called for bids from suppliers of metal springs, neoprene washers, plating, assembly, and boxes. Selecting the best supplier in each case, we ordered all parts in quantities of 500,000 lots to benefit from volume price discounts. However, each supplier was instructed to deliver and bill to the die-casting factory ordering from him, instead of making deliveries and billings to us. And as the die-casting plants required additional supplies, they ordered direct from the various suppliers.

As compensation to the four die-casting factories for the extra bookkeeping and inventory control this situation entailed, we allowed them to add 10 percent to parts and services purchased from suppliers. However, in each case, the die-casting plant was directly responsible for payment to the supplier as well as inventory and quality control on the parts and services ordered. Consequently, each plant delivered to us completed, boxed Spud Guns, packed in master shipping cartons . . . all at a fixed price.

This procedure gave us the tremendous price advantage of mass production and parts purchases, without the headaches of stocking inventory, hiring additional help for assembly and packing, renting additional warehouse space, and worrying about losses or shortages.

3. USE THE TALENTS, BRAINS, AND FACILITIES OF YOUR SUPPLIERS

We've seen companies spend days and weeks on production problems that could be solved in minutes or hours by checking with suppliers or manufacturers. In most cases, your supplier is a trained expert in his field and has at his disposal top-notch men to design, produce, and advise. They'll gladly assist you in the development of your idea in return for potential business.

For example, most box companies have designers on their staff who will design a sample box for your product. Many plastics factories employ trained engineers who can help you with technical problems. Manufacturers of the raw materials that go into your product will be glad to help you solve problems that might cost a great deal of your time and money if you were to try to get the answer elsewhere.

You have literally thousands of dollars worth of talent and brains at your disposal—use them!

4. USE THE YELLOW PAGES FOR HARD-TO-FIND SUPPLIERS

As stated previously in this chapter, there is a surprising difference in bids from suppliers, and this is mainly due to a company's facilities and method of business. At times, you'll find yourself using the wrong supplier or manufacturer simply because he doesn't have the know-how or equipment to properly service your particular job on a competitive basis. The trick is to find the right man or company for the job involved. It takes a bit of detective work, but it is well worth the effort. For example, when we look for die-casting plants for a specific part, instead of contacting die-casting factories direct, we call manufacturers of die-casting machines and ask them to recommend a good factory with the proper equipment. These manufacturers know the field better than you and are happy to suggest a company which is properly equipped to do the job.

So the next time you want a job done in the best way for the least money, check your Yellow Pages and contact the manufacturer of the basic machinery used in the production you need. You'll save time, money, and production headaches.

5. CONTACT THE CHAMBER OF COMMERCE IN YOUR CITY

Many times the particular manufacturer you require is difficult to locate—even in a telephone directory. If this is the case, the Chamber of Commerce has a list of all manufacturers in your area qualified to turn out your particular product, and they'll be glad to assist you.

6. TRADE PUBLICATIONS IN YOUR FIELD ARE A PRIME SOURCE OF CONTACT

These valuable publications usually carry a classified section listing manufacturers in your particular field. A letter to the editor will bring a prompt reply telling you who to contact for a specific manufacturing job.

7. WORK ON A ROYALTY BASIS

If you don't want to get into production and merchandising, turn your product over to an established company on a royalty basis. The royalty rate for a new product is usually a small percentage of the net sales and is paid to you once every three months. It is best to associate with an attorney who is well equipped to protect your interests.

8. CONTROL YOUR PRODUCTION

Many times you'll be tempted to have something manufactured out of the country because it's cheaper and you can save dollars on production. However, think twice before you let production out of your control. We know one company that came out with a beautiful line of hobby kits. Their lines was so well made they captured a major part of the market by displaying the product at a current hobby show. They took thousands of dollars in advance orders for promised fall and Christmas delivery. But to save a few dollars, they had the tooling and manufacturing completed out of the country. Due to labor trouble, shipping strikes, and inexperienced help at the manufacturing level, they couldn't make the promised deliveries. As a result, the item was never launched, and the company lost every dollar they put into the product.

Manufacturing outside the country is being done today by many American companies, but you must always run the risk of troublesome delays when you do not have control of your production.

9. FAMILIARIZE YOURSELF WITH THE VARIOUS COURSES THAT CAN BE TAKEN IN MANUFACTURING

Many times a product can be made in any one of a dozen different materials. It can be manufactured in various kinds of plastic, or it can be metal-fabricated or even made in rubber or synthetic materials. Before you decide what material to use, make a brief study of the many manufacturing processes at your disposal. Again, you'll find excellent descriptions of these processes at your local library.

As an example . . . if you intend to make your product in plastic, you have several choices, including extrusion, injection molding, blow molding, vacuum formed, or pressure molding. Each of these processes has its own advantages and disadvantages. In some cases, the initial tooling is quite expensive, but the cost per piece is much less. The same is true if you intend to manufacture your product in metal. Among many methods, you have a choice of die-casting, stamping, or metal forming. Manufacturing in rubber or plastisol, you can use the flotational molding method or the slush molding method. Acquire a brief working knowledge of these various methods of manufacture, and you'll be better equipped the next time you have a product to be produced.

10. LOOK AT ALL THE ANGLES ON YOUR PRODUCT

Are you overlooking anything? Especially the obvious? In chapter 4, I told you about a cat-food manufacturer who forgot to test his product on the ultimate consumers—cats. It seems incredible, but many such mistakes happen in business. Here's another one, which I believe is a classic:

A company I know invested over $75,000 in plastic injection tooling which manufactured a giant plastic telescope set to retail for $15. The telescope was a work of art in design and extremely well made. The company received thousands of dollars in advance orders and made shipments to all parts of the country in late summer so that jobbers would have stock on hand for the all-important Christmas season. Subsequently, a large part of these shipments was returned to the manufacturer marked "defective." The complaint? The telescopes would not function properly. It seems that the manufacturer had used a plastic lens instead of a ground glass lens, and when the units were shipped in the late summer season, the heat warped the plastic lens making the telescopes virtually useless. This simple and easily overlooked error had caused the manufacturer to lose his entire market on that product.

Another story is about a friend of mine who made a trip to Mexico and discovered he could buy live Mexican burros at a very low price. He ran an ad in a magazine stating he would ship a live burro to any point in the United States for $98, prepaid. The test ad pulled a tremendous number of orders, and he began running the offer in publications all over the country. Flying to Mexico, he set up a shipping system that would make Sears, Roebuck & Company envious. Everything was going along smoothly: Orders were pouring in, the burros were being shipped by Railway Express, and it looked like he had a real winner on his hands. But one day he received a frantic call from the Express agency asking him what they should do with all the burros piling up in Chicago. "What do you mean," my friend asked, "every burro has its address tag tied to its neck. All you have to do is ship it to the name and address written on the tag!" "We hate to tell you this, mister," they replied, "but all that's hanging on your burros' necks are frayed cords. The burros were shipped forty to a freight car, and during the ride up from Mexico, they ate each other's address tags!"

It was some time before my friend straightened out the mess, but now he sees to it that each tag is placed in a tightly closed tin can and then strapped around the burros' necks!

We, ourselves, got into a little bit of a mess when we first came out with the Ant Farm. We introduced the Ant Farm at the March Toy Show and took hundreds of orders for fall and Christmas delivery. By October 15 of that year, we had shipped well over 50,000 Ant Farms and orders were pouring in at the rate of several thousand units each day.

Then we began getting complaints . . . the ants would die a few hours after they were placed in the Ant Farm! We couldn't understand this for we had been testing the Ant Farm for the previous six months and had never experienced this difficulty. In fact, we had several Ant Farms on display in our office and the ants were thriving quite well in their new farms. Nevertheless, we couldn't deny the fact that we were getting complaints on dead ants, and we knew we were in trouble.

We called in one of the chief entomologists in the Los Angeles area and explained our problem to him, but he could not tell us why the ants would live in the Ant Farms in our office but would die as soon as they were placed in Ant Farms elsewhere.

It was now late October and we were at the height of our Christmas season. By this time we were several thousand Ant Farms behind in our shipments, but production was called to a halt until we could solve the problem. Then our consulting entomologist gave us an idea. Why not airmail an Ant Farm to ten of the leading entomologists in the United States and offer a thousand-dollar reward to the first who could tell us why the ants were dying. This we did, and within twenty-four hours we received a phone call from New York from a happy entomologist who advised us to send him the thousand dollars! When we finally learned why the ants were dying, the answer was so simple that we wondered why we hadn't guessed it ourselves.

The Ant Farm consisted of two sheets of clear plastic held together with a perimeter of four strips of outside plastic "clamps." Because these plastic "clamps" did not fit tightly around the clear plastic sheets, the girls in the factory were putting a spot of glue at the four corners of the Ant Farm. The glue being used to hold the strips in place created a chemical reaction with the plastic, which, in turn, poisoned the soil in the Ant Farm, killing the ants in contact with the soil! The display Farms in our offices had not been affected because these particular units had not been glued!

We immediately reworked the tooling, which solved the problem. But I shudder to think how close we came to losing a wonderful product simply because we didn't look at all the angles!

6 | Selling Your Products

"The successful man is one who makes hay from the grass growing under the other fellow's feet."

After you've found your product, tested it to your satisfaction, developed, and produced it—you are now about 25 percent "home." In our opinion, selling and promoting the product is the other 75 percent. If you don't believe this, walk into any factory, die-casting plant, or other manufacturing concern, and you'll see dozens of products that have reached the selling stage and stopped. There is no doubt that the product itself is important—that quality and workmanship are requisite in a good item—but without sales knowledge, you may as well throw in the sponge.

What do we do when we reach this stage? We have developed a procedure that is practically foolproof in selling a product. We've used this procedure dozens of times, and it has never failed us. Here's our step-by-step approach to selling a new product to the American public:

1. THERE ARE SEVERAL CHANNELS THROUGH WHICH WE SELL

These include selling through a jobber, direct to dealers, house-to-house organizations, direct mail to the consumer, mail order ads in magazines and newspapers, as a premium, or even as a supplement to another product already on the market. To sell to any one of these outlets, selling tools are most important, and the best is an effective and hard-selling circular.

When we're ready to hit the market with a new item, two or three artists are called in, and each one submits to us a rough layout of an 8½" × 11" circular. Each artist gives his impression of our product in the layout, and we usually end up with a final circular that is a combination of all layouts submitted.

The approved circular is then printed in one color: black on white paper. This circular will serve several purposes ... a catalog sheet for your jobbers and representatives, a mailing piece for your direct mail, a giveaway at trade shows, an information sheet to send in response to inquiries, a catalog sheet to send to an editor when he requests additional information.

2. WE REQUIRE A TOP-NOTCH PHOTOGRAPH OF THE PRODUCT

We never cut corners money-wise by making the photograph ourselves. Instead, we employ the best commercial photographer available and have him "shoot" the product. Long ago we discovered that the money paid for a good photograph is one of the best investments we can make in our promotion.

3. A NEWS RELEASE OF OUR PRODUCT IS THE NEXT IMPORTANT STEP

What is a news release? Magazines all over the country are hungry for news about products that will interest their readers. Pick up most any magazine, and you'll find illustrations of new products with accompanying copy that gives a description of the item, the price, and usually the name and address of the person or organization selling the product. A news release is free . . . the magazine does not charge you for printing it. In most cases, it is better than a paid ad, for it is located in the best position on the magazine or newspaper page. Here's the procedure:

As soon as we have a good photograph of our product, we send that photograph to a company specializing in quantity photographs. Instead of the larger 8" × 10" print, we use the 4" × 5" single weight, glossy print for two reasons: (a) No special envelope or stuffer is required, as the 4" × 5" photograph fits into a standard business envelope together with a news release and sales letter, and mail weight is less than one ounce; (b) The 4" × 5" photograph we use is much cheaper. By having four of the 4" × 5" photographs printed on each 8" × 10" sheet—we get four photos out of each 8" × 10" sheet. If we ordered four hundred 4" × 5" separate prints, the cost would be almost doubled.

While waiting for the photos to be delivered, we write a good, short description of the product, covering its best points. This will develop into our news release, so we keep it as factual as possible. You can get an indication of the type of copy we use by checking the shopping columns of most any magazine. After the news release is written and approved, it is then reproduced. In addition to the news release and photograph, a short letter, typed to the attention of the editor, is enclosed. Here is our letter and news release to the editor used for our Ant Farm.

Dear Editor:

Did you ever watch a little child hovering over an ant hill, fascinated by the scurrying lines of tiny insects?

The interest of children in all living things has prompted us to produce a new type of ant house . . . in unbreakable plastic . . . that will entertain the kids for hours.

Through the transparent walls of this unusual toy, the youngsters can see what ants do when they go underground as well as above ground. They can watch the preparation of nests . . . construction of tunnels . . . all the details of an ant's daily life.

Because we feel that the ant house should be of interest to your readers, we are enclosing a press release and glossy photo for your use.

Any space you may devote to this unusual product will be appreciated.

Sincerely,

EJC:sh

E. JOSEPH COSSMAN & COMPANY

FASCINATING ANT HOUSE $2.98

A house for ants? An ant house for kids? Yes, and mother and father have fun, too, watching the ants after they go underground, as well as above ground. See the busy worker ants, digging tunnels, carrying their loads. Watch the feeder ants storing away supplies for the rest of the colony . . . the nursemaids caring for the ant babies. An ant's entire world seen through the clear plastic walls of this fascinating house. Only $2.98 including sand, sandbar, stand. Cossman Co., P.O. Box 4480, Palm Springs, CA 92263.

Now comes the important and little-known fact regarding news releases. Ask any agency in the country where you should send your news release, and it will tell you to send it only to those magazines who may be interested in your particular product. This advice is 100 percent wrong! Under no condition should you attempt to be selective in your choice of magazines. Use a "shotgun" approach—not a "rifle" approach. If you can afford it, send your news release, photograph, and letter to the editor of *every* magazine listed in *Standard Rate & Data*. As mentioned in chapter 2, you can find the *Standard Rate & Data* in your local library or in most advertising agencies.

It is possible to send your news release to every magazine in the United States for a total cost of about $2,000. This takes in consumer magazines, trade publications, and farm magazines. This is standard practice for us when introducing a new product, and we've never failed yet to receive the equivalent of $3,000 or more in "free space" as a result of our "shotgun" approach. Surprisingly enough, a good part of the magazines which publish our releases would never be suspected of showing interest in our type of product, and conversely, magazines which should be interested in our items often do not accept our release!

On one occasion, we were stuck with several thousand burglar alarms—our first product—but were fortunate in selling the entire inventory to an American exporter who bought the item for resale to South America. Where did he hear about the burglar alarm? From a small news item appearing in the *Woman's Bowler*, a magazine with a total circulation of 1,500! He just happened to pick up his wife's copy and saw our news item. It's true . . . you never know where your business will come from.

Remember, solicit every magazine you can regardless of its format, category, or classification. You will seldom lose a penny following this advice.

4. SELECT YOUR MERCHANDISING CHANNELS

If we've turned out a newsworthy release, an interesting letter to the editor, and a professional photograph, it's almost certain that our release will be published in several magazines throughout the country. These releases will now serve a threefold purpose:

(a) In cases where the release is published by consumer magazines, such as *Elks, Redbook, Better Homes & Gardens*, you more than likely will get retail orders direct from consumers. As a rule, they will be accompanied by payment, although some orders may request C.O.D. shipment.

(b) Where the release was published by trade journals, you will receive inquiries and orders from both dealers and jobbers.

(c) Also, from trade journal releases, you will receive inquiries from representatives who would like to represent your product in their area. Quite often, you'll also get inquiries from other companies requesting the use of your product as a premium or for some other purpose.

Orders and inquiries you receive from the consumer make excellent sales ammunition when offering your product to mail order houses. Nothing speaks louder to a mail order house than proof that a product is pulling orders from a news release.

Inquiries and orders received from dealers as a result of trade journal releases are turned over to jobbers as a means of interesting the jobber outlets to handle your product. There are times, however, when you should hold all inquiries and orders received from dealers and jobbers until you've appointed a sales representative for the product in a particular territory and then turn these leads over to him.

Another excellent bonus from news releases is the acquiring of new markets opened up for the product . . . markets not necessarily anticipated by you. As an example, when we introduced our Home Sprinkler, we sent the following letter and release to every magazine editor in the country.

Dear Editor:

Since most of your readers have lawns and gardens, here's a new invention that will save many man hours (and woman hours, too) of their time.

After many months of serious research we have developed a revolutionary type of garden sprinkler. This sprinkler is now ready for national distribution, and we'll soon be conducting a national advertising campaign on this NEW product.

If you consider the HOME SPRINKLER newsworthy, we'll appreciate your giving it a write-up in your publication.

A photograph and publicity release are enclosed.

Thank you.

> Sincerely,
> SPRINKLER SYSTEM COMPANY
> E. Joseph Cossman, President

For Immediate Release

50 FOOT SPRINKLER WEIGHS 1 POUND

This double, lightweight, plastic sprinkler can spray an area more than 12 feet wide by 50 feet long at average water pressure! You can drape it over your hillside, twine it around your flower beds, shape it to any contour of your landscaping, or just lay it straight on your lawn . . . it will do a perfect sprinkling job in any position. Turn it over and it becomes a soaker! The HOME SPRINKLER will not rot or mildew, even if stored wet. The spray is so fine, it's gentle on flowers. Complete with brass connector. 20 ft. length $2.50; 50 ft. length $4.75, postpaid. HOME SPRINKLER, P.O. Box 4480, Palm Springs, CA 92263.

You'll note that it is a specific, factual description of the item, yet many editors discovered unique and practical uses for the Sprinkler which we had not thought of. For instance, the editor of a poultry magazine gave us a half-page write-up on the Sprinkler, emphasizing its practical use for air-conditioning chicken coops by placing the Sprinkler over the coops and turning on the water. Another imaginative editor of a dog magazine gave the release a half-page spread showing the Sprinkler in use for wetting down dog runways so that dust would not accumulate. Of course, we immediately began soliciting poultry ranches and dog-kennel owners as potential customers for our Sprinkler.

On another occasion, we were introducing a product called "Fix-So." It was an adhesive product used to mend clothing. The normal procedure would have been to send news releases on this clothes-mending product to a select group of magazines catering to women who sew. However, we used our shotgun approach as usual and received editorial stories on this new product from the most incredible outlets. A mortician magazine picked up the news release and gave us excellent publicity on the product. How could a funeral director use Fix-So? The editor of the mortician magazine brought out the fact that Fix-So was practically indispensable in the embalming room! It made an excellent adhesive where quick repairs had to be made on a body. A rather macabre use for a home product, but his news release resulted in several hundreds of dollars in business from funeral directors all over the country.

5. OTHER WAYS WE SELL OUR PRODUCTS

(a) *To mail order houses.* We make up a list of names and addresses of top mail order houses from ads that they run in magazines such as *House Beautiful, Better Homes & Gardens, Redbook,* and many others. Our habit is to buy the October and November issues of each of these publications each year, as any mail order house worth its salt will always have an ad in one or more of these publications at this time of year. In this way, we're able to compile a "fresh" list of 500 or more good companies each year.

When offering our product, we keep in mind that mail order houses need at least 50 percent and 10 percent off the list price of a product. This means that if our item sells for $10 retail, the mail order house cannot pay more than $4.50 for it. To encourage mail order houses to run paid advertising on our product, we offer them exclusives for any magazine they choose. And if our item is really good, they may want advertising exclusives for all magazines. A good example of this is our product, Cossman's Fly Cake. The first year we sold this item, a large mail order house took $108,000 in paid ads for newspapers and magazines. Because they put forth this effort for our product, we gave them exclusive mail order sales rights on the product for that year.

The type of letter we use to solicit mail order houses on new products follows:

THE PROOF IS IN THE PROFITS . . .

and we can point with pride to our customers who have chalked up profits with our mail order merchandise during the more than ten years we have served them!

Manufacturing mail order products is our business. As you will note from the enclosed catalog, we not only manufacture the mail order product . . . but also "manufacture" the mail order ad . . . ready for your catalog or space advertising.

And when you look over our *tested* products, please remember that:

- You get our products individually packaged in a self-mailer container, ready for your address label.
- You get "exclusive protection" on your space advertising . . . just let us know where and when.
- You get TOP discounts of 50% and 10% off the list prices.
- You get FULL freight on all orders of 100 lbs. or more . . . with immediate deliveries assured even during the busy Christmas season.

Make this year one of your best mail order years by latching onto our products. Write us today . . . tell us what products you like . . . and we'll immediately airmail to you glossy photos and ad copy for your space ads and/or catalogs.

Sincerely,

EJC/ctl

E. JOSEPH COSSMAN & COMPANY
E. Joseph Cossman, President

P.S. You may order samples at your cost price, but please include payment and save us the trouble of invoicing for this small amount. A postage-paid envelope is enclosed for your convenience. Thank you.

(b) *We offer our product to radio and television stations on a commission basis.* These outlets keep 40 percent of monies received from orders, and they send us the orders. We realize 60 percent of the monies and for that amount furnish the merchandise and ship directly to the customer. The year we put our Cowboys and Indians figurines on the market, we sold more than half a million sets at $1 a set through this method. And here is the letter we sent to all radio and television stations soliciting their advertising of our product on a commission basis:

Gentlemen:

We're selling 50 Wild West Toys for a dollar . . . Yes, all 50 Toys for a single dollar . . . and the results to date have been slightly short of terrific. Each set consists of BUCKING BRONCOS . . . HOLD-UP MEN . . . SHERIFFS . . . COWGIRLS . . . INDIAN CHIEFS . . . WIGWAMS . . . LOG CABINS . . . CHUCK WAGONS . . . COWBOYS . . . INDIANS . . . and many others . . . all beautifully colored . . . all made of strong durable plastic . . . and each toy a FULL TWO INCHES HIGH.

Each set of 50 toys comes packed in an attractive GIFT BOX . . . and included FREE . . . with each order . . . an INDIAN TEPEE and a SCENE OF WILD HORSES . . . and the whole deal COMPLETE for just one buck!

We've just started! And from three five-minute programs daily on Station WPIT here in Pittsburgh, Pennsylvania, our first four days' mail pull ran 85, 167, 243, and 377 . . . and they're STILL coming in! Bob Connelly or Bill Ewing of WPIT will verify this, and also verify the quality of the toys . . . and I know what you're thinking about other toys of last Christmas.

We can ship any number sold up to December 20th. We're the principals in this deal and shipping is made from our warehouse, here in Pittsburgh. You can thoroughly check us through D & B, or any accredited bank.

Now, we want to do a volume job and haven't time to go out and do a "wise" buying job . . . so we're asking a carefully selected group of stations to take the offer on a per inquiry basis of 40¢ NET . . . no agency discounts involved.

If you're interested . . . and this is the greatest mail puller we've ever had . . . and all orders will go out the same day received . . . then do the following!

1. Get in touch with Bob Connelly or Bill Ewing at WPIT, Pittsburgh, Pennsylvania, to verify the quality of the toys. If you want a sample (but don't lose valuable time) then we'll airmail a set to you.
2. Run the attached copy verbatim . . . no ad lib . . . no changes. If you want, we'll send you an electrical transcription.
3. Send all orders same day received direct to us via registered mail. We'll pay you direct on each week's business. Remember . . . the 40¢ per order is NET to your station . . . yes, it's small, but this is a tight deal . . . and because of this, we purposely by-passed an agency in order to give you the fullest profit possible.

Wire us if you're interested and if you want to make any changes in the suggested setup. If not, send us your best suggestion for a three-day trial of the "Cowboys and Indians" offer . . . and give us your best "knockdown" deal.

But let's go . . . this is REALLY the greatest.

Sincerely,
E. JOSEPH COSSMAN & COMPANY
E. Joseph Cossman

Ejc;sr
Encl.

P.S. WCKY of Cincinnati, Ohio, pulled a total of 3,006 mail orders on their FIRST TEN SPOTS . . . or an average of 300 ORDERS PER SPOT . . . and the Xmas season hasn't even started yet!

(c) *We appoint sales representatives throughout the country.* These men are established brokers who work on a commission basis. As a rule they sell the product to jobbers and distributors in their territory and receive anywhere from 5 to 10 percent commission for their services. They're usually paid monthly and receive commissions on all business originating from their assigned territory whether they are directly responsible for that business or not. Sales representatives are the fastest and most economical source of national distribution. To compile our list of sale representatives, we write to trade magazines specializing in the field our product fits. For example, if we're manufacturing a toy, we write to magazines like *Playthings*—and they furnish us with a current list of toy representatives. If our product is a food item, we write to food publications for broker lists.

Just one more point before we leave the sales representation field. If your product will sell to different trade categories . . . use our method of "cross-pollination." Cross-pollinating a new product in a given area is one of the most effective ways of exposing it to several merchandising channels at one time. There is no necessity for giving your product exclusively for all categories to any one trade representative. For example, when we put on representatives for our Fly Cake product, we had four separate organizations covering *each* state. One covered the dairy and agricultural field; one covered the grocery field; one covered the housewares field, and the fourth covered the industrial and commercial field. As most good representatives stay within narrow, confined channels of trade, there was very little, if any, overlapping or conflict between them. Cross-pollinating the sales potential of your product is good business, for it exposes your item to hundreds of accounts that one single representative cannot possibly cover. Illustrated here is the type of letter we use in soliciting good representation for our products in all fields:

Dear Sir:

We are looking for representation on our product, FLY CAKE, which is fully described on the enclosed brochure.

If you would be interested in representing our firm on this product, please furnish us with the following information:
1. What territory do you cover?
2. What lines do you now carry?
3. How many men in your organization?
4. How often do you cover your territory?
5. How long have you been in business?
We will appreciate your prompt reply.

Sincerely,
E. JOSEPH COSSMAN & COMPANY
E. Joseph Cossman
EjC:jb
Encl.

6. TRADE SHOWS

A trade show is one of the most effective methods of selling. We attach so much importance to this medium, we've devoted an entire chapter to a thorough exploration of this great sales potential. In that chapter you will see the step-by-step method we use for selling our products through this all-important outlet.

7. HOUSE-TO-HOUSE SALES—DIRECT TO THE CONSUMER

If your product requires demonstration, this is a great merchandising medium. You may contact house-to-house salesmen by advertising in one of two publications, *Opportunity Magazine* or *Specialty Salesman*. Next to sales representatives, house-to-house salesmen can be the second quickest distribution channel open to a new firm just getting started. In addition to books, cosmetics, greeting cards, toys, and vitamins, millions of dollars worth of housewares are sold each year through this channel. Items from gadgets to electrical appliances, from pots and pans to plastic housewares, from food supplements to shoes and clothing . . . they can all be sold through the more than 300,000 active independent salesmen and saleswomen who are constantly on the lookout for new and profitable items to add to their lines.

House-to-house-selling companies are responsible for creating the demand and consumer acceptance for many of today's most commonly retailed items, such as sewing machines, vacuum cleaners, and home food freezers. Both turnover and sales personnel are enormous. One company reports that it recruits as many as 15,000 sales people a year to maintain a selling organization of 7,000. We ourselves have never been successful in this form of merchandising.

8. DIRECT MAIL TO THE CONSUMER

Some products are best sold to the consumer by direct mail order. The mailing usually consists of a letter; a circular describing the product; a self-addressed, post-paid return envelope; and an order form. There are several excellent list brokers throughout the United States who rent out names and addresses in any category of buyer.

Generally, the names are furnished to you on multi-sticker labels and cost from $30 to $60 a thousand depending on the type of list, The vast number of categories available is surprising, and with a little imagination and ingenuity you can sell your product to the most improbable list of names.

A friend of mine had been selling mink coats by mail order ads and, lately, orders had fallen off in volume. He was searching for a new source of advertising and we told him to contact a list broker and rent lists of names and addresses of new mothers; then to send his fur coat offer to every name on that list addressed to the attention of the new *father*—not the new mother. We suggested that the letter accompanying the offer be one of congratulation, incorporating the idea that the father show his love and appreciation by presenting his wife with a new mink coat!

This direct mail promotion pulled more orders for my friend than all previous ads put together, and he is still running the promotion. This is one of the best examples we know of offbeat selling through mail order. And an interesting sidelight to this story is that when my friend ordered his mailing list of new mothers, he was offered the choice of mothers with babies one month old, two months old, three months old, all the way up to one year old! This will give you an idea of the tremendous selectivity available in good mailing lists.

You should work with a list broker for your mailing list. They don't charge anything for their advice, service, or experience. Actually, the list broker is paid his fee by the owner of the list, and not by the mailer who is renting the list.

The names and addresses of a few mailing list brokers are:

ADVANCE-FRIEDMAN DIRECT MAIL SERVICES, INC., 756 N. Maclay St., San Fernando, CA 91340 (800) 423-5898; (213) 343-2111. "MASA Member."

AMERICAN MAILING LISTS CORPORATION, 7777 Leesburg Pike, Falls Church, VA 22043 (703) 893-2340.

ASH BUSINESS LISTS, 8040 Remmet Ave., #1, Canoga Park, CA 91304 (213) 992-8010.

BELTH ASSOCIATES, INC., 971 Richmond Rd., East Meadow, NY 11554 (516) 483-3030.

BERNICE S. BUSH CO., 15052 Springdale St., Suite A, Huntingdon Beach, CA (714) 891-3344.

21st CENTURY MARKETING, 750 Zeckendorf Blvd., Garden City, NY 11530 (516) 877-1420.

CELCO (CAROL ENTERS LIST CO.), 381 Park Ave. So. #919, New York, NY 10016 (212) 684-1881.

CONSUMER'S ADVERTISING & MARKETING ASSOCIATES, INC., 403 Mercer Street, P.O. Box 930, Hightstown, NJ 08520 (609) 443-1330.

COMPILERS PLUS INC., 2 Penn Place, Pelham Manor, NY 10803 (914) 738-1520.

COMPUTER MARKETING SERVICES, A Harte-Hanks Communications, Inc., Co. 2830 Orbiter, Brea, CA 92621 (714) 996-8900.

THE COOLIDGE CO., INC., 25 W. 43rd St., New York, NY 10036 (212) 730-5678.

CONRAD DIRECT, INC., 406 Conrad Rd., Englewood, NJ 07631 (201) 567-3203; Washington DC (202) 234-6194.

DEPENDABLE LISTS, INC., 1825 "K" Street N.W., Washington, DC 20006 (202) 452-1092.

DEPENDABLE LISTS, INC., 333 N. Michigan Avenue, Chicago, IL 60601 (312) 263-3566.

DEPENDABLE LISTS, INC., 33 Irving Place, New York, NY 10003 (212) 677-6760.

DIRECT MEDIA, INC., 90 S. Ridge St., Portchester, NY 10573 (914) 937-5600; 310 Madison Ave., Room 1717, New York, NY 10017 (212) 661-7370; 3414 S. Broadway, Edmond, OK 73034 (405) 348-8651; 406 Chestnut Lane, Wayne, PA 19087 (215) 688-9130.

THE ALAN DREY CO., INC., 333 N. Michigan Ave., Chicago, IL 60601 (312) 346-7453; 600

Third Ave., New York, NY (212) 697-2160.

MARY ELIZABETH GRANGER & ASSOCIATES, INC., P.O. Box 16836, Baltimore, MD 21206 (301) 882-5588.

THE GUILD COMPANY, 171 Terrace St., Haworth, NJ 07641 (201) 387-1023; 121 Nashua Road, Bedford, NH 03102 (603) 472-8456.

LEON HENRY, INC., 455 Central Ave., Scarsdale, NY 10583 (914) 723-3176 (800) 431-2525.

INPUT-DATA; 506-61st St. STE. 410, West New York, NJ 07093 (201) 864-0032.

THE KLEID COMPANY, INC., 200 Park Ave., New York, NY 10166 (212) 599-4140.

E.J. KRANE, INC., P.O. Box 2245, Princéton, NJ 08540 (609) 896-1900.

WALTER KARL, INC., 135 Bedford Road, Armonk, NY 10504 (914) 273-3353, (212) 324-8900.

THE LIST EMPORIUM, 2000 Johnson Drive, Suite 150, Mission Woods, KS 66205 (913) 236-6830.

LIST REVIEW, INC., P.O. Box 439, Jericho, NY 11753, (516) 931-2442.

MAIL DUNN ASSOCIATES, 159 Madison Ave., New York, NY 10016 (212) 683-2032; 221 N. LaSalle, Suite 3306, Chicago, IL 60601 (312) 782-0977; 7 A Meacham Rd., Cambridge, MA 02140 (617) 491-0375.

9. AS A PREMIUM

Many times, your product will make an excellent premium for other companies. Here again, imagination can dig up offbeat uses for your product. For instance, we sold thousands of Shrunken Heads to various companies throughout the United States. They were used mostly in gag mailings to the company's accounts. The following letter shows the use one organization made of this unique product.

You are now the proud possessor of all the mortal remains of Pablo Pedro Salvatore Guchelberger. Pablo was once superintendent of a beet sugar factory.

One day one of the prize customers, a bottler of beverages, returned a shipment and cancelled all orders. Seems they discovered floc in some returned soft drinks and traced it to impurities in their beet sugar.

Pablo's board of directors took a very dim view of losing this business. They discovered that Pablo had not been using Darco activated carbon to assure the highest standards for color, odor, and purity, and promptly reported him to the company's chief head shrinker. Poor Pablo!

In their candy, baked goods, ice cream, and beverages, food processors demand neutral sweetness free from undesirable impurities of every type, and they expect the same high quality standard in every shipment. That's why so many beet sugar producers are now using Darco which costs little and requires a minimum of equipment. Regardless of beet conditions, it assures high yields of refined sugar that will meet the very highest standards for color, odor, and purity.

It's too bad that Pablo Pedro Salvatore Guchelberger didn't know these facts. Poor Pablo wasn't on our mailing list and did not receive the Darco Beet Bulletin or T.M. Rinehart's Darco Digest. If Pablo had been so informed on the benefits of Darco, he would have kept his head, and at the right hat size. He would not have wound up as the ideal gift for "the man who has everything."

DARCO SALES

On another occasion, we had finished a Christmas promotion on a set of circus toys which consisted of 41 plastic figurines retailing for $1 a set. We sold several hundred thousand sets before our promotion ended, but at the close of the promotion, we still had eighty thousand sets in stock. We offered them to a cereal company who bought our complete inventory as a self-liquidating premium. They printed an illustration of the circus set on the back of their cereal box and offered this dollar value for one box top and fifty cents. Not only did they sell the entire eighty thousand sets, but we had to manufacture several thousand *new* sets to fulfill the demand the premium offer created.

10. RESIDENT BUYERS

Many people in business do not know of this lucrative sales source. A resident buyer's job is to locate new products for his customers who are generally large department stores or chain store operations. Resident buyers are located in most large cities, and you'll find a list of them under the heading, "Resident Buyers," in your local Yellow Pages. As a rule, they will ask you to furnish them with a few hundred circulars on your product, which they will distribute to clients. By contacting a half dozen resident buyers, you have an opportunity to expose your product to department and chain stores throughout the entire country. A book listing the Resident Buyers of the United States, plus the stores they represent, may be purchased from Phelon, Sheldon and Marsar, Inc., 32 Union Square, New York, NY 10003.

11. THE YELLOW PAGES

Each year we order the Yellow Pages of the twenty-five major cities in the United States from the telephone company. This is one of the cheapest and most accurate mailing list sources you can find and one of the most inexpensive. We use these out-of-town directories for many purposes but primarily for an accurate mailing list to various categories of trade.

12. EXPORT SALES

American products are in great demand in overseas markets. If your product lends itself to a foreign market, you can develop a tremendous sales potential through this outlet. The Consular Offices in most large cities are also good sources, and many foreign governments maintain commercial attachés for the sole purpose of developing trade between their countries and ours. A commercial attaché is most helpful in giving information and getting your product established in his country. As to quantity of business from this source . . . the first year we sold Fly Cake, Australia was responsible for 10 percent of our total sales volume!

TO SUM UP

When looking for new markets for your product, don't be fenced in by restrictions of conventional trade channels. Developing a sales program just a little better or more original than your competitor makes an incredible difference in the final sales result. And don't be unduly influenced by statistics or research figures. Sometimes an inexperienced person can be more successful than an experienced businessman because he doesn't know any better and exposes his product to channels the experienced man would never consider. When you're on the lookout for new markets, depend a great deal on your own judgment, and don't be swayed by others who believe your product must stay within accepted channels.

In the business world, many so-called "proven results" are merely the opinion of one individual whose judgment may be no better, or worse, than yours. When you're presented with a set of facts or conclusions reached by self-styled experts, just remember the story of the researcher who was employed by a large advertising agency to dig up material on the lowly cricket. He placed the small creature in front of him, yelling, "Jump!" The cricket leaped about ten inches, a fact which was duly noted in the researcher's notebook. As his next test, the researcher tied down one of the cricket's front legs and again yelled, "Jump!" This time the cricket leaped only eight inches; a fact which the researcher again jotted down in his book. He then tied down another leg of the cricket, yelling, "Jump!" and noted that his subject made only four inches this time. This, too, was put down carefully in his record book, and as a final test, the researcher tied down every leg the cricket owned, and yelling, "Jump!" observed that the cricket did not move at all. The test being completed, the researcher wrote up a nine-page report on his experiment, summing up his findings with this sentence: "Crickets become progressively more deaf as you tie their legs down, and if you tie down all their legs, they can't hear at all!"

7 | Promoting Your Products

"To catch lions, you must think in terms of lions—not mice."

In this wonderful, amazing, impossible-to-saturate country, there are literally hundreds of ways to promote your product. And promote you must, if you want your product to sell. With a little ingenuity and originality on your part, you can promote your product on a national basis and get results which will equal, or even surpass, those obtained by large professional sales promotion houses.

Some time ago, we were approached by one of these large sales promotion companies. They wanted to service our account on a retainer basis and would handle all of our sales promotion and publicity for a yearly fee. Just for the fun of it, we outlined several publicity objectives on our Ant Farm and asked them to quote us a price. They came up with an annual fee of $25,000. We had already accomplished these publicity objectives on our Ant Farm for a total cost to us of less than $1,000. By using the merchandising and publicity tools at your disposal, it's amazing what you, too, can accomplish with just a few dollars and a bit of original thinking.

Here are listed some of our promotional activities which you might use as a guide:

1. YOUR LOCAL PRESS

Contact your local press for special feature stories about your products or business. They are always willing to cooperate with a local boy. In some cases, UPI and AP pick up such columns and, as a result, they appear in hundreds of papers throughout the country.

2. THE WORKING PRESS OF THE NATION

Buy *The Working Press of the Nation*, published by the National Research Bureau, Inc., 310 South Michigan Avenue, Chicago, IL. This three-volume directory is a complete listing of the newspapers, magazines, and radio stations active in the United States. It also provides the most comprehensive listing of key personnel in all communications media. Each directory volume is broken down into categories so that you can direct any promotional literature to the exact editor in any field. Say you're thinking in terms of radio and television. The radio and TV directory lists not only all major radio and television stations in the United States, but it also gives complete and detailed information on specific types of programs, such as name of program, description of program, name of master of ceremonies, and information as to whether or not guests are used.

3. TELEVISION GIVEAWAYS

Many TV programs are constantly on the lookout for free merchandise as giveaways on their programs. Most audience-participation shows fall in this category. In return for free merchandise from you, they will give your product a short commercial at no charge. As a rule, it is a good idea to write these brief commercials yourself and send them along with your letter. Here's a typical approach letter and a list of advertising commercials which accompanied it. Also illustrated is a letter we sent to our representatives as a follow up on the television plugs.

Dear Program Director:

How would you like to give away, FREE, without any cost or obligation, the smallest pets in the world? We're inviting you to use them on any shows of your choice.

These pets are California Red Harvester Ants . . . living and working in their own California Ant Farm.

And What Is an Ant Farm?

It is a large, clear, see-through, unbreakable plastic case, containing a barn, silo, windmill, trees, house, white sandy soil, and of course—live ants!

The Ant Farm is a nationally accepted item. It recently received a front-page feature in the *Wall Street Journal* and soon will have a big "story" spread in a national magazine.

What makes Ant Farms so fascinating is that they are a living replica of the human race. There are worker ants, soldier ants, and lazy ants. They all talk and laugh together, have hospitals, and even make war. It will be a wonderful giveaway item for you to use on children's programs and for Santa Claus show promotions coming up later this fall.

While it is used primarily by children, including classrooms in schools, we have sold a surprisingly large percent to adults for their own entertainment . . . and even to hospitals for therapy uses. At any rate, I believe you'll discover that they can also be given away on adult shows as a "laugh" gift.

Just write and let us know!

1. On what show you would like to give away the Ant Farms.
2. Date and time.
3. The monthly quantity of Ant Farms you'll need.

We will ship them directly to you at no charge and at no obligation!

We are not asking you to give us a commercial, except of course, to call them by their name, COSSMAN ANT FARMS, and mention that they are unbreakable:

> ". . . and we're giving you the smallest pets in the world; a genuine, unbreakable COSSMAN ANT FARM complete with a colony of live ants . . ."

As this is a fascinating product, you may get some inquiries over your switchboard about them. It would be a good idea to give the name of one of the retail stores where they are available. When things get rolling, we will give you the names of some of these retail outlets.

Sincerely,
E. JOSEPH COSSMAN & COMPANY
E. Joseph Cossman, President

EJC:jb
Encl.

P.S. Remember . . . you're under no financial obligation for Ant Farm giveaways. They are FREE to you. Just write and let us know what your schedule is and how many you wish.

Suggested Copy for Ant Farm Giveaways
. . . and here are the world's smallest living pets, California Red Harvester Ants living and working in their very own *escape-proof*, *see-thru*, COSSMAN ANT FARMS. These COSSMAN ANT FARMS *are available now at* ....store here in town.

. . . and we have a very unusual gift for you, an authentic *escape-proof, see-thru,* COSSMAN ANT FARM *complete with a colony of California Ants. For their size, these pets lift enormous amounts of weight. More than any other living creature, including the elephant! They dig tunnels, build bridges, move mountains, communicate, work, and play, right in the* COSSMAN ANT FARM *where you can see them!* COSSMAN ANT FARMS *can be found at* . . . . *store.*

. . . *and we're going to give you a miniature living TV set! A genuine escape-proof* COSSMAN ANT FARM *complete with a supply of California Red Harvester Ants! These pets will entertain you and your family for hours on end. They dig tunnels, build bridges, store food, move mountains! If you watch them closely, you'll notice each ant has an individual personality. There is a boss ant, lazy ants, worker ants, and even busybodies!* COSSMAN ANT FARMS *can be found at* . . . . *store.*

. . . *I don't know if there are any Republicans watching the show right now, but if so, they'll be glad to know we are giving away some Democrats! These Democrats are Ants . . . not the relative variety, but genuine California Red Harvester Ants working in their own escape-proof, see-thru,* COSSMAN ANT FARM. *They are the nation's newest hobby craze for kids and adults alike . . . and they're going to perform for you hours at a time . . . because they live, work, and play just like the human race! That's a* COSSMAN ANT FARM *from* . . . . *store.*

Letter to Our Representatives

HERE'S GOOD NEWS
ON THE ANT FARM!

This fall, Ant Farms are going to have the biggest, nationwide promotional publicity campaign ever held for any type of item on the market . . . and it is all FREE TO YOU!

This promotion is designed to presell Ant Farms . . . first to the retailers and then to the public. Here is the idea:

1. We are offering the Ant Farm to TV and radio stations in every major city in the country with many secondary markets covered as well.
2. The Ant Farm will appear on children's shows as free giveaways and also as entertainment prizes on adult participation shows.

The campaign is now underway, and we are asking each TV station to give a "credit" to a local retail store where the Ant Farms can be purchased. The announcement will go something like this:

"... and here are the world's smallest living pets, California Red Harvester Ants, living and working in their unbreakable, clear, see-thru Cossman Ant Farm. They are available here in town at . . . . *store* . . ."

This campaign is going to make the whole country "Cossman Ant Farm Conscious" and will build up sales for all of your accounts. As soon as possible, send us the name or names of your favorite retailers that you want to receive this free publicity plug. The name and addresses are all we need . . . we'll do the rest!

We will try and let you know show times and dates so that you can monitor the programs. In the meantime, the announcements will go ahead without any local tie-in until we hear from you . . . so hurry and get those names to us, as the campaign is starting now.
EJC:jb   E. JOSEPH COSSMAN & COMPANY

4. GET ON TELEVISION SHOWS WITH YOUR PRODUCT

Several TV shows are eager to present interesting, non-professional personalities on their programs. You might just fill the bill. Many of these shows, which are national network programs, are worth thousands of dollars in free publicity to you and your product.

Some time ago, I appeared on the Merv Griffin show. I had a great time, and the Ant Farm got the equivalent of over $60,000 worth of free time.

Armed with a Spud Gun, I appeared on Bill Leonard's "Eye on New York" show, which was carried by the CBS network to 140 or more stations from coast to coast. This adventure gave the Spud Gun over $50,000 worth of television advertising—for free. On behalf of our Home Sprinkler, I appeared as a guest on dozens of gardening programs.

5. MAKE A VIDEOTAPE OF YOUR TELEVISION APPEARANCE

It would cost several thousand dollars to make a film about your product. However, if you have an opportunity to appear as a guest on a television show, you can order a videotape of the show for as little as $200. This tape can be useful to you in many ways:

1. You can have reprints made and send them to your representatives who, in turn, may be able to get a re-run of the tape on a local television program in their area.

2. You can also use this tape at trade shows. How? Rent a videotape player in the city where the show is being held and play this videotape in a continuous showing at your booth. One thing to remember, however: If any other person or persons appear in the film, you must obtain a release from them before you make commercial use of it.

6. GIVE YOUR PRODUCT A "TWIST"

When we discovered the Shrunken Head, we knew we had a potential blockbuster on our hands. But how do you go about selling a shrunken head? We decided to use a light and humorous touch in all of our promotions, but just how does one treat a shrunken head with lightness and humor? First, we sent this letter to novelty dealers.

WHAT??? SHRUNKEN HEADS???

Yes . . . SHRUNKEN HEADS . . . But please read on . . .

These Shrunken Heads were introduced to the public for the FIRST TIME at the recent Los Angeles County Fair . . . and they created a real sensation! In fact . . . they sold so fast that we were forced to take a bigger booth after the first day . . . people just kept crowding and jamming to get to our booth.

And surprising as it seems . . . no selling efforts were made . . . We merely hung a few heads from the top rail of our booth with a small sign giving the price of $3.95. Yet we took in $632 the very first day of the Fair . . . a sales record that wasn't equalled by ANY two other exhibitors in our area! We know . . . for we were the talk of the show.

Actually . . . we couldn't believe our success . . . imagine selling more merchandise than any two other exhibitors . . . with no more sales effort than hanging a few heads from our booth! So we tested further . . .

The next day we took 36 heads to a local drugstore . . . had the owner hang a few by his cash register . . . and he was COMPLETELY sold out of the three dozen by the next morning . . . with orders taken for 9 more!

To our further amazement, the same thing happened at the station where we buy our gasoline. A few heads hung in the gas station window moved more than two dozen overnight . . . each at $3.95 per head.

What we're trying to say is . . . here's one of those rare items that sell and sell . . . wherever it can be seen by the public. At first we sold them retail for $3.98, but when we had to make more molds to meet the demand, our production costs dropped substantially.

We now suggest a retail of $2.98 each . . . your cost is $21.60 per dozen with terms of 2/10/30 to rated accounts. They're packed three dozen heads to the box. Order today from your local jobber . . . or if he can't supply you, order direct from us. We can make immediate deliveries.

EJC/ea
Sincerely,
E. JOSEPH COSSMAN AND COMPANY

This letter was followed up by several cartoon postcards similar to the one pictured below.

CAN YOU JUST <u>SHRINK</u> HER MOUTH?

We had still another inspiration: Every shipment of shrunken heads that left our warehouse had a large label boldly plastered on the outside of the carton. This label warned, "FRAGILE, SHRUNKEN HEADS, HANDLE WITH CARE!" Incidentally, this label brought us letters from postmasters all over the country, and also served to bring the unique item to the attention of the thousands of people who saw our shipments en route. Still developing this levity-themed promotion, we publicized an article, "How to Shrink a Head."

Here is another effective letter which we sent to gasoline stations all over the country accompanied by a letter of testimony. It was an offbeat approach which resulted in a substantial amount of business and made the Shrunken Head as important to the teenage driver as his license.

GENTLEMEN . . . WE MANUFACTURE SHRUNKEN HEADS!

How does this concern you? Well . . . read the attached letter and see what one small gas station did with this amazing product!

This station bought 163 heads at $1.80 each . . . sold them all in two weeks at $2.98 retail . . . and made a profit of $192.34 for the 14 days . . . all on one item!

Want more proof of success? The enclosed form letter and circular were mailed to 3,000 independent gas stations. Two hundred four sent in a sample order for one dozen or more . . . but best of all . . . REPEAT ORDERS came in a few weeks later.

And this was a "first time" mailing to a list of 3,000 gas stations we picked at random from different telephone directories throughout the country . . . not regular and steady customers of ours, mind you, but customers we had NEVER contacted before with any product!

As our circular says, we really don't know why most people want a Shrunken Head, but it seems that every other car in Los Angeles has one of our heads dangling from the rearview mirror . . . and the fad is spreading fast!

The Shrunken Heads retail for $2.98 . . . your cost is 50% and 10% off list of $1.35 each, individually gift-wrapped and boxed 36 to the shipping carton. We pay freight on orders of two gross or more.

Since you have several stations under your jurisdiction, here is a perfect money-maker for you AND your accounts. Believe us, the average gas station can pay its monthly rent with the profits possible on this unique item.

Send us your order today . . . and your station will be one of the first to offer these heads to your accounts.
An order envelope is enclosed for your quick convenience.

Sincerely,
E. JOSEPH COSSMAN & COMPANY
E. Joseph Cossman, President

EJC/ss
Encl.

E. JOSEPH COSSMAN AND COMPANY

Dear Sir:

As soon as possible, please send me 72 more Shrunken Heads. I own the Union Oil Gas Station at the corner of Orange Drive and Sunset Blvd. Two weeks ago, I bought three dozen Shrunken Heads from your company and practically sold out of them the first two days.

I reordered immediately, and my station has sold 163 heads to date.

I thought you would like to have this information for your records. This is one of the fastest selling items we have ever handled!

Sincerely,

H. Doerfle

7. MAKE YOUR REPRESENTATIVES WORK

Always remember that your product is just one of many carried by your various sales representatives. Very few of them will exert the additional effort needed to make your product stand out from the other items they are carrying. In the final analysis, it's the energy and promotion you put into your product that will bring orders from a territory. Although most carefully chosen sales representatives know how to do their job, we try to put our own promotional "muscle" into a campaign. As soon as we appoint a sales representative for a territory, we immediately request and receive from him a list of all accounts in his territory. We then barrage these accounts with direct mail pieces at least once a month. These direct mail efforts bring in more than 60 percent of the business from an average territory. Most of this business would not normally be received if we depended entirely on the representative.

8. OFFER JOBBERS AN INCENTIVE

If a product is to sell, it must be displayed where it can be seen. A good promotion insures this by giving something to the jobber, the jobber salesman, or the dealer who puts your product out in front where the customer can see it. Nothing pleases a jobber, a jobber salesman, or a dealer more than good hard cash. The trick is not to offer them money, but to make them earn it for services rendered.

Many manufacturers spend thousands of dollars in an effort to get their products placed in choice locations in the store. They offer valuable prizes, cash incentives, and other rewards, but if the offer is not interesting to the people involved, it will not be successful.

We developed the following plan to get our merchandise displayed in prominent locations in stores. The plan was so successful in stores all over the country that we have used it for product after product. Basically, it offers the dealer a certain amount of free goods in return for a simple snapshot of the display of the product in the dealer's store. Our psychology is that if the dealer is going to take the picture, he will, as a matter of pride, set up the display of our product in a prominent location and certainly leave it there for several days after the picture is taken. Store checks by our representatives throughout the country have proved our theory correct. Storekeepers everywhere gave us top exposure on our Ant Farms, and we were soon flooded with thousands of photographs from dealers. To keep the jobber happy in his promotion, we gave him the full jobber commission on free merchandise we shipped to the dealer. We later convinced the jobber to turn his commission over to his jobber salesman and everybody was happy.

Letter to the Jobbers

A LOVE LETTER TO

A WIDE-AWAKE JOBBER!

How would you like to make your full 25% profit on orders you don't stock, ship, or bill?

HERE'S ALL YOU DO

1. Give circulars like the enclosed to *all* of your retail accounts . . . we'll furnish free of charge as many as you need with your name and address shown as the jobber.

2. When *any* of your accounts send us a snapshot of his Ant Farm display, we send directly to that account, FREE and POSTPAID, 6 Ant Farms . . . a true and honest $18.00 retail value!

3. At the same time, we airmail a credit to you for $2.70 to cover YOUR 25% PROFIT on the free goods.

● The retailer loves you for giving him a chance to pick up an easy $18.00 with no strings attached.

● You love us because we know from past experience that if the Ant Farm is displayed, it will sell! And you're sure to come back to us for repeat after repeat order from now till Christmas . . . you'll have to . . . your dealers will demand it!

To get your share of all this love, send in the enclosed order card today. Be sure to print your name and address exactly as you'd like it to appear on the circulars.

HURRY NOW!

E. JOSEPH COSSMAN & COMPANY
"The Ant Farm People"

EJC:jb

P.S. Send us a list of your salesmen and we'll write to each and everyone . . . to tell them about this $18.00 in FREE GOODS. We'll also send them a Sales Kit . . . including a Live Ant Farm, too!

9. TAKE ADVANTAGE OF ALL PUBLICITY BREAKS

You will receive many unsolicited letters of testimony from satisfied jobbers. Get written permission from the jobber and make copies of the letter to send to other jobbers as a promotional piece. If a photograph is involved, have the person sign the following model release.

Model Release

I hereby authorize and give full consent to ....
.... to copyright, publish, and display all photographs taken by him in which I, ...
...., appear. It is further agreed that he may use, or cause to be used, my photographs for any and all exhibitions, public displays, publications, commercial art, and advertising purposes, without limitation or reservation or any compensation other than that receipt of which is hereby acknowledged.
Signed:

....

Address:

....

Witnessed:

....

....

Once in a while other publicity breaks come your way which make natural promotional programs. Some time ago, we received a phone call from the producer of "Queen for a Day." He wanted one of our Ant Farms as a premium gift. An Ant Farm had been requested by the winning candidate on that day. We not only gave him the Ant Farm but took full advantage of this break by putting out the following letter to all of our key jobbers.

THIS IS A TRUE STORY!

What is one of the most wanted toy gifts for Christmas giving and receiving?

Dolls? Wagons? Guns? Space Items? Science Kits?

We have a national television program that originates in Hollywood, California. It's called "Queen for a Day." Five or six women are called to the stage and are asked, "What do you want more than anything else in the world?" The audience then votes for the woman who has made the most appealing, most unique, or most popular request. The winner is given her wish . . . and becomes the

"Queen" for that day. She's chauffeured around in a gold Cadillac, wined and dined, and is generally made to feel like royalty for twenty-four hours.

Imagine our surprise when that gold Cadillac swung into our driveway, and the "Queen" came into our office with her escorts. Seems that her request was for . . .
"an Ant Farm for the children."

It isn't strange that she requested an Ant Farm. Two million people can't be wrong and that's how many Farms have been sold to date. What got us was the fact that the TV audience (at least 500 people) voted this request as the winner for the day! Proof positive of the Ant Farm's appeal!

Yes . . . what is one of the most wanted Christmas toy gifts today? Can it be the Ant Farm? At least a complete TV audience thought so!

Have you checked your stock lately? An order card is enclosed!

Sincerely,
E. JOSEPH COSSMAN & COMPANY

EJC:jb

P.S. The Queen's request? We gave her a gold-plated GIANT ANT FARM with a supply of our most intelligent ants!!!

Promotion can sometimes be so successful that the waves of publicity roll you in the sand. We once received an order for one of our Ant Farms from the White House. We quickly called in the local papers and planted a story on the incident. We then had the letter reproduced and proudly sent it to our representatives to show to their accounts. We had the letter framed and hung in a place of honor in our office. Two months later we received a second letter from Washington, DC. This one asked in firm language why they never received their Ant Farm. In our hustle-bustle to get publicity out on the important order, we forgot to ship the merchandise!

10. BE VERSATILE

Fight against stereotyped thinking. In addition to selling your item to obviously normal channels, try to think of offbeat markets. Throughout our business history, we have successfully sold all kinds of products and have cultivated all kinds of marketing channels. To quote a few:

1. We sold about two million Home Sprinklers. The usual chan-

nels were nurseries and garden-supply houses. Most of our sales, however, were made through grocery supermarkets.

2. We sold thousands of Shrunken Heads to the obvious novelty and gag shops, but the majority of our sales were to auto-accessory stores. Teen-age motorists bought them to hang from their rearview mirrors!

3. Our Ant Farm moves by the tens of thousands to toy and hobby outlets, yet we developed a very lucrative market through schools and hospitals.

4. Radio and television mail-order sales sold over three hundred thousand toy train sets for us.

5. Over a quarter of a million circus sets were sold as a box-top premium.

Yes, many times the most "un-obvious" market can develop into your biggest outlet. Ergo, keep your thinking daisy-fresh!

11. TAKE ADVANTAGE OF THE PRODUCT'S UNIQUENESS

To supply the daily in-season demand for our Ant Farm, we buy about a million live ants a week. We pay a penny-an-ant, and if you figure that out, that's a weekly "ante" of $10,000! More than 35 persons devote themselves to our ant-hunting expeditions. To take full advantage of the news value in this unique product, we are constantly mailing out publicity releases on the Ant Farm. These releases result in numerous feature stories in newspapers and magazines.

12. SWAP YOUR CUSTOMERS WITH THOSE OF OTHER MANUFACTURERS

Every company has a list of prize accounts which can move large quantities of merchandise. Many times we have literally swapped the names and addresses of some of our top accounts for the names and addresses of top customers of other manufacturers with non-conflicting lines. Here is a letter we used with great success in accumulating other customer lists.

Dear Fellow Exhibitor:

We manufacture Shrunken Heads, and we exhibited them at the recent AAMA Show in New York City. As you know, these Shrunken Heads were the talk of the show, and we did a tremendous volume of business during the four days.

Prior to this show, however, our only contact with trade was through our direct mail efforts. When you consider that we sold more than 300,000 heads during December and January . . . all through direct mail . . . then you realize that we are contacting the right people.

During the past few years, we have built up our own private mailing list of approximately 15,000 of the top automobile accessory jobbers in the U.S.A., and our direct mail to these people has brought in this tremendous amount of business to us.

The thought struck us that you might be interested in exchanging your list of accounts with ours. Since your product is noncompetitive with ours, we believe it would be mutually profitable. What do you think?

> Sincerely,
> E. JOSEPH COSSMAN & CO.
> E. Joseph Cossman, President

EJC:ss

8 | Ten Secret Rules of Mail Order Success

"Training means learning the rules. Experience means learning the exceptions."

Everyone in business has certain guideposts or rules he follows. We are no different. Our rules developed as a result of our diversified activities. We've been using them from the beginning of our business and find ourselves practicing them even today. As we look back on our many years of successful mail order promotions, we realize that the ten rules I'm now setting forth have been, to a large extent, responsible for our success in business. Here they are:

1. EXPOSE YOURSELF

Most of the money we made did not come from ventures that we originally started but from opportunities that came about as a result of our original ventures. As an example, one of our most lucrative products came into existence because we had exposed ourselves to an entirely different item.

A few years ago, I was in New York having lunch with a couple of business friends. One of them dropped a chance remark that had all the possibilities of a good mail order promotion. It seemed that a large art foundation in the United States wanted to bring art to the masses. The time was 1937 and people were just coming out of the

Depression. The art foundation figured the time was ripe to introduce a complete art course to the public. They voted a million dollars for the project, selected a committee of leading art critics, and had them choose forty-eight of the greatest paintings of all time, including works by Michelangelo, van Gogh, Renoir. The art foundation then spent thousands of dollars having these paintings photographed in their true colors. Since the original paintings were located in many parts of the world, you can well imagine the expense involved getting these photographs made.

They then selected the finest craftsmen in Europe and had printing plates made for the project. The project consisted of 60,000 printed sets, each set containing the complete forty-eight paintings.

What excited me was the fact that nothing had ever been done with these 3 million prints! They had been stored in a warehouse in Brooklyn in their original cartons, and for some unknown reason the prints had never been merchandised. I immediately took a cab to the Brooklyn warehouse and examined a set of the paintings. They were beautiful reproductions and still held their original colors, even after being stored for more than twenty years.

Tracking down the owner of the prints and negotiating a deal with him, I took an option on all 3 million prints at a cost to me of 4¢ a print. I flew back to Los Angeles with 500 sets of the paintings.

I called in my printer and showed him one set. He told me that the paper alone was today worth more than 15¢ a sheet. I called in two art critics and had them look at the paintings. They told me they had never seen such true fidelity in color printing and that some of the prints had as many as ten different imprinted colors. I then went shopping in retail art stores, and where I could find comparable prints in quality, I discovered that they were selling for two to three dollars a print. Then I really got excited!

Making up an attractive circular describing the prints, we put out a direct mail campaign to the consumer. It flopped! Not the least bit discouraged, we then sent a direct mail campaign to companies throughout the United States offering the prints as a giveaway premium. This also flopped! We ran a few test ads in newspapers and magazines offering the prints for $10 a set. This, too, flopped!

To shorten a sad tale, about $5,000 and six months later, I still had the prints. Of course, many times I came close to selling the entire lot. For instance, at that time color television was just coming into its own, and I had one of the largest television manufacturers ready to buy the 3 million prints at 10¢ each, or $4.80 for the set. The company had a promotion completely mapped out whereby their eight thousand dealers from coast to coast would each take six sets of the prints and offer them to the first six people who walked in to see their new color television sets. Well, color TV did not catch on that year, and the promotion never materialized!

One valid offer did come my way. I could have sold 60,000 units of one print. A motion picture depicting the life of Vincent van Gogh had just been released, and the studio wanted the 60,000 van Gogh prints for their promotion. But my option to buy covered all 3 million prints. To accept the studio's offer would mean tying up more than $100,000, and my recent experiences in "carrying art to the masses" left me with no inclination to gamble!

Nevertheless, I still had faith in those prints, and as a last resort, I took a booth at the Pomona County Fair. This is one of the largest county fairs in the United States, and it runs for seventeen days with more than 3 million people attending. My plan was to sell the prints for 50¢ each, direct to the consumer at the fair. If it worked out, I would then sell the prints in fairs throughout the country.

Renting one of the best locations at the fair, I decorated my booth like the interior of an art gallery, framing forty-eight prints and hanging them throughout the booth. It was probably one of the most beautiful booths at the show.

While I was decorating my booth, I noticed the fellow in the booth next to me hanging "shrunken heads" all over his walls. Their grotesque faces were made of black rubber, the lips were sewn together with heavy cord, and each head was covered with long silky "hair" made of black nylon. I couldn't imagine anyone wanting a shrunken head, especially at $3.98 each! Frankly, I felt sorry for my neighbor, for it looked like he had put money into a bad proposition.

Well, two hours after the fair opened, you couldn't get near my booth. People milled and pushed in front of it, and this crowd continued for most of the day. The only trouble was that all of these people were an overflow from the booth next door to me. All day long I watched my neighbor sell shrunken heads at $3.98 each, while nary a customer came over to buy one of my paintings for 50¢ each. The fair lasted seventeen days. I took in $14.50, and my neighbor took in over $5,000! After the fair was over, I engaged him in conversation and discovered that he made the heads in his garage. I negotiated a deal with him, took over the product, and sold more than 1.5 million shrunken heads that year.

If I hadn't exposed myself to the paintings, I would never have run into the shrunken heads. Eventually, we sold all of the prints to savings & loan associations, who used them as premiums. Remember this rule—expose yourself!

2. DON'T RELY ON THE OPINIONS OF OTHERS

People will not give you an honest and frank opinion of a product, a plan, or a promotion. Not because they wish to be misleading—only because it's human nature to disguise a true feeling and strive to be either conservative or enthusiastic.

To illustrate: right after World War II, before we moved to California from Pennsylvania, there was a series of rape cases throughout the city of Pittsburgh. In two months' time several women had been molested in their homes and a few babysitters had been attacked. Studying the situation, we believed an inexpensive burglar alarm would make an excellent item to sell at the time. We checked hardware stores in the city and discovered that the cheapest burglar alarm was a complex affair selling for over a hundred dollars.

We hired an engineer and had him design a system that could be sold for $1.98 and would work with an ordinary flashlight battery. Making up a hand model, we called it "Alert Alarm," and took it around to more than five hundred private homes in the Pittsburgh area for a "consumer" test. Almost everyone we spoke to told us the item was definitely needed and that they would buy it as soon as it came on the market. Since one "Alert Alarm" was needed for each door and window, evey home would require at least a dozen or more alarms to keep it burglar-proof. Based on the wonderful comments we received from consumers interviewed, we financed tooling to the tune of $6,000 and made ten thousand complete units. We were in for the shock of our life, because when we put the item on the market, the only people who bought the alarm were those who had been molested within the past week!

It was a costly lesson, but we learned one thing: Do not put too much faith in the opinion of others. Not until they actually plunk their dollar down on the counter to buy your product do you know their *real* opinion. Fortunately, we were able to sell the ten thousand units for export to South America, but we didn't move more than one hundred alarms in the American market.

3. BE PERSEVERING. KEEP DIGGING!

This is one of the most important rules in mail order. I've seen people within inches of success suddenly quit. When I arrived in New York and found no soap, my first inclination was to turn around and go home. It was only by digging and digging for a soap supplier that I was able to turn failure into success.

4. BE HONEST

This may sound pompous, but the world is smaller than you think. Embarrassing exposure awaits the businessman involved in shady affairs. On the other hand, if you build a reputation for honesty, people freely come to you with their ideas, for they have no fear of your intentions. We have hundreds of products offered to us every year because people know we'll give them a fair and honest deal.

5. DON'T GET EMOTIONAL ABOUT YOUR PRODUCT

I have seen many people lose thousands of dollars because they fell in love with a product and allowed emotion to sway their clear judgment. A case in point is a good friend of mine who has sunk thousands of dollars into model train dies simply because he likes model trains. He's been doing this for the past ten years and hasn't sold enough to date to recoup any part of his original investment. Yet, he continues to pour money into new tooling because his emotional feeling for his hobby sways his common sense. If you do something successful, let your ego be satisfied, but don't do things merely to satisfy your ego!

6. KEEP GOOD RECORDS

Keep your reds and blacks on their proper sides of the ledger. Mail order money can be most tempting . . . in many cases, you get it in advance before you ship the merchandise, and it is easy to forget that a part of the money must be used to pay for the advertising, the merchandise, and other expenses before you can call the balance your own.

7. BE ENTHUSIASTIC

If you don't effervesce, you're just plain water. Being enthused with your work and looking on the optimistic side of your daily activities, you subconsciously prepare a climate conducive to progressive and successful thinking. Enthusiasm is a habit and easy to develop.

You might want to try a little trick I learned some time ago. When I awake in the morning, I lie in bed for five or ten minutes and think of the workday ahead with optimism. Of course, none of us always wakes up on the right side of the bed, and there is an occasional morning when I find myself grouchy and grumpy. However, this mood will quickly pass if you make a mental effort to appear happy. Difficult as it seems, whistle or hum a song upon arising even if it is against your nature at that time to do so.

I learned this trick on my very first job. Before World War II, I worked at the Singer Sewing Machine Company selling sewing machines door to door. Although our workday started at 9:00 A.M. each morning, we had to report to the office thirty minutes earlier and sing songs for the half hour. This thirty-minute activity seemed rather silly to me at first, but it was surprising how quickly it put everyone in a happy and enthusiastic frame of mind.

8. LOOK AT YOUR PRODUCT WITH "NEW" EYES

At one time, we ventured into the mail order jewelry field. Selling gemstone necklaces by mail, we quickly realized the line was not for us. That year, at the end of the Christmas season, we found ourselves "stuck" with 5,000 necklaces, each necklace containing seven "gem" stones. It was the year of the "Bridey Murphy case"—a fantastic story about hypnotism and reincarnation that broke in newspapers all over the country. Books on the subject of hypnotism couldn't be kept on booksellers' shelves, and being curious about everything, I enrolled in a hypnotism course just to see for myself what it was all about. My instructor told me that the first thing needed to induce a hypnotic state was a "point of fixation."

I suddenly realized that I had 35,000 "points of fixation" stored away in my warehouse, since each "gem" stone could be classified as a hypnotic stone! I took my teacher down to the recording studio and had him make a recording on self-hypnosis. All during the recording, he referred to the hypnotic stone. We made up a mail order package consisting of the hypnotic course on a long-playing twelve inch record, the hypnotic stone (which was, of course, our "gem" stone!), and a book of instructions on hypnosis.

Simply by looking at 5,000 useless necklaces with new eyes, a brand new, salable idea emerged, and to date we have sold and shipped well over 100,000.

Another case in point is our Ant Farm. We learned that the U.S. Science Building at the Seattle World's Fair had a giant ant house on display large enough for children to walk through and observe the ants in action. I flew up to the fair and made arrangements to have our Ant Farm listed as an official World's Fair souvenir. However, we went a step further. Our regular Ant Farm consisted of a panoramic dimensional scene with farm house, barn, and silo. We took this farm scene out of the Ant Farm and replaced it with three landmarks of the Seattle World's Fair . . . the U.S. Science Building, the Monorail, and the Space Needle. Now the ants literally walked out of the U.S. Science Building, crawled over the Monorail, and climbed up the Space Needle! This gave us an entirely different product to promote and we introduced the "Ant Fair" to a brand new set of customers.

9. PUT IT IN WRITING

Misunderstandings are created and fortunes are lost because agreements hurriedly reached by two people are not reduced to writing. A dollar spent on a legal document today may be worth thousands of dollars tomorrow. Remember, the best memory in the world is a signed contract.

Someone once said, "A man who acts as his own lawyer has a fool for a client," and this certainly holds true when you are making a contract in business. If you insist on wording your own agreement or contract, at least have your attorney check it over before you sign it. Many times the *addition or omission of a single word* can change the entire concept of the agreement. Also remember that all contracts must have the following elements in them to make them valid.

1. There must be an offer and an acceptance with a definite agreement between the parties. In other words, one party must make a clear offer, and the other party must accept it.

2. Both parties must be legally competent to enter into the contract. This excludes people under the legal age, insane persons, and drunkards.

3. There must be a consideration involved. A consideration is something of benefit to the person making a promise or something of detriment to the person to whom the promise is made. It can be the price, motive, or matter inducing the contract as long as it is something of value in the eyes of the law. However, the value of the consideration given to support the promise is generally immaterial.

4. The subject matter of the contract must be legal. Gambling agreements, for example, are generally held to be illegal, and in some states, any contract entered into on a Sunday is illegal.

And remember one more thing . . . the contract as such does not have to be a formal document. A contract can be made orally, by letter, or by other informal agreement, and these contracts are just as binding upon the involved parties as if they covered a formal document of many printed pages that was duly signed and executed before a notary. As long as a contract or agreement has the four elements mentioned above, it can be considered a legal and binding arrangement between two parties.

10. BE CURIOUS

Curiosity may have killed the cat, but it's a healthy trait for a mail order man. Always keep your eye open for new ideas, new products, and new trends.

A few years ago I started on a fishing binge, and being a clumsy fisherman I always had trouble baiting the hook. The bait would splatter, or fall off the hook, or be stolen by the fish. It continually annoyed me. For months I thought about the problem. I examined many lures on the market, but they were all static and none gave the action of live bait. However, my curiosity wasn't satisfied, and I made it a point to keep looking for an answer to the problem.

Then a few months later I heard about a patented application for a toy submarine. A tablespoon of baking powder would keep the submarine "swimming" through the water for a half hour or more. I contacted the inventor and asked if he could use the same application on a fishing lure. He liked the idea and replied, "Sure, it's just a matter of a change in design." I told him to make a prototype at our expense, and we'd talk after I saw the model. When the model was ready, we tested it in water and the lure's performance exceeded my expectations. It "swam," it dived, it surfaced . . . at last the "lazy man's bait" had been invented. I signed the inventor to a 5 percent royalty arrangement and began marketing the "Swim-N-Lure."

Our first test ads proved there were many fishermen like me in the country, for although the ads ran in the middle of winter, they paid out handsomely, and we sold close to 100,000 units the first six months.

This sales volume necessitated our ordering baking powder in large quantities. In fact, we ordered over ten tons of baking powder the first three months. Incidentally, an amusing incident developed from our baking powder orders. We bought the product from an Eastern concern, and they apparently showed our orders to their advertising agency. The agency got excited when they saw this large volume of business in such a short time period and came to the conclusion that home baking was enjoying a revival on the West Coast! They planned an extensive advertising campaign for the Los Angeles area with home baking as the central theme but, fortunately, before breaking with the campaign, they sent an account executive to Los Angeles to interview us—the people buying all this baking powder! The account executive walked into my office one day, showed me the campaign layout, and wanted to know how we used our baking powder. I stated simply that we packaged the baking powder in plastic bottles and sold it with our Swim-N-Lure. He replied, coldly, "If I'd wanted a funny answer, I would have asked a funny question!" It took quite a while to convince him that I wasn't joking, and that ended the plans for the home baking campaign!

This last rule—BE CURIOUS—is one of the most important rules we have listed. Curiosity turned a toy submarine into a swimming lure and gave us another mail order winner.

9 | How to Get the Most from Trade Shows

"Not doing more than the average is what keeps the average down."

There is far more opportunity in this world than there is ability, and the opportunities wasted at trade shows prove this saying to be true. I've devoted this entire chapter to trade shows, for the advantages they presented to us have been most important in developing our business. The direct mail order practices which have proven successful in other facets of our business have been applied to the trade show, and with great success.

Participating in a trade show is a bit more complicated than merely putting your merchandise in a booth and waiting for a customer to give you an order. For example, before you consider going into a trade show, be sure your budget will stand the total expense of participating. The cost of renting a booth at a trade show can actually be the smallest expense involved. Usually, most national trade shows are held in Chicago or New York, and you must consider the travel expense of getting there, plus the hotel and living expenses of staying in the city while attending the show. Also, the cost of shipping your merchandise to the show and back to your home base must be considered. Then there is the cost of special promotions, models, additional personnel to work the booths, plus several other little expenses that seem to creep in before you realize it. However, if you handle the trade show properly, it should prove one of your most profitable methods of moving merchandise. Just remember that the rental for the booth can be the smallest expense in the overall picture, so don't try to cut corners by selecting a booth in a poor location because it is $50 or $100 cheaper than one in a better location.

There are trade shows for every category of business—from Accounting to Zoos—being held each year in the United States. No matter what your product, there are literally dozens of shows you can use for its promotion.

Exhibits Schedule (Successful Meetings Magazine, 633 Third Avenue, N.Y., NY 10017) contains a complete directory of shows and exhibits covering all industries, trades, and professions. This publication is in three sections and lists each show by industry, by city, and by date. Over 10,000 events are listed, covering trade shows, industrial expositions, technical exhibits, fairs and public shows, foreign fairs and expositions, and medical and scientific exhibits. It also gives information on dates of the shows, executives in charge, contact addresses, sponsor organizations, and expected attendance. All shows are listed two years in advance.

Just reading the list of these 10,000 scheduled shows can stimulate many ideas on how to promote your product. Although our Spud Gun was basically a toy, we exhibited it at food shows, sporting goods shows, premium shows, housewares shows—as well as the more pertinent toy shows. Each show opened up a new market for our product.

However, merely exhibiting at a trade show does not insure success for your item. We discovered that at least 50 percent of our success in trade shows depended upon work done *before* the show . . . work in which mail order practices are utilized to the fullest.

When pre-show promotions are prepared in the proper way, they can be a most profitable method of getting national distribution for your product. A good trade show enables you to appoint sales representatives, to personally meet your jobbers and dealers, to evaluate your competition. It also offers you a chance to test new products and at the same time write enough business at the show to more than pay for expenses involved.

Here is our step-by-step procedure practiced before and during a trade show:

1. WE ATTEND ONLY NATIONAL TRADE SHOWS . . . that have been operating for five years or more. The reason is obvious. Many times

an unscrupulous promoter will try to cash in on the popularity of an established trade show by promoting one of his own simultaneously or perhaps a week or two earlier. These "fly-by-night" promoters will print costly brochures and develop tremendous fanfare about the advantage of displaying your product in their show. Unfortunately, they spend all their time, money, and effort promoting their show to the exhibitor, but neglect to publicize it in the all-important dealer and jobber area. As a result, the exhibitor finds himself in a trade show well attended by other exhibitors but very light in buyer traffic. After being stung a few times with these "one-time-only" trade shows, we made it a point to exhibit *only* in well-established exhibitions.

2. WE RENT THE BEST POSSIBLE DISPLAY LOCATION. Location is of paramount importance in a trade show. Get the very best location you can afford. You are much better off with a small booth in a good location than with a large booth in a bad location. Avoid taking booths that are off the main traffic aisles of the show. People, like sheep, tend to follow each other.

3. WE PUBLICIZE OUR PARTICIPATION IN THE SHOW. A few months before the trade show opens, send press releases to all trade publications in the field. The release should describe any new products you intend to introduce at the show and also any new features you may be adding to your regular line.

4. WE HIT THE LOCAL PRESS. About ten days before the show opens, we send releases to newspapers located in the town where the trade show is to be held. Each letter sent to trade publications and newspapers is slanted to the particular publication or editor receiving the release.

5. WE ALWAYS MAIL "REMINDER LETTERS." About a week before the show opens, we mail a letter of invitation to every jobber on our mailing list and remind him to visit our booth at the show. Most trade shows today are such vast affairs that the average buyer is confused before he covers half of the exhibits. Any impression you can make on him *before* the show is more effective than any attempt to get him to your booth during the show. Here is a typical invitation letter we send to our jobber accounts.

AN INVITATION TO
VISIT US, MR. BUYER . . .

Yes . . . please accept this letter as an invitation to visit us at the National Pest Control Show in the Mayo Hotel, Tulsa, Oklahoma, October 17th through October 20th. We'll be in Booth Number 31.

At the Show we'll be introducing an incredible NEW PRODUCT called . . . COSSMAN'S FLY CAKE . . . as described in the enclosed circular.

You'll see actual demonstrations of this newly patented product. Flies killed in seconds, as soon as they touch the cake! Believe us . . . you won't believe your eyes when you see the Fly Cake in action!

See you at the Show.

> Sincerely,
> E. JOSEPH COSSMAN & CO.

EJC:jb
Encl.

P.S. If you can't make the Show, you can still be one of the first in your area to offer this NEW product to your accounts. Just mail the enclosed airmail order envelope today. We make immediate deliveries.

P.P.S. Going to the Show? You can *also* send in your order now, and the merchandise will be at your place of business on your return!

6. WE SEND A LETTER TO ALL TELEVISION AND RADIO STATIONS IN THE SHOW TOWN. We tell them some unique facts about our product and offer to appear on their shows at their convenience.

Radio-TV

Date

Name
Address
City, State, Zip
Dear Sir:

From breeding ants to killing flies! Does that sound like unusual occupations for one man?

Well, E. Joseph Cossman, the man who does both, is unusual. He breeds and buys billions of ants a year to supply Ant Farms to youngsters all over the country. He made a fortune selling shrunken heads. His mail order business is the largest of its type in the world. He now has a product which paralyzes a fly's nervous system and kills it on the spot!

Cossman will be in New York City at the Park-Sheraton, October 8 through 22, where he will attend the National Hardware Show which runs at the Coliseum October 10 through 14.

Since his present worldwide business had its meager beginning in New York, we thought you might be interested in contacting him for possible use on one of your shows.

He has appeared on many network radio and television shows originating in Los Angeles. Enclosed are several reprints which will give you additional information on Cossman.

If you have the opportunity to visit the Hardware Show, be sure to stop by Booth 11238, meet Cossman in person, and pick up your gift Ant Farm for the youngster in your family.

Thank you for your kind attention.

Fay Carlson, Public Relations

7. RELATED BUSINESSES ARE APPROACHED. We double, triple, quadruple the results of our out-of-town shows by writing to "fringe" accounts in the show city. This is a procedure we developed within our company, and it has been responsible for a great deal of extra business. Here's how it works: Order an out-of-town Yellow Pages from your local telephone company. Look up "fringe" categories—possible prospects for your particular product who would not normally attend the trade show in question. Write these people a letter, inviting them to the show. A very successful letter we have used for this purpose was this one:

Acme Janitor Supplies
426 Brush Street
Brooklyn, New York

Gentlemen:

We'll be exhibiting at the National Pet Supply Show being held in New York City . . . September 9 through 11 . . . at the New Yorker Hotel. We'll be in Booth 43.

What does this have to do with the Acme Company? Well . . . even though you're probably not interested in pet supplies, we know you'll be very interested in the new product we're introducing at the show.

This new product is called FLY CAKE and is fully described in the enclosed brochure. It's been on the market only a few short weeks, but we've already sold and shipped over a million FLY CAKES to accounts on the West Coast.

If you'd like to be one of the first in the east to offer FLY CAKE to your trade, drop over to our booth for a free sample. I'll personally be there to meet you and to give you more details on this incredible product.

Sincerely,
E. JOSEPH COSSMAN & CO.

EJC:le

P.S. I'll be registered at the New Yorker Hotel if you want to contact me before or after show hours.

At the time we were displaying our Fly Cake at the National Pest Control Show in Tulsa, we sent this letter to every bakery supply jobber in that city.

Avon Bakery Company
1218 Oak Street
Tulsa, Oklahoma

Gentlemen:

Please accept this letter as your invitation to visit us at the National Pest Control Show being held at the Mayo Hotel in Tulsa, Okla., from October 17 through 20. We will be in Booth No. 31.

What does a Pest Control Show have to do with the Avon Bakery Company? Well, at the show, we will be introducing a revolutionary new product called FLY CAKE. Fly Cake kills flies instantly, and each cake lasts an entire season.

We know this product will fit into your present merchandising setup. Come over toour booth, pick up a free sample, and be one of the first in the bakery supply business to offer this newly patented item to your trade.

Sincerely,
E. JOSEPH COSSMAN & COMPANY
E. Joseph Cossman
EJC:sh

One big bakery supply jobber accepted our invitation and visited our booth at the show. His visit resulted in the largest order we wrote at the show, and he is now one of our best accounts. Normally, he would not have attended a pest control show, since it isn't related to his line of business, but the letter we sent provoked his interest and brought him into our booth.

When we exhibited our Ant Farms at the National Toy Show in New York, we put out a similar letter to every pet supply jobber in the area. This mail order solicitation resulted in vast sales of Ant Farms to pet supply jobbers, buyers we would not have contacted otherwise.

Acme Pet Supplies Company
418 Oakdale Avenue
Brooklyn, New York

Gentlemen:

Please accept this letter as your invitation to visit us at the coming National Toy Show being held at the Hotel New Yorker from April 10 through 19. We will be in room number 1241.

What does a Toy Show have to do with a pet supply business? Well, at the Toy Show, we will be introducing our Ant Farm as described in the enclosed circular. We originally brought this product out for the toy field, but have found a tremendous market on the West Coast with pet supply dealers.

If you have a chance, drop over to our room and pick up a free sample. Once you see the product, we know you will want to be one of the first to introduce it to your trade on the East Coast.

Sincerely,
E. JOSEPH COSSMAN & COMPANY
E. Joseph Cossman
EJC:sh

8. AT THE TRADE SHOW, WE MAKE A DETAILED STUDY OF ALL THE OTHER EXHIBITORS. Are any of them prospects for our product? Occasionally, another exhibitor has a complete national sales setup that does not conflict with ours, and at the same time can take our product and give us national distribution overnight.

A few months after we introduced Fly Cake, we exhibited the product at the National Poultry Show in Memphis. Although this was our first exposure to poultry people, Fly Cake was an immediate hit. Our booth was constantly crowded with customers, and it didn't take long for the other exhibitors to see that we had one of the best moving products at the show.

With Fly Cake so enthusiastically received by the poultry trade, we needed some means of getting quick, national distribution in this field. Inspecting all the other booths at the show, we noted that one of the largest exhibitors was a manufacturer of basic poultry equipment. The last day of the show we called at his booth and were fortunate enough to meet the sales manager and vice-president. We told them that we had written over $5,000 in business during the few days of this show and would be willing to turn over all these orders to them in return for their taking Fly Cake for national distribution to the poultry trade only. They had seen the tremendous reception the product had at this show and were, therefore, quite willing to add the item to their existing line of poultry supplies.

As luck would have it, most of their salesmen were in attendance at their booth. Immediately after the show, we rented a small hall in the vicinity and invited their entire sales staff to a sales briefing on Fly Cake. Meanwhile, we had called our office in Los Angeles to air-express additional literature and samples direct to us in Memphis. After talking to the salesmen and briefing them on the different sales points of Fly Cake, we then loaded each and every one of them with Fly Cake samples and literature. The result of this sales meeting was an enthused group of salesmen who, overnight, gave us national coverage in the poultry field. Because we made this connection at a three-day poultry show, we enjoyed the services of a national sales force that would normally have taken several months to activate.

9. IN MY OPINION, ONE OF THE MOST IMPORTANT REQUIREMENTS FOR A SUCCESSFUL EXHIBIT CAN BE SUMMED UP IN TWO WORDS . . . BE DIFFERENT! Walk through any exhibit hall of any national convention and within minutes most of the exhibits begin to look alike. Originality and ideas are more important than expensive exhibits and costly literature. The following article tells how we got attention for our Ant Farm at the National Toy Show in New York. Note that every facet of our promotion was designed to make our product, our exhibit, and our company different from all others.

HOW TO GET ATTENTION AT A TRADE SHOW

When we first put the Ant Farm on the market, sales on the West Coast were exciting, but when we arrived at the American Toy Fair in New York, we discovered that nobody, but nobody, east of the Mississippi River had ever heard of the product. We had no publicity staff and we had no budget for publicity. All we had was a room reserved in the New Yorker Hotel for the show, and we had to compete with approximately 1,500 other exhibitors who were showing their products at the Hotel New Yorker, the Hotel Sheraton McAlpine, and the Fifth Avenue Building. Our only chance was to make such a big splash with the Ant Farm during the nine short days of the fair that every toy buyer would be convinced that the Ant Farm was the hit of the show. Here's what we did:

1. Front-page ad space was taken each day in the Toy Trade News, which was published especially for the show.

2. More than 10,000 stickers, 2″ × 1½″, saying "See the Cossman ANT FARM, room 1241, Hotel New Yorker," appeared on the mirrors of hotel rooms all over New York. A buyer couldn't shave without seeing an Ant Farm sticker! This was accomplished with the cooperation of numerous bell boys. (Later in the week, when business got so heavy, and everybody was trying to corner me, a joke went around the show, "Look for a fellow peeling stickers off a wall . . . the man behind him ready to put on another is Cossman!")

3. A cartoonist, working in the lobby every evening, was paid to keep a large caricature of the Ant Farms attached to his easel.

4. Models in tight satin dresses with Ant Farms stenciled fore and aft, caught all eyes as they walked from floor to floor of the hotel.

5. Thousands of "I bought Cossman Ant Farms" blue ribbons were distributed, and worn.

The results of all this promotion went beyond the wildest expectations!

The Ant Farm booth was at the end of the hall on the 12th floor. Every day there was a lineup of people, from the elevators to the door, waiting to get in! The room itself was so mobbed that another room had to be taken across the hall.

At 3:55 P.M. Friday afternoon, five days after the show opened, a clanging was heard in room 1241. It was so loud that it could be heard all over the 12th floor. People rushed out of every room asking, "Where's the fire?"

The alarm was the biggest clock I could find in a second-hand store.

It announced that sales had tipped the 100,000 mark on Ant Farms.

Perhaps some of these promotional ideas sound corny, but on or off the cob, Americans love corn, and a good sense of humor, as can be proven by these results.

Ant Farms not only walked off with a king-size portion of all sales, but it can honestly be said that it was the only "live" item there! (No pun intended)

10. EVERY TRADE SHOW YOU ATTEND SHOULD BE DIVIDED INTO THREE AREAS OF ACTIVITY: PRE-SHOW, SHOW, AND POST-SHOW. For post-show, send a report to all of your representatives to brief them on what happened at the show.

Most trade shows today provide each exhibitor with a registration list of the names and addresses of all the dealers and jobbers who attended the show. Make good use of this list by immediately contacting them by mail after the show. Many times this mailing piece can be your "second chance" to sell the buyers you missed or couldn't sell at the show.

To sum up, a trade show can be one of the most important merchandising tools for the promotion and sale of your product. Actually, a trade show is about the only place in mail order where your customers come to you. No other single activity will afford you the opportunity to make such tremendous sales progress within the span of a few days.

10 | The Spud Gun: A Case History

"Today's ideas are tomorrow's success stories."

The month was January and everyone in the office walked around with a long face. It was a time of crisis. The National Toy Show was only three months away and we had nothing new to exhibit! Three years before, we had been the hit of the show with our Toy Soldiers; a year later, we topped that performance with our Shrunken Heads; the next year, we literally stopped the show with our Ant Farm. But for this year . . . nothing! Somebody had to whip up a miracle . . . and fast.

Our miracle arrived just in time via the telephone. A metal die casting shop called and wanted to know if we'd be interested in buying a set of tooling that originally cost $6,000. Their asking price was $600.

"What does the tooling make?" we asked.

"Spud Guns," they replied.

"And just *what* is a spud gun?" we wanted to know.

"A toy gun that shoots potato pellets fifty feet. Plunge the tip of the gun into a potato, scoop out a little nib, squeeze the trigger, and the pellet goes flying through the air. It's harmless," they added, "because a potato pellet is almost 90 percent water."

Our instinct told us that this could be "it." We asked for the history of the item and were told they had made an original run of 100,000 units some ten years ago and had, at that time, put the gun on the market. It was a big flop, and at this date—ten years later—

they still had 90,000 guns in their warehouse. They also had the original tooling. On a hunch, we sent our truck to their factory and picked up 200 samples of the gun.

One sample gun and a letter was sent to each of our toy representatives, and another sample and letter went to all leading toy jobbers in the country. The letter was short and stated simply that we were thinking of reviving the Spud Gun and would appreciate their comments.

Well, we got back plenty of comments, but not one of them was encouraging. Several jobbers bemoaned the fact that they still had Spud Guns lying around their cellars after ten years; they wouldn't touch the product. Many of our toy representatives remembered the gun and were very expressive in their way of telling us to forget it!

Despite the barrage of negative reactions, we had a "hunch" and continued to investigate the Spud Gun's possibilities. Our first real break came from—of all places—the United States Department of Agriculture! That department told us that the country was faced with the biggest potato "glut" in twenty years. Every section of the United States had a bumper crop and the price of potatoes was down to a new low. Here was the something "big" we needed to hang a promotion on.

Beginning with this idea, we followed our "hunch" and bought the tooling for $600. We immediately sent the following reproduction of a mimeo letter and "fact sheet" to each of 100 potato associations throughout the country.

This mailing was called "Project Potato" and its main purpose was to influence the potato associations. In essence, the mailing bluntly asked each of them to ship a few pounds of their best potatoes to the New York Toy Show. Frankly, we expected five or ten associations to cooperate by shipping perhaps 500 pounds of potatoes each. This would give us a "roomful of potatoes" and start our Spud Gun campaign moving.

> Gentlemen:
>
> We have just been in conference with Francis Pusateri of the Kern County Potato Growers Association and also Burt Purtle of Bakersfield, and they have given us your name and address to help put across the biggest national potato publicity campaign in years.
>
> Here's the idea . . . we are a Toy and Novelty Manufacturer who have just invented a Spud (potato) Gun. The Spud Gun shoots harmless potato pellets, and it will not hurt even the smallest child.

The Spud Gun will be introduced for the first time at the National Toy Trade Show to be held in New York, March 9 through 14. This show is one of the biggest trade shows in the world, and it will be attended by an impressive representative group of every major newspaper, magazine, and television station in the country. The publicity potential is terrific! The press is going to be looking for a clever "human interest" story and with your help, we're going to give it to them. We want to show a roomful (hotel size) of potatoes represented from every section of the country . . . complete with a list of the names of the people they came from!

The photo and story slant will be built around the idea that the potato is now America's most important vegetable! *But to put the idea across, we must have potatoes represented from every area in the nation.* Send any quantity you like . . . large or small . . . but send something so your state will be represented.

TIME IS DESPERATELY SHORT. WE MUST HAVE THE POTATOES DELIVERED BY NO LATER THAN MARCH 10, IN NEW YORK, TO THE COSSMAN COMPANY ROOM 1241, AT THE HOTEL NEW YORKER.

Enclosed is a "fact sheet" to give you full information. If there are any questions in your mind, please call us here in Los Angeles.

Sincerely,
Fay Carlson, P.R. Director
E. JOSEPH COSSMAN & COMPANY

FC:st

FACT SHEET ON
"PROJECT POTATO"!

- The world famous National Toy Trade Show will be held in New York, March 9 through 14.

- The Public Relations Department of the Toy Association has arranged to have members of the press, newspaper syndicates, national magazines, and television station representatives attend.

- We, here at the Cossman Company, have arranged our own complete press campaign! We're asking potato associations all over the country to send in a sackful of potatoes directly to our exhibit room at the New Yorker Hotel! We want to show the press a "roomful of potatoes" from all over the country. The press will know about the potato samples even before they arrive at the Toy Show. Here's the plan . . .

- A potato sack will be filled with a potato, Spud Gun, editorial release, and nutritional fact sheet and sent to:

    (a) Every city desk of every newspaper and news service in New York.

    (b) Every human interest feature writer on each newspaper

(c) Every home economics editor of each newspaper.

(d) Every television station in New York.

- The News Editor of each television and radio station in New York will receive the same promotion material as the newspapers plus a "news story" that can be used over the station.

- Time, Newsweek, and the New Yorker magazines are receiving special letters on the idea.

- United Airlines' Publicity Department is working with us! In Los Angeles, Peter Gunn of TV fame will be shooting potatoes with his potato gun at the airport . . . and in New York we hope to get Richard Boone of "Have Gun, Will Travel" western fame. Glossy photos and a story will hit every newspaper and wire service in the nation.

- Every gossip columnist will be given exclusive story items.

- We're well on our way to lining up two national television shows: "What's My Line?" and "To Tell the Truth." They'll give potatoes and potato guns a terrific plug.

- More than 18,000 sets of potato and potato gun "teaser cards" (six cards to a set), have been mailed out all over the nation inviting people to see the potato display and potato gun at the Hotel New Yorker.

- Twenty-five window display areas have been purchased in New York City to show potatoes and potato guns.

- More than 5,000 potato guns and potatoes will be given away free.

- Advertisements have been taken in the Toy News trade magazine for all six days of the show.

- More than 100,000 potato gun circulars have been printed.

- Girls in potato sacks will advertise the promotion in the hotel all during the six days of the show.

- Nutritional chart sheets and pamphlet giveaways on potatoes will be displayed in the Hotel New Yorker.

- Honorary Sheriff's badges for the "Spud Gun Patrol" will be given away to every person who comes into the hotel.

- And! . . . when the New York show is over, we are going to help promote potato sales at your National Convention to be held here in California starting March 15.

From our research we discovered that potato sales have dropped 50% in the last 20 years. We estimate conservatively that each child will use at least six pounds of potatoes with each gun. We're going to sell a minimum of two million potato guns and that adds up to twelve million pounds of additional potato sales. Of course, we can't even estimate how many additional million pounds of potatoes will end up on the dinner table, too, from all the publicity.

But remember, success hinges on *good representation* from all potato people!

TIME IS SHORT! WE MUST RECEIVE ALL POTATOES BY MARCH 10!

The potatoes should be tagged with the name and address of the donor and the name "type" of potato and sent to: E. Joseph Cossman & Co., Room 1241, National Toy Show, Hotel New Yorker, New York, New York.

Arriving in New York, I found 50,000 pounds of potatoes waiting for me! Potatoes at the express office, potatoes at the airport, potatoes at the post office, potatoes at the trucking docks—potatoes everywhere—all consigned to me in care of our show room at the Hotel New Yorker!

Fortunately, I was in New York one week before the opening of the show and had seven full days to lay my plans. I had my "taters," but I needed the magic ingredient: Kids! So I called a New York orphanage and asked if they wanted 50,000 pounds of potatoes after the Toy Show. They certainly did, they said, for that would represent a big saving in food. I asked if they would, in return, "lend" me twenty-five of their charges and bring them to the Hotel New Yorker the following Saturday at noon. They liked the idea, and that Saturday at twelve o'clock sharp, twenty-five small boys and girls stared gleefully at a twenty-four-foot trailer-truck as it ceremoniously pulled up and stopped in front of the Hotel New Yorker. The truck was covered with big signs reading "Another Car Load of Ammunition for the Cossman Spud Gun," and was loaded with 8,000 pounds of potatoes. Crowds of curious, smiling people began to gather by this time, and a big yelp of excitement went up from my kids as the trailer dumped *all* 8,000 pounds of potatoes on the sidewalk right in front of the hotel! My twenty-five orphans, each with two Spud Guns strapped arond his waist, lost no time in getting the Battle of Potato Mountain underway. Potato pellets flew fast and thick all over the Manhattan District! Sidewalks were covered with pellets. This was the first time the Hotel New Yorker had ever served mashed potatoes on the sidewalk!

Television stations and newspapers had been alerted and at least two dozen cameramen, reporters, and publicity people showed up for our "Project Potato." The promotion made most of the Sunday papers, and the next day I was tapped by Bill Leonard, the producer of the television show, "Eye on New York," to appear on his program that can be seen on 140 CBS stations from coast to coast. This was the break I'd been waiting for! That evening I lugged a half dozen sacks of potatoes to the studio and was given the run of the show for ten minutes. Here I was, talking about the national potato surplus and demonstrating the Spud Gun to millions of people from coast to coast. It was a salesman's dream come true!

The payoff on the stunt came the next day—the opening date of the Toy Show. Our display rooms were on the twelfth floor of the Hotel New Yorker, about twenty-two rooms away from the elevators. Within the first hour of the show, every toy buyer in New York City, it appeared, was fighting to get to our rooms. We had four lovely models dressed in potato sacks, each with two Spud Guns strapped around her waist, and they were kept busy most of the day serving coffee to the long line of people stretching from the elevator to our room. When buyers finally got inside, they came face to face with a mountain of potatoes. We had rented an extra room next to our display room and had filled it to the ceiling with potatoes. At the far side of this room we had placed a life-size "Pinup" of a popular movie actress. When a buyer entered the room, he was handed a potato and a Spud Gun and asked to take a "pot shot" at the girl on the poster. If he hit her, he got three pounds of potatoes. If he missed, he had to take six pounds! This gimmick spread through the Toy Show like wild fire, and everyone made it a point of honor to visit our room and try their luck at the target.

In addition to this "fun" promotion, we rented display windows throughout a triangle area formed by the conjunction of the New Yorker Hotel, the Hotel McAlpin, and the toy building at 200 Fifth Avenue—the three buildings in which the Toy Show was being held. One week before the show, we scouted stores along this triangle, renting window space and filling these display areas with potatoes, Spud Guns, and a sign inviting the buyer to our room for a free sample. These displays gave us more outside exposure than any other form of advertising, because all visitors to the show had to walk from one building to another in this triangle. If the stores where we rented space sold hardware, lingerie, or greeting cards, it made no difference. In fact, the more unrelated the store, the more effective our window display.

Another promotion incorporated six comic postcards sent out on six consecutive days a few weeks prior to the show. A sample of these cards, which were mailed to jobbers throughout the country, appears on page 141.

Toys and Novelties, the trade magazine of the toy industry, publishes a daily magazine during the toy show which is distributed to buyers visiting the show. We ran an ad each day in this publication using the cartoons which were printed on the postcard mailing. Any buyer seeing the ads immediately remembered receiving our postcards, thereby giving us double mileage on this one promotion.

All this related activity created such a demand for the Spud Gun that we were oversold by 400,000 units five days after the show opened. And by the end of the ten-day show, we were oversold close to 600,000 guns! Suddenly, our $600 set of tooling was worth its weight in gold, but unfortunately, it made only 2,000 guns a day, and we were in trouble.

Searching for additional tooling, we learned that the potato gun had originated in England. Placing a person-to-person call to a leading toy magazine editor in London, England, we held the line while he thumbed through back issues, trying to locate the original potato gun manufacturer. He found the information in an issue about twelve years old, and we placed another person-to-person call to the manufacturer.

Luckily for us, he had another set of tooling, which we bought and had flown to Los Angeles. The London manufacturer called us back a little later and said that a few years ago a third set of tooling had been sold to a party in Brooklyn. After several hours of searching for the Brooklyn owner, we finally contacted him and asked to buy his tooling. He told us the item had been such a "dud" when first introduced that he'd been using the tooling for the past four years as an anchor on his boat in Long Island Sound!

Our only alternative, now, was to make more tooling ourselves. We contacted four tool makers in Los Angeles and gave each of them an order for two sets of tooling. We were getting from 15,000 to 20,000 Spud Gun orders a day, and we needed production! To top it all, the week following the toy show, we received a call from a large food chain in the East placing an opening order with us for 9,000 dozen Spud Guns. I asked what a grocery chain would do with that many toy guns, and was told that although the produce department is one of the most profitable sections of a supermarket, it seldom has anything to promote in order to bring in traffic. They intended using the Spud Gun as a promotion gimmick, giving one away with every

ten pounds of potatoes. We changed their promotion around and had them sell the gun for 98¢ and give away ten pounds of potatoes. Based on the tremendous success of this one chain store promotion, we offered the unit to other national food chains.

Before the Spud Gun had "died" completely, we sold well over 2 million units. And this was the product that had been a total flop ten years before.

As an incentive to our toy representatives, a complete report on the Spud Gun operation, from start to finish, was sent to them. Here is a brief description of the report.

The *Spud Gun Report* was made up in brochure form and ran close to fifteen pages. We bound the reports in attractive folders and sent them airmail to our sales representatives all over the country.

The report itself gave our representatives the factual story of our success in the Toy Show and included glossy photographs, illustrations, and actual samples of sales aids. We broke the report down into the following order:

REPORT ON THE COSSMAN SPUD GUN

(a) *The Problem*
Here we told of our phenomenal success at the show and the fact that we had oversold ourselves by more than half a million units! We spoke briefly of our production problems and what we were doing about them.

(b) *The Solution*
Here we gave our company a well-deserved "boost" in the eyes of our reps by telling them how we had overcome the problems and what was happening daily to the Spud Gun program.

(c) *Promotional Aids*
On the next ten pages of the brochure, we listed our advertising schedule and sales aids, such as extensive TV exposure (giving programs, dates, areas where the spotlighting of the Spud Gun could be seen, etcetera), complete listing of TV stations, addresses, TV personalities, etcetera. We also suggested that if any of our reps had additional ideas for future promotions to immediately contact us.

We listed in detail all the promotional aids they could receive from us immediately, simply by requesting them . . . attractive, "sight-selling" aids, such as gaily colored window streamers, envelope stuffers, dump displays, catalog sheets, special local TV lists of scheduled programs, and glossy photos. We also included additional sales aids, such as printed toy balloons and toy sheriff's badges . . . all advertising the Spud Gun and giving that "something extra" to the consumer. We even had a short record cut with original lyrics and melody entitled "Spud Gun Rock!"

(d) At the end of the report brochure, we headed the final page with a summation that in truth was a "push" to our reps to get going on this "hot" item. Short, but to the point, we stated:

". . . as you can see, we are going all out to make Spud Guns a dictionary name in the United States. From now on, nothing should stand in your way, for we have the production facilities to make almost immediate delivery, plus the promotional aids to get the gun moving off the dealer's shelves.

"For your own confidential information, we received an opening order from a leading food chain for 9,000 *dozen* Spud Guns! With action like this on an *opening* order, you're sitting on one of the hottest numbers in the country today!"

11 | Our 35 Best Mail Order Letters

"Words should be like windows . . . you should be able to look through them and see the product."

In mail order, letters are your salesmen. Just as an honest, home-spun salesman can outsell a professional slickster, so can an honest, sincere letter outsell a fancy, misleading one.

This chapter illustrates 35 of our best mail order letters. Most of them pulled fabulously well. They all had what I call "the three C's of letter writing." Here they are:

1. *Be Convincing.* If you are convinced of the truth of what you say—if you are honest, sincere, and enthusiastic in what you write—then your letter will be better than any professional letter that you can purchase.

2. *Be Clear.* How often have you received a letter that you had to read three or four times before you could grasp the writer's meaning? See that your letters are concise and complete, so that what you are trying to say is instantly conveyed to the reader.

3. *Be Conversational.* If you write the way you think and let your letter reflect your particular personality, then don't worry too much about split infinitives, grammar, or the proper spacing of paragraphs. A simple letter with your personality in it will work far better than a letter that is technically and professionally perfect, yet impersonal.

Of course, the greatest letter in the world cannot sell if your product is not basically appealing, if your market is not there, and if your price is not right. But if these three factors are in your favor, then your own honest and sincere approach is the best ingredient you can put into a letter designed to bring in the orders.

The following letter campaign on our Home Sprinkler sold over 1.5 million units within a very short period of time. Our first plan was to place all advertising and sell these units exclusively by ourselves, but the product offered so many other channels of distribution that we reconsidered and decided to offer mail order houses throughout the country first crack at it and then merchandise the Sprinklers' sales success from there.

To test the mail order possibilities of the product, we ran a small ad in the *Los Angeles Times*. Although the ad ran during the rainy season, it proved the product had mail order potential by pulling $963 and over 30 percent repeat orders. A small reprint of the *Los Angeles Times* ad was sent to 4,800 mail order houses along with Letter 1. This letter not only brought in orders, but also helped to book more than $80,000 worth of advertising through the mail order houses.

We then sent Letter 2 to 5,000 homes on an occupant list and also to 5,000 active customers obtained from a leading West Coast mail order house. Both mailings went to the same cities at the same time. While the occupant list pulled $803.74 in orders, the list of regular mail order buyers doubled it, bringing back a total of a little over $1,600. We sent copies of this mailing to mail order houses once again, accompanied by Letter 3, which convinced many mail order houses to make exclusive mailings to their own customer lists.

With complete coverage of the mail order field assured, we now concentrated on jobber distribution. With rented lists, we mailed weekly letters such as Letter 4 to 75,000 jobbers. This Letter 4 was printed by offset and no attempt was made to personalize it.

Jobbers who responded to the offset letter by requesting a sample order were sent a follow-up series of auto-typed letters. These personalized follow-up letters turned many sample requests into large orders. With the orders, jobbers received point-of-purchase material, radio, television, and other promotional aids.

Letter 5 was sent out as an acknowledgment of the sample order. Letters 6, 7, 8, 9, and 10 were to the same jobbers spaced one week apart . . . and Letters 11 through 14 were used to begin the campaign the following year.

Letters 15 and 15A were sent to newspapers and magazines, asking them to run cooperative ads on the Home Sprinkler. As you'll note from this series, we hit all bases with this powerful campaign!

We recently conducted a survey of 1,000 storekeepers who maintain a record on salesmen's calls. We learned that 48.2 percent made one call and quit; 24.4 percent made two calls and quit; 14.7 percent made three calls and quit; 12.7 percent made four calls and quit. But here is the twist: 60 percent of the merchandise purchased by these storekeepers was made on the fifth call or after! And so it is with direct mail. Although a lot of business came in from our early letters, most of our Home Sprinklers were sold to the jobber *after* they had received the third or fourth letter in the series.

LETTERS 1–15

Letter 1

Dear Buyer:

There are mail order items and mail order items . . . but here's one that's H O T ! This one answers that age-old problem of watering the lawn with the least amount of time and effort.

And value? Imagine a Home Sprinkler System for only $2.50! That's right . . . a 20 Ft. Home Sprinkler is what your customers get for only $2.50 postpaid. What a leader for your catalog!

And what a profit maker! The enclosed ad pulled more than $900 . . . BUT IT ALSO PULLED OVER 30% REPEAT ORDERS! And it ran in November on a test!

The 20 ft. sprinkler lists for $2.50 and the 50 ft. sprinkler lists for $4.75. Your discounts off the list are:

12 or more sprinklers	40% F.O.B. Los Angeles, Calif.
144 or more sprinklers	50% Delivered (we pay freight)
288 or more sprinklers	50% and 5% Delivered (we pay freight)
720 or more sprinklers	50% and 10% Delivered (we pay freight)

Terms are 2/10/30 to *well rated* accounts. *All others* cash with order.

If you want to run any ads, please let us know the publication and date . . . we'll see that no other mail order house runs in competition with you. Glossy photographs for your newspaper and magazine ads (and your catalog) furnished free.

Send us your order NOW, before the rush starts. We can make prompt delivery.

Sincerely,
SPRINKLER SYSTEM COMPANY
E. Joseph Cossman
President

Ejc/vb

Letter 2

A Dear Friend

of ours actually enjoyed having his lawn watered the old-fashioned way . . . that is, standing outside holding a hose for an hour or more.

That's because his wife takes care of the lawn and garden!

So if the job of keeping your lawn beautiful is YOURS . . . the NEW Home Sprinkler was made for you.

Take a moment to read the enclosed circular . . . then don't wait a moment . . . clip the order blank . . . use the postpaid envelope . . . and get YOUR Home Sprinkler by return mail.

The Home Sprinkler will save you lots of time and money!

Sincerely,

SPRINKLER SYSTEM COMPANY

Lee M. Milton
Sales Manager

LMM/eft

P.S. Our friend's wife is very glad she ordered one!

Letter 3

John H. Jones
Acme Supermarket
418 Oak Street
Akron, Ohio

Dear Mr. Jones:

We didn't believe it! In fact, we asked our bookkeeping department to recheck the figures. Here's why, Mr. Jones.

The enclosed test mailing went out to 5,000 "occupants" and 5,000 regular mail order buyers. After 10 days we enjoyed the amazing pull of 5% of the occupant list and 11% on the regular list.

AT AN AVERAGE OF $4.18 PER ORDER!

You'll note the mailing piece is simple and inexpensive. The circular and letter are printed on an offset press. No costly plates or artwork are necessary.

We'll be glad to furnish a reproduction proof, ready to shoot, of the circular. No obligation or cost to you, of course.

Just pencil your request at the bottom of this letter and remail it to us in the enclosed reply envelope.

Sincerely,

Sprinkler System Company

E. Joseph Cossman, President

EJC:im

Encl.

P.S. And orders from both lists on the test mailing are still coming in!

....

O.K. Joe: Send me the reproduction proof.
                                (Signed)....................................

Letter 4

Dear Buyer:

Here's the Home Sprinkler that everybody's reading about . . . and buying . . . for it answers the age-old problem of watering the lawn with the least amount of time and effort.

Imagine a Home Sprinkler System for only $2.50! That's right . . . a 20 ft. Home Sprinkler is what your customers get for only $2.50 postpaid. What a leader for your catalog!

AND DOES IT SELL?

A Mail-Order House pulled 11% . . . yes, ELEVEN PERCENT . . . on a direct mailing to their customer list!

A dealer put the Home Sprinkler in his catalog of 98 items. The Home Sprinkler outpulled EVERY other item in the catalog . . . by two to one!

A house-to-house salesman averaged 8 sales out of every 10 calls made . . . and several of the sales were for more than one sprinkler!

The Home Sprinkler is racking up fabulous success stories . . . it sells *itself* through mail order . . . over the store-counter . . . at fairs and home shows . . . house-to-house . . . direct mailings . . . or through any number of merchandising ways.

And best of all . . . we'll furnish PROVEN sales aids to you . . . tested ads, glossy photos, mats, samples of successful mailings, window streamers, display cards, etc.; just let us know what you need with your order. But hurry and get your order in . . . this is really the Top Item of the Year!

Sincerely,
SPRINKLER SYSTEM COMPANY
E. Joseph Cossman

EJC:ss

P.S. The 20 ft. sprinkler lists for $2.50 and the 50 ft. sprinkler lists for $4.75. Your discounts off the list are:

36 or more sprinklers	40% (we pay freight)
144 or more sprinklers	50% (we pay freight)
288 or more sprinklers	50% & 10% (we pay freight)

Terms are 2/10/30 to well-rated accounts. *All others* cash with order. We can make immediate delivery.

Letter 5

John H. Jones
Acme Supermarket
418 Oak Street
Akron, Ohio

Dear Mr. Jones:

Many thanks for your sample order, dated April 26, covering three dozen Home Sprinklers.

The merchandise is being shipped today via Parcel Post.

We believe our Home Sprinkler is perfect for your type of distribution, Mr. Jones, for we purposely designed the package into a self-selling product.

Each Home Sprinkler is factory wound on its own individual steel storage reel and comes complete with an attractive five-year factory guarantee card.

Last year, we sold more than half a million of our Home Sprinklers and 75% of our sales were through outlets like yours. This year we've added the FREE reel which makes the package doubly attractive for consumer satisfaction.

We can make immediate delivery on all of your orders. If you require any further information, please let us know.

Sincerely,

SPRINKLER SYSTEM COMPANY

E. Joseph Cossman, President

P.S. Your discounts off list are 50% and 10% with Full Freight ALLOWED ON ORDERS OF ONE GROSS OR MORE.

Letter 6

Dear Buyer:

Did you hear about the beautiful blonde who received a diamond ring about the size of an overripe grapefruit?

It was big . . . it was dazzling . . . and she was proud.

But no matter how she waved her hand or twiddled her fingers at the bridge club meeting, her ring went unnoticed. Finally, in exasperation, she stood up and exclaimed, "My, it's hot in here. I think I'll take off my ring!"

Well, we're a little like that blonde . . . for we, too, have something we're proud of . . . something that wants to make us get up and shout. Yes . . . we're proud of the way our Home Sprinkler has been accepted by the trade throughout the country.

Enclosed is a copy of a letter we received from the Racine Mfg. Company . . . it explains better than we can just what we're trying to say.

The enclosed circular gives full information and list prices. Your discounts off list, COMPLETE WITH THE STORAGE REEL, are 50% and 10%.

Terms are 2/10/30 . . . and remember . . . on orders of one gross or more, we pay freight to your door. Send us your order today . . . and you'll sell more in dollar value than any other item in your line.

Sincerely,

SPRINKLER SYSTEM COMPANY

E. Joseph Cossman, President

P.S. The enclosed postage-paid order label is for your convenience. Merely paste it on your order envelope. Mail it today . . . and we'll ship tomorrow!

Letter 6A

Mr. E. Joseph Cossman, President
Sprinkler System Company
Sunset Boulevard
Hollywood, California

Dear Mr. Cossman:

We have looked at 8 different lines of plastic Sprinklers for our Spring catalog and have come to the conclusion that you offer the best value.

I discovered, however, that the photographic print that we have on hand is the one from last year and it does not show the new free reel that you furnish. Therefore, please rush Air Mail Special Delivery, the up-to-date glossy print.

Sincerely,

RACINE SPECIALTY MFG. CO.

President
RFWentsel:bb

Letter 7

John H. Jones
Acme Supermarket
418 Oak Street
Akron, Ohio

Dear Mr. Jones:

Did you ever drop a stone over the edge of a cliff, and wait for the echoing sound to come back to you? If you heard nothing at all, then your curiosity really was aroused and you wanted to find out what was at the bottom of the cliff and how deep it was.

We are in the same position today . . . but the stone we dropped was a sample of our Home Sprinkler. It was dropped in your direction on March 20 and since then we have heard . . . nothing.

Frankly, the sample Home Sprinkler was sent to you as per your request and we're a bit puzzled as to why we haven't heard from you.

The enclosed literature describes this fast-moving product and we invite you to read it . . . keeping in mind that we kept your type of account in mind when we designed the package into a self-selling, over-the-counter product.

Now that a second stone has been dropped in your direction, Mr. Jones, we will listen intently for the echo. When can we count on getting your order?

Sincerely,

SPRINKLER SYSTEM COMPANY

E. Joseph Cossman, President

P.S. Each Home Sprinkler is factory wound on its own individual steel storage reel and comes with its own individual five-year factory guarantee card. Your discounts off list are 50% and 10% with full freight allowed on orders for one gross or more.

Letter 8

John H. Jones
Acme Supermarket
418 Oak Street
Akron, Ohio

Dear Mr. Jones:

When your name was placed on my desk this morning, it meant just one thing . . . that your order for Home Sprinklers has not been received.

That tempts me to do the customary thing . . . to write you a long letter, telling you how good our Home Sprinkler is and how we've sold over half a million of them, just through accounts like yours. But you probably know what I'd say . . . so to save you time, we'll skip that part—

—The important questions are: "Did you overlook anything when we sent you our sample and price quotations? Is there anything more we can do to justify your business?"

Will you kindly let me know the other side of this letter? We sincerely value accounts like yours, and would be proud to have you for a customer.

Sincerely,

SPRINKLER SYSTEM COMPANY

E. Joseph Cossman, President

P.S. Each Home Sprinkler is factory wound on its own individual steel storage reel and comes with its own individual five-year factory guarantee card. Your discounts off list are 50% and 10% with full freight allowed on orders of one gross or more.

Letter 9

John H. Jones
Acme Supermarket
418 Oak Street
Akron, Ohio

Dear Mr. Jones:

We know you're a clever merchandiser, or you wouldn't be in your present position.

You must also be a very busy man, else you would have seen the literature we've been sending you on our Home Sprinkler.

We've sent you pictures of our Home Sprinkler on the lawn . . . we've shown you how it gently waters a hillside . . . how it makes a perfect spray for narrow strips and parkways . . . but as we've said . . . you must have been too busy to notice.

So . . . we're taking desperate measures NOW to attract your attention. This time we're placing our Home Sprinkler on the knee of Miss Home Sprinkler of the Year! If you don't see it now, you're REALLY too busy!

And why are we so anxious to show you our Home Sprinkler? Because we know that once you see our product, you'll place an order. Hundreds of other smart buyers before you have done so . . . and their repeat orders substantiate their judgment.

Just attach the enclosed airmail label to your order envelope, Mr. Jones . . . and be assured you made a wise move.

Sincerely,

SPRINKLER SYSTEM COMPANY

E. Joseph Cossman, President

Letter 10

Dear Buyer:

Once upon a time there was a man in the same business that you're in.

He received the same return card that is enclosed with this letter. The exact same return card.

He filled it in, as I hope you will.

As a result, this man sold a total of 1,200 Home Sprinklers . . . all within a five-week period! His first order was for 600. His second order was for 180. His third order was for 420.

That's a total of 1,200 Home Sprinklers . . . all within a five week period.

Along with the return card, I'm also enclosing a copy of this man's three orders.

Look them over . . . then follow his example.

Sign and mail the enclosed card today.

Do it NOW . . . and you'll be glad you did!

Sincerely,

SPRINKLER SYSTEM COMPANY

E. Joseph Cossman, President

P.S. Your discounts are the same as his . . . 50% and 10% off list. Terms are 2/10/30 and we pay freight to your door on orders of one gross or more. How can you miss?

Letter 11

Dear Buyer:

Just a few names as convincing evidence that our Home Sprinkler is leading the country in sales.

T aft-Thriftway Company, Des Moines, Iowa.
H acknew Wholesale Grocery Company, Athens, Tennessee.
E ggleston Supply Company, Medford, Massachusetts.
Y akima Grocery Company, Yakima, Washington.

A ssociated Grocers of San Antonio, Texas.
L irosi Importing Company, Schenectady, New York.
L ewis, Alfred M. Company, National City, California.

B eeson Hardware Company, Highpoint, North Carolina.
O rlando Drug & Novelty, Orlando, Florida.
U lry-Talbert Company, Grand Island, Nebraska.
G roce-Wearden Company, Victoria, Texas.
H udson's Bay Company, Canada.
T ex-State Auto Supply, Houston, Texas.

H ackney, H. T. Company, Athens, Texas.
O hio Markets, Inc., Columbus, Ohio.
M ayfield Company, Tyler, Texas.
E conomy Stores, Inc., Norfolk, Virginia.

S piegel Bros. Paper Company, Kingston, New York.
P ayless Stores Company, Prairie Village, Kansas.
R io Stores, Albany, Georgia.
I ndependent Wholesale Grocers, Billings, Montana.
N ash-Finch Company, Bozeman, Montana.
K elly Bros. Nurseries, Inc., Dansville, New York.
L evy-Ward Grocer Company, South Bend, Indiana.
E vangeline Wholesale Company, Ville Platte, Louisiana.
R agland Bros. Co., Chattanooga, Tennessee.
S afeway Stores.

We'd like to add your name to our long list of money-making customers. Won't you send us your order today? A postage-paid airmail label is enclosed for your convenience.

Sincerely,

SPRINKLER SYSTEM COMPANY

E. Joseph Cossman, President

Letter 12

Dear Buyer:

Imagine a Home Sprinkler stretching across the country . . . from New York City to Los Angeles . . . and you'll have an idea of how many Home Sprinklers were sold last year! Yes . . . more than half a million of our Sprinklers . . . the equivalent of fifteen million feet . . . were sold last year!

And that was only the beginning . . . for this year we've added something NEW . . . something that will mean MORE SALES and MORE PROFITS for you . . . for this year each Home Sprinkler will be factory wound on its own individual handy steel reel . . . at NO increase in your cost . . . at NO increase in your selling price. The reel is given FREE to the customer with each Sprinkler purchased.

The enclosed circular gives additional features that mean more sales for you . . . each Home Sprinkler is made of the finest vinyl plastic . . . comes complete with a solid brass connector and sliding end clip for adjustable length . . . and each Home Sprinkler carries its own 5-year factory guarantee card, for customer confidence.

And to help you do a volume job, list prices are low . . . discounts are high. List prices, COMPLETE WITH THE STEEL STORAGE REEL, are $2.50 for the 20 ft. unit and $4.75 for the 50 ft. unit. Jobbers discounts off list are as follows:

Less than 1 gross   50% & 10% F.O.B. Los Angeles
1 gross or more   50% and 10% Delivered
                      (we pay freight)

Terms are 2/10/30 to well rated accounts. All others, cash with order. Remember . . . on orders of one gross or more, we pay freight to your door.

Send us your order today . . . and you'll sell, sell, sell!

Sincerely,

SPRINKLER SYSTEM COMPANY

E. Joseph Cossman, President

P.S. And delivery? We ship all orders same day received, and airmail reaches us overnight. Just paste the enclosed postage-paid airmail label on your order envelope. Mail it today and we'll ship your order TOMORROW!

Letter 13

AN OPEN LETTER TO
WIDE-AWAKE BUYERS!

Do you sell to grocery stores, supermarkets, variety stores? If you do, then our Home Sprinkler is for you!

According to a recent grocery market survey, an ideal product must stack easily, stay clean and sanitary, pilferage must be minimized, and the product should be seen without having to open the package. Also, the product should provide a hang-up hole for display purposes.

Since 90% of our last year's sales were sold to Grocery Jobbers, (more than 500,000 Home Sprinklers!), we naturally kept this recent survey in mind when we designed our new package for this year.

Yes, our Home Sprinkler is perfect for grocery store merchandising, for we purposely designed the package into a self-selling unit. Each Home Sprinkler is factory wound on its own individual steel storage reel . . . and comes complete with an attractive five-year factory guarantee card . . . your assurance of customer satisfaction.

The enclosed circular gives full information and list prices. Your discounts off list, COMPLETE WITH THE STEEL STORAGE REEL, are 50% and 10%. Terms are 2/10/30 . . . and remember . . . on orders of one gross or more, we pay full freight to your door. Send us your order today with the enclosed postage-paid airmail order label.

Sincerely,

SPRINKLER SYSTEM COMPANY

E. Joseph Cossman, President

P.S. One thing the survey didn't mention . . . the product must be a fast-moving repeater. Enclosed is a copy of a reorder we received from the Fleming Company which proves what our Home Sprinkler can do.

Letter 14

Dear Buyer:

Do you know the pretty lass on the enclosed photograph?

She's Miss Home Sprinkler!

And do you know what she's doing? She's stretching a Home Sprinkler across the country . . . from New York City to Los

Angeles, California . . . just to give you an idea of how many Home Sprinklers were sold last year.

Yes . . . more than a million of our Sprinklers . . . the equivalent of 3,000 miles . . . were sold last year! And at the rate orders are coming in this year, we'll stretch around the world by the end of this season!

The enclosed circular gives full information and list prices. Your discounts off list, COMPLETE WITH THE STORAGE REEL, are 50% & 10%.

Terms are 2/10/30 . . . and remember . . . on orders of one gross or more, we pay full freight to your door. Send us your order today . . . and you'll be ready to reorder before you know it!

Sincerely,

Sprinkler System Company

E. Joseph Cossman, President

Letter 15

Dear Editor:

How would you like to get double your advertising rate?

Sounds impossible, you say? Well, just listen . . . run any size ad you wish on the Home Sprinkler . . . use one of your own box numbers so the mail will come directly to you . . . then send all orders to us for shipping . . . and we'll pay you:

$1.60 for each 50 ft. Home Sprinkler order.
.75 for each 20 ft. Home Sprinkler order.

How does this double your advertising rate? Well, we ran a TEST 3-inch ad on the Sprinkler in the *Los Angeles Times* last November. The ad cost $80 . . . it pulled 51 orders for the 20 ft. and 83 orders for the 50 ft. Sprinkler. If we had paid the *Los Angeles Times* on the above commissions, they would have received, instead of $80, the sum of $171.05 . . . and the ad is STILL PULLING!

With a record like that, you're probably wondering, "Why don't these blokes buy at space rates and run the ads themselves?" Well, the truth is . . . this is a NEW product we have . . . an honest-to-goodness necessity for every homeowner, rich or poor . . . and we're out to do a volume job of selling. We haven't the time to do a "wise" buying job, so we're asking a carefully selected group to take this offer. Since we're the principals, there are no agency discounts involved and all commissions are net to you.

If you're interested . . . and the Home Sprinkler will be the greatest mail-puller this year . . . and you can run ads with immediate deliveries constantly assured . . . then drop the enclosed card in the mail today. It will bring you a sample of the Home Sprinkler along with glossy photos and copy.

Sincerely,

SPRINKLER SYSTEM COMPANY

E. Joseph Cossman
President

Letter 15A—Fact Sheet (with Letter 15)

THE COMPANY:

Please check us thoroughly through Dun & Bradstreet, any accredited bank or any Better Business Bureau. We're one of the largest mail order companies in America with an enviable reputation for clean deals.

THE PRODUCT:

We manufacture two . . . The Home Sprinkler and the Water Sweeper. The Home Sprinkler was introduced by us last year and fast became one of the leading mail order products in the country. The Water Sweeper is a *new* product and this is its *first* season.

THE OFFER:

Many fine publications ran our ads on a cooperative basis (and will run again this spring and summer) and we'd like to do the same with you. Here's our offer . . . run our ad on the Water Sweeper and/ or the Home Sprinkler in your publication . . . under your address or one of your own box numbers so the mail will come directly to you . . . then send all the orders to us for shipping . . . and we'll pay you:

    $1.60 for each 50 ft. Home Sprinkler order.
     .75 for each 20 ft. Home Sprinkler order.
     .60 for each Water Sweeper order.

These payments are *net* to you . . . no agency discounts.

SUCCESS STORY:

Imagine a Home Sprinkler stretching across the country . . . from New York City to Los Angeles, California . . . and you'll have an idea of how many Home Sprinklers were sold this year! Yes, more than a half million of our Sprinklers . . . the equivalent of fifteen million feet were sold . . . and most of our sales were through mail order advertising! . . . Many publications received more than double the cost of the space they used . . . and this was *without* the free reel! And now we have *two winners* . . . the Home Sprinkler and the *new* Water Sweeper . . . how can you miss?

DELIVERY:

All orders are shipped same day received . . . we maintain a constant inventory on hand for immediate shipments.

STARTING DATE:

You can run either or both products as soon as you get reproduction proofs and glossy photos . . . and we'll airmail them to you as soon as we get your card. Mail it today!

These following eight letters contributed to the overall success of our Ant Farm. We present them together so that you may note that each letter is designed to entertain as well as to give information.

LETTERS 16–23

Letter 16

A + MEANS "EXCELLENT"
IN ANY LANGUAGE

whether it's a mark given on a 10th grade English composition or a mark given for an excellent sales promotion.

My daughter wrote the enclosed composition for a school assignment (without my knowledge), and I was tickled pink to see her get an A+ on her work.

If you have a moment, read her composition . . . it's most interesting. And when you read it, please note that 35 people make a nice living raising ants . . . but only because Ant Farms are selling in such tremendous quantities that we need 1,000,000 of the cute little creatures each week.

Our Ant Farms come in two sizes:

#H15B ANT FARM . . .   measures 6″ × 9″ and retails for $2.98. Your jobber cost is $16.20 per dozen and we pay full freight on orders of 1 gross or more.

#H33 GIANT ANT FARM . . .   measures 10″ × 15″ and retails for $6.95. Your jobber cost is $37.80 per dozen and we pay full freight on orders of 6 dozen or more.

Our terms are 2/10/30 and we make immediate deliveries on all of your requirements.

Get your share of this wonderful business and send us an order today.

A postage-paid airmail reply label is enclosed for your convenience.

Sincerely,

E. JOSEPH COSSMAN & COMPANY

E. Joseph Cossman, President

Letter 17

HOW COME YOU'RE NOT BUYING OUR ANT FARMS?

The above isn't good English . . . but it's certainly good business . . . 'specially when:

- More than 500,000 Ant Farms have been sold in the past six months!
- We give you top discounts . . . along with prepaid shipments!
- We make immediate delivery on all of your requirements!
- 'Most every key jobber in the United States is selling the Ant Farm . . . that is, 'most every key jobber except you!

Why not send us a trial order today?

An airmail reply label is enclosed for your convenience.

Sincerely,

E. JOSEPH COSSMAN & COMPANY

EJC:bd   E. Joseph Cossman, President
Encl.

P.S. The #H15B Ant Farm is $2.98 retail. Your jobber cost is $16.20 per dozen and we pay full freight on orders of 1 gross or more. Terms are 2/10/30. Each Ant Farm is packed in a colorful display carton, six dozen Ant Farms per case.

E.J.C.

Letter 18

Here are some STRANGE . . . BUT TRUE facts on our Ant Farm . . .

1. We buy about one million ants each week for a penny each. That's about $10,000 in ants . . . but we need this many ants to just keep up with the demand for Ant Farms!

2. More than 35 people make a very good living in Southern California by just raising ants for us.

3. We ship only one species of ant . . . the harmless Harvester ant of California.

4. Each vial of ants we ship must be from the same colony. Ants from two different colonies will war with each other.

5. More than 300 varieties of soil were tested before we found the type best suited for the Ant Farm.

6. You can use any species of ant in the Ant Farm . . . as long as they come from the same ant hill.

7. Many jobbers report that their dealers are selling Ant Farms as gifts for shut-ins and convalescents . . . in fact, we're surprised at the number of hospitals and rehabilitation centers now buying the Ant Farm in quantity. Schools, too.

8. 'Most every key jobber in the country is selling the Ant Farm . . . that is, 'most every key jobber except you!

Yes . . . these are all STRANGE, BUT TRUE facts . . . but the strangest of all is fact number 8! How's about sending us a trial order today?

Sincerely,

E. JOSEPH COSSMAN & COMPANY

EJC:bd

P.S. Your jobber cost is $16.20 per dozen with full freight prepaid by us on orders of one gross or more.

Letter 19

(This letter was typed on graph paper.)

AN OPEN LETTER TO
A WIDE-AWAKE BUYER . . .

Your first impulse when you opened this letter, no doubt, was to ask, "Why a letter on graph paper, usually associated with engineering?"

Well . . . we are the manufacturer of the famous Ant Farm . . . and since ants are the world's tiniest (and best) engineers, this paper is most appropriate.

However, our ants not only excel in construction building . . . they are also terrific builders, and just a quick look at the enclosed brochure will prove this to you . . . 'most every leading department store in the country is doing a wonderful, wonderful job on the Ant Farm!'

The Ant Farm is $2.98 retail. Your cost is $21.60 per dozen, less 10% advertising allowance rebatable upon proof of ad. We pay full freight on orders of 1 gross or more. Terms are 2/20/30. Each Ant Farm is packed in a colorful display carton, six dozen Ant Farms per case.

Send us your order today and cash in on one of the most fascinating products to hit the market in a long time. We make immediate deliveries.

> Sincerely,
> E. JOSEPH COSSMAN & COMPANY

EJC:ctl   E. Joseph Cossman, President
Encl.

PS. And best of all . . . your customers get a supply of ants, but you don't stock them! A "Stock Certificate" is packed with each Ant Farm. The customer mails the certificate to us and we airmail a FREE supply of ants direct to him.

> E.J.C.

Letter 20

OPEN LETTER TO
ALL TOY BUYERS:

We are the only toy manufacturer who can accurately report to you the day-by-day retail sales of our line. Each time we receive a certificate for ants, we *know* another Cossman ANT FARM has been sold. It's just like hearing the cash register ring.

The Christmas buying rush is over . . . and *again* the popularity of Cossman ANT FARMS has been proven! We worked our people 'round the clock to "express" hundreds of thousands of ants from coast to coast.

However, the really IMPORTANT FACT is that our business does *not* "die" after the holiday rush. We keep right on shipping thousands of ants *every day* . . . *all year!* No other proof is needed that Cossman ANT FARMS are still the *No.* 1 regularly selling toy.

We invite you to check our records. If you're enjoying regular ANT FARM sales, we're confident you will continue to take advantage of a line that provides this steady sales picture. If, on the other hand, you are among the few who have overlooked your potential share of this constantly tremendous market . . . don't put off getting on the band wagon any longer. Order a supply of Regular size and Giant size Cossman ANT FARMS . . . TODAY!

Sincerely

E. JOSEPH COSSMAN & COMPANY

EJC:jb
Encl.

P.S. Remember . . . we *know* they're selling . . . *we* ship the ants!

Letter 21

HERE'S GOOD NEWS FOR SMART BUYERS!

The Cossman Ant Farm is now in a *new full-color package* that almost JUMPS off the shelf! Just take a look at the enclosed full-color box wrap and you'll agree!

We know it's great because recent market research tests show the new package outselling the old one 5 to 1 . . . yet more than two million Cossman Ant Farms were sold in the old package!

Just look at these reports:

> A Retail Dealer told his Jobber: "I had Cossman Ant Farms last season, but my customers tell me they didn't see them in my store until I displayed the new box."

> A Pet Supply Jobber called and said: "The new package on the Cossman Ant Farm is like having a new item. The dealers are selling them like hot cakes."

> A Department Store Toy Buyer stated: "The customers stopped dead in their tracks when we put up a display of the new package. We're doubling our sales on Cossman Ant Farms."

Yes, we've received glowing reports and compliments from almost everyone except the ants! . . . and even they're proud of this new package! Best of all, there's no increase in price . . . The Cossman Ant Farm is still only $2.98 retail. Same liberal discounts, too . . . your jobber cost is $16.20 per dozen and we pay full freight on one gross or more. Terms are 2/10/30.

Send us your order today and cash in on one of the biggest money-makers to hit the market in a long time. We can make immediate deliveries!

Sincerely,

E. JOSEPH COSSMAN & COMPANY

EJC:jb

P.S. Don't forget our GIANT Ant Farm . . . $6.95 retail . . . your cost, $37.80 per dozen. See enclosed order blank for the *"New Box Special Offer."*

EJC

Letter 22

There's no need for a long letter when our message is brief. So we'll just skip—
—down to here and say "Ant Farms are selling, selling, selling! Do you have enough in stock?"

Sincerely,

E. Joseph Cossman & Company

P.S. Your cost? Still only $16.20 per dozen with full freight prepaid on one gross or more. Order today.

Letter 23

WHAT? A FARM FOR ANTS?
AN ANT FARM FOR CHILDREN?

Yes . . . and it looks as though the main crop of this unique Ant Farm is making MONEY. If you have not ordered our Ant Farm as yet, here are three good reasons why you should do so now:

1. National publicity is pouring in from Coast to Coast . . . from newspapers, radio, magazines, and television. It seems that everybody is talking about our Ant Farms!

2. In our 12 years of manufacturing, we have never seen a product sell so fast. We have several accounts on our books who are already on their fourth and fifth repeat orders . . . even though the product has only been on the market a few short weeks!

3. If you order now, you, too, will be reordering again and again.

The Ant Farm is $2.98 retail. Your cost is $21.60 per dozen less 10% advertising allowance rebatable upon proof of ad. We pay full freight on orders of one gross or more. Terms are 2/10/30. Each Ant Farm is packed in a colorful display carton, six dozen Ant Farms per case.

Send us your order today and cash in on one of the most fascinating products to hit the market in a long time. We make immediate deliveries.

Sincerely,

E. JOSEPH COSSMAN & COMPANY

E. Joseph Cossman, President

EJC:ctl

P.S. And best of all . . . your customers get a supply of ants but you don't stock them! A "Stock Certificate" is packed with each Ant Farm. The customer mails the certificate to us and we airmail a FREE supply of ants direct to him.

Letter 24 is the one we used to introduce our Fly Cake to the trade, and Letters 25 through 27 were the start of our Fly Cake selling campaign.

LETTERS 24–27

Letter 24

HERE'S NEWS ON A NEWLY PATENTED PRODUCT . . .

We are now producing a revolutionary new product called FLY CAKE. Frankly, we are so excited about this new product, we don't know where to begin. Now, for the first time . . . a fly killer has been invented that . . .

- Lasts all season . . . yes, each cake is effective for a complete season and controls up to 100 square feet of area.

- It kills flies on contact . . . the fly does not have to eat the cake; actually, it dies within seconds after alighting on the cake.

- Fly Cake kills other insects also . . . it has been used effectively for cockroach control, ants, or other crawling insects. However, its chief value is its effectiveness with fly control.

- Common sprays or aerosols disperse their poisons in all directions throughout living areas. Fly Cake's special insect-destroying chemicals are safely sealed within a solid cake—can't taint food, clothing, furniture. Pets are not attracted to Fly Cake and it is not harmful if touched or even tasted by humans.

Fly Cake is a product that homeowners, farmers, and industry have needed for a long time. A test order will convince you.

We can make immediate delivery on any quantity. Send us your order today.

Sincerely,

E. JOSEPH COSSMAN & COMPANY

E. Joseph Cossman

EJC:jb
Encl.

P.S. Your costs are on the enclosed postage-paid order envelope.

Letter 25

DO WE HAVE A WINNER?

Sure . . . when you introduce a new product, you're bound to get a lot of sample orders.

Sure . . . when you run national advertising in trade publications, many companies will at least try out a test shipment.

- But when the product has been on the market for a few short weeks . . .

- And you ship over a million units in that time . . .

- And most of these sales are a result of *repeat, repeat,* and *repeat* orders from the trade . . .

THEN YOU KNOW YOU HAVE A WINNER!

To prove our point, just look over the enclosed letter we received from a leading local account. He's already on his fifth repeat order . . . and is so enthusiastic about the product, he just had to write us about his results!

If you're not handling FLY CAKE, you're losing money right now. Study the enclosed circular . . . read all about this incredible product . . . then send us your order today!

We can practically guarantee that in a few weeks you, too, will want to sit right down and write us a letter about this effective, fast-selling, money-making product—FLY CAKE!

Sincerely,

E. JOSEPH COSSMAN & COMPANY

EJC:jb
Encl.

P.S. The enclosed postage-paid airmail order envelope gives your costs and packing information. Mail it today . . . and we'll ship tomorrow. Airmail reaches us overnight.

Letter 26

Kockos Brothers, Ltd.
220 Shaw Road
So. San Francisco, California

Gentlemen:

There are over fifty thousand dead flies in the enclosed photograph . . . and they were all killed by one Cossman FLY CAKE!

Although FLY CAKE came on the market as late as last June, we have already sold, shipped, and delivered over two million cakes. And since a large part of this business were repeat orders, this is proof-positive of FLY CAKE'S effective fly control and acceptance.

Because of the unprecedented demand for FLY CAKE last year, there were times when many of our accounts had to wait for delivery . . . we just couldn't make the product fast enough!

If you carried this incredible product last year, may we suggest you place your order now so your company will have FLY CAKE available when your customers begin demanding it this spring. If you didn't carry it, may we suggest you place a trial order now for immediate delivery. An order envelope is enclosed for your convenience.

Sincerely,

E. JOSEPH COSSMAN & COMPANY

E. Joseph Cossman

EJC:jb
Encl.

P.S. Take advantage of our "Early Bird Special" . . . order FLY CAKE within the next 30 days and you can have dating terms of 2%/ 60 days. To qualify, your order envelope must be postmarked any time within thirty days from the date of this letter.

Letter 27

A LETTER OF THANKS

Yes, thank you for your opening order of Cossman FLY CAKE. We are very glad you ordered at this time, for it gives you an opportunity to be the first in your area to offer this newly patented product to your accounts.

Frankly, we have a most incredible product in FLY CAKE . . . it has been on the market only a few short weeks and we've already sold and shipped over a million cakes. Imagine how this product will sell when the fly season is in full swing!

Enclosed with this letter is a sample of our envelope stuffer. The last page provides a space for your name and address imprint. If you wish, we can supply you with these stuffers at $4 per thousand. They make an extremely effective selling tool and will more than pay for themselves with the results you'll get from them. If you would like to try a few hundred, we'll be glad to send them to you at no charge.

Remember . . . we can make immediate delivery on all your FLY CAKE requirements. We'll be looking forward to some healthy repeat orders from you in the very near future.

Sincerely,

E. JOSEPH COSSMAN & COMPANY

Encl.

P.S. Also enclosed is a postage-paid airmail order envelope for your convenience in reordering.

Letters 28 and 29 were used most effectively for getting business from mail order houses.

Letter 30 was used to sell a telephone amplifier, and Letter 31 was used to introduce a new soft drink to the fountain trade in Los Angeles.

We used Letter 32 to get mail order houses to run an ad on a product selling for more than $100!

LETTERS 28–32 ·

Letter 28

IMAGINE GETTING A ONE GROSS INITIAL
ORDER FROM A MAIL ORDER HOUSE . . .

and one week after his catalog was out . . . getting an urgent phone call . . . 3,000 more pieces. And then, only five days later, another reorder for 3,000 more! That's what happened with our Ant Farm!

Imagine running a test ad on a new mail order product and receiving 14 orders from the newspaper staff BEFORE the ad was even published! That's what happened with our "World's Greatest" Trophies.

These are just a few of the unique experiences we've received with our latest mail order items. Look over the enclosed brochure carefully, as we believe it contains some of the best products we have ever offered during our eleven years of manufacturing mail order merchandise.

And when you look over these 23 *tested* products, please remember:

- Our products come to you individually packed.
- You get "exclusive protection" on your space advertising.
- You buy at extreme jobber discount prices.
- You get full freight on all orders of 100 lbs. or more.

Start a successful selling year NOW! Write us today . . . tell us what you like . . . and we'll immediately airmail to you glossy photographs and ad copy for your space ads and/or catalogs.

Sincerely,

E. JOSEPH COSSMAN & COMPANY

E. Joseph Cossman, President

EJC:ctl

P.S. You may order samples at your cost price, but please include payment and save us the trouble of invoicing for this small amount. A postage-paid airmail label is enclosed for your convenience. Thank you.

Letter 29

NOW YOU CAN CARRY A $100,000 INVENTORY

FOR THE COST OF A POSTAGE STAMP!
. . . and every product in this tremendous stock is a proven, tested Mail Order best-seller for you!

Here's all you do:

- Insert a copy of the enclosed mailing piece with every order you're now shipping.

- Or send this mailing piece to your regular lists of customers.

- Or sell these products to fund-raising groups or organizations.

WE DO THE REST . . . AND YOU MAKE A 40% NET PROFIT!

Our company has manufactured products exclusively for the mail order trade for the past 12 years and the enclosed mailing piece represents the 16 most popular items in our line. This mailing piece can become YOUR very own catalog . . . it can be imprinted with your name and address to actually look like a custom catalog for your own business.

And when your customers order from this catalog, you deduct 40% PROFIT FOR YOURSELF, send us the balance, together with the order and your OWN addressed mailing label . . . and we do the rest. Yes, we do all the packing, shipping, handling, and pay postage . . . and your customers get their orders with your own label attached to the package.

How do you get these catalogs? We supply them to you at our cost as listed on the enclosed price list. Send us your order for catalogs today . . . you'll be glad you did, for it puts extra dollars in your pocket as soon as you mail them out.

Sincerely,

E. JOSEPH COSSMAN & COMPANY

Encl.

P.S. Did you know our customers include most of the leading mail order houses throughout the country? Let us add your name to our list of accounts NOW making money!

Letter 30

WILL YOU GIVE YOURSELF
AN EFFICIENCY TEST?

Just take a pencil and answer these 5 questions:

	Yes	No
1. Did you ever need both hands free while talking on the telephone?	( )	( )
2. Were you ever left "hanging" on the phone while waiting for your party to answer?	( )	( )

3. Have you ever had occasion for a conference call in your office? ( ) ( )

4. Did you ever want to look for a paper, a file, or some other information but you were chained to the telephone? ( ) ( )

5. Did you ever want to "move about" your office while talking on the phone? ( ) ( )

If your answer to any of the above questions is "yes" . . . then the EXEC-U-PHONE is for you. And to introduce EXEC-U-PHONE to you, we'll be very happy to let you try it in your own office on a seven-day free trial basis.

We absolutely guarantee that EXEC-U-PHONE will do everything we say it will . . . or you can return it to us in one week with no obligation.

Fair enough? Then order one today . . . and "unchain" yourself from your desk.

Sincerely,

E. JOSEPH COSSMAN & COMPANY

EJC:jb

P.S. EXEC-U-PHONE also makes a wonderful gift for the home. If you order two, take a 10% discount for yourself on both. Same 7-day free trial offer.

Letter 31

WOULD YOU GIVE US 15 INCHES OF YOUR COUNTER
FOR $231.80 PER MONTH?

Frankly, we are being conservative. Most of our dealers are making much more! They are making it simply by selling the purest, most delicious, the "business-buildingest" fruit drink in the country . . . Reymer's LEMON BLENND!

Reymer's Lemon Blennd is a non-carbonated drink, made of 100% pure California orange and lemon juices. Gives you better than 300% profit! Look at these facts:

1. Give us only 15 inches of your counterspace and we'll install, absolutely without charge to you, our smart, modern electric JET SPRAY DISPENSER—a $300 value which serves BLENND so beautifully and deliciously!

2. BLENND outsells 4 out of 5 other popular soft drinks in the East—has for years. In recent tests in Los Angeles, it outsold our most optimistic estimates.

3. BLENND will be a household word to Southern Californians in no time, thanks to a powerful advertising campaign. We'll supply free to every BLENND dealer a full assortment of bar and window banners, stickers, counter cards and caps for the crew, to tie in with the overall advertising.

Cash in on this "FOUNTAIN OF GOLD" by returning the enclosed postage-free card, or by calling us now at the above phone number. Frankly, we will be able to get only 1,000 JET SPRAY DISPENSERS this year, so it will be first come, first served. Call now for your Dispenser, or for additional information.

Sincerely,

E. JOSEPH COSSMAN & COMPANY

E. Joseph Cossman, President

Encl.

Letter 32

HOW WOULD YOU LIKE TO MAKE
$1 PROFIT ON EVERY SALE YOU MISS?
AND
$20 PROFIT ON EVERY SALE YOU MAKE?

At last . . . the perfect mail order item:

- A standard product, backed by years of national advertising, with a large market already created because of its brand name alone.

- No inventory to carry.

- $1 profit *on every application you receive.*

- No orders to process . . . no ads to write . . . no postage, handling, or shipping . . . we do *everything* with absolutely no cost to you!

Here's all you do:

Run the enclosed ad in your forthcoming mail order catalog. Keep the dollar the customer sends to you. As soon as your customer's credit application is approved, we send you $19 additional. That's all there is . . . it's as simple as that!

For further particulars, read the enclosed fact sheet. If you need more information, phone me collect. In the meantime, be sure to give this offer top space in your next catalog. In addition to lending prestige to your catalog, it will pay you off in dollars and cents.

Sincerely,

E. JOSEPH COSSMAN & COMPANY

E. Joseph Cossman, President

EJC:cs

P.S. Be sure to let us know when your next catalog closes, so we can send you the necessary glossy photos, art work, etc.

Letters 33, 34, and 35 are three excellent collection letters which have helped us keep our credit losses low.

LETTERS 33–35

Letter 33

Gentlemen:

Re: Your past-due account of $............
Invoice #............ Dated ....

Got a pencil handy?

Here's a fast and easy way to take care of the above past-due account. Just check one of the spaces below and mail this letter back to us.

[ ] Just overlooked it. Here's full payment.

[ ] Will pay it all in the next .... days.

[ ] Just overlooked it. Here's full payment.

[ ] Am short of money. I'm sending part of it now and you'll get the rest on ....

[ ] Just overlooked it. Here's full payment.

Best regards,

E. JOSEPH COSSMAN & COMPANY

EJC:ctl

Letter 34

Gentlemen:

There's an old saying that goes:

"Wealthy people miss one of the greatest thrills in life . . . paying the last installment!"

Enclosed with this letter is a list of other good sayings and stories to put you in a good mood.

If you want to put us in a good mood . . . please pay your past due account in the amount of $ .... covering Invoice # .... dated ....

Send us your check today and we'll send you another list of sayings immediately. Okay?

Many thanks.

Sincerely,

E. JOSEPH COSSMAN & COMPANY

EJC:ctl

With Letter 34, we sent the following "list of sayings" referred to in the letter:

1. What this country needs is a good five-cent dime.
2. Psychiatry is the only business where the customer is always wrong.
3. The best way to a man's wallet is to build a better gadget for his wife.
4. Women's intuition is nothing more than man's transparency.
5. Suspicion is a mental picture seen through an imaginary key-hole.
6. A bachelor girl is one who is still looking for a bachelor.
7. The world needs more leaders with stars in their eyes instead of in their helmets.
8. Worry often gives a small thing a big shadow.
9. Your calendar shows the passing of time. Your face shows what you're doing with it.
10. Some families can trace their ancestry back 300 years, but can't tell you where their children were last night.
11. The nice thing about old age is that you can whistle while you brush your teeth.

* * *

Says a local cynic: "The only reason a great many families don't own an elephant is that they never have been offered an elephant for $1 down and $1 a week."

* * *

12. When your Outgo exceeds your Income, your Upkeep is your Downfall.
13. There is no better exercise for the heart than reaching down and lifting somebody up.
14. Destiny may shape your end but your middle is of your own chewsing.
15. Heaven may forgive your sins, but your nervous system won't.
16. Many things which seem simple at twenty are impossible at sixty, and vice versa.
17. Diplomacy is the art of saying "Nice doggie" until you can find a rock.
18. Today it costs more to amuse the child than it did to educate the parent.
19. Since the discovery of elastic, women take up one-third less space.

* * *

Overheard on the cocktail circuit: "One thing about the speed of light—it gets here too early in the morning."

* * *

20. Husband-hunting is probably the only sport in which the animal that gets caught has to buy a license.
21. Don't put it off until tomorrow. Tomorrow there may be a law against it.

Letter 35

Letter 35 consisted of the following words—

... and you owe us since ....
What's your excuse?

EJC

P.S. Enclosed is an envelope. Mail us your check today. Thanks.

EJC

—which were handwritten on one of my personal memo-pad sheets and attached to the list of excuses below:

EXCUSES!   EXCUSES!

- A Buffalo (New York) bakery-truck driver told police he was speeding "so that the whipped cream on the cupcakes wouldn't turn sour."

- In Pittsburgh (Pennsylvania) an ex-convict, discovered trying the doors of a rectory with a bunch of keys, stated: "I was just looking for a place to pray."

- A Davenport (Iowa) man, arrested for having in his possession an expensive pair of sandals, claimed: "I happened to fall through the store window and the sandals somehow became attached to me."

- An East Chicago (Indiana) man asked the mayor to get a job for his steel-striking brother-in-law, explaining: "He supports my mother-in-law. If he doesn't, I'll have to."

- A Montreal (Canada) motorist, failing to signal a left turn, told police that because it was a local election day, he was afraid to put his hand out lest a candidate run over and shake it.

- A St. Louis (Missouri) man considered he was entitled to a divorce because his wife's dumplings stuck to the roof of his mouth.

- A San Antonio (Texas) driver, fined for driving without a license, protested he couldn't get one because of poor vision. His job: car jockey in a parking lot.

Sometimes a cute or novel letter will backfire. As an example, when we sent out Letter 35 on "Excuses," we received a reply from one of our delinquent accounts. His excuse? He claimed that he found our series of collection letters so entertaining that he wasn't going to pay his bill until he received the entire series! He promised to send us the full amount due if we would send him, by return mail, the balance of our collection series. This we did, and his check was received within a few days.

12 | 22 Trade Secrets and Ideas

"The more you know . . . the more luck you will have."

This chapter lists a collection of trade secrets and ideas that are known to only a few businessmen. It took us several years to learn most of them, and the ideas listed here have literally saved us thousands of dollars. We defy anyone to read through this chapter without picking up at least one new idea that can be applied to his own business.

1. HOW TO PROTECT A SALABLE IDEA

Many times in your business career you will develop an idea that cannot be protected by copyright or patent. Yet the idea is so simple that once you divulge it, anyone can take it away from you. How to protect such an idea? The best way we know of was fully described in Annual No. 3 of *Management Aids for Small Business* issued by the Superintendent of Documents, United States Government Printing Office, Washington, DC. The book sold for less than one dollar, but this particular article, "How to Protect Salable Ideas," was worth many times the book price. The article gave several test-case examples and provided a guidepost of rules to follow in protecting an intangible idea.

A wide variety of business innovations are developed daily—affecting such diverse items as hairpins and farm implements, household articles and large industrial equipment. Ideas also occur for improving business methods or streamlining operations. Innovations may be classified as tangible and intangible. In the first class are those which affect mechanical items, designs, chemical compounds, works of art, and the like. The intangible kinds include business plans, systems, advertising campaigns, and so on.

● *Marketable Ideas.* Many new ideas are basically intellectual property. But, if put into practice, they could be profitable both to the originator and to the businessman who adopts them. Improvement in the design or in the appearance of an item already patented or available to the public falls into this class. Also, the redesign of an article, popular years ago, to make it acceptable again may prove profitable. Likewise, the substitution of superior materials for inferior ones may enhance the salability of a product.

Ideas for improving various compositions, including formulas, by the mere addition of a new flavoring, a new scent, or the like, may make it possible to offer a superior product to the public, and thereby increase profits. The important questions are: How can the ideas man or businessman promote these valuable unpatentable ideas? How can they be protected? What steps can be taken to profit from them?

● *Growth of Legal Opinion.* As far back as the early English courts, it was held that a man had title to his originations, but, unless protectable by established law, those ideas became public property as soon as divulged. This old common law has been passed down to become part of our present code. Many ideas men, therefore, are led to believe that their ideas cannot be protected in any way. As a result, numerous potentially profitable concepts have been abandoned. There is little, if any, actual statutory law governing the exchange of ideas, but a large body of court decisions in this field has been accumulated. Much can be learned from the more important cases.

● *Cases in Point.* The requirement that the possessor of an idea must be able to prove that it was actually original with him was brought out by the suit of *Moore v. Ford Motor Company*, 43 Fed. (2d) 685. Moore had conceived a thrift purchase plan adapted for use in the sale of automobiles. He wrote to the Ford Company that he would like an opportunity to submit the plan, which he believed would increase the sale of their automobiles. Ford replied:

"If you will kindly write us in detail regarding the plan which you have in mind for increasing the sale of Ford cars, understanding that in doing so there will be no obligation on our part, we will be very glad to give the matter our careful attention and advise you whether or not we would be interested in the plan."

Thereupon, Moore submitted his plan in a letter, concluding with the following paragraph:

"The above is a general idea of what I have in mind. I understand it is subject to amendments and eliminations, but if it is usable I would very much like to aid in perfecting it. However, as called for in your letter, I am writing to you with the understanding that there is no obligation on your part."

The Ford Company subsequently returned Moore's letter stating that it would not be interested in the proposition. At a later date, Ford put into effect a weekly purchase plan which became nationally known. That plan was similar to the one submitted by Moore except as to specific differences in detail.

Moore then brought suit, contending that his plan had been appropriated by Ford. In the trial, Moore relied on his own evidence; namely, the correspondence between himself and the Ford Company, plus the copy of the plan as presented to Ford, which the latter had returned, marked "not interested." Ford called in witnesses testifying that various Ford dealers throughout the country had already been using similar plans; that is, weekly payment schemes whereby terms of purchase could be made easier.

The court held that there was no piracy because there were too many differences in detail between Moore's plan and the one put into effect by Ford. Furthermore, said the court, the basic idea appeared to have been used in Christmas savings club plans, which were known throughout the country prior to Moore's proposal. Because the inventor could not establish that he was the first and true originator, nor prove definitely that the Ford Motor Company had appropriated or copied his idea, Moore did not have any ground on which the suit could be sustained.

The requirement for protecting an idea with a contract was brought out in the case of Bowen v. Yankee Network, Inc., 46 Fed. Sup. 63. Bowen contended that William Wrigley, Jr. Company pirated his valuable and novel idea for a "radio presentation." Bowen had submitted his plan to Wrigley, which after some delay returned it as unacceptable. Wrigley later disclosed the idea to Yankee Network, Inc. Soon, a weekly radio presentation entitled "Spreading New England Fame," containing the features and ideas set forth in Bowen's proposal, was produced on the network.

In court it was brought out (1) that Bowen voluntarily submitted his idea to Wrigley; (2) that because of the voluntary submission there was no breach of trust or contract; and (3) that there was no correspondence or other evidence to show that the disclosure of the idea to Wrigley had been done with the understanding that there was any limitation upon the use of it by the company. As a result it was held by the court that Bowen could have protected his idea by contract, but that he failed to do so when he voluntarily communicated it. Whatever interest he had in the idea therefore became public property.

From this case we learn: (1) An idea made public, by word of mouth or in writing, immediately becomes common property, and unless the plan is revealed under contract or by confidential disclosure, anyone can make use of that property without infringing any rights; (2) the voluntary submission of an idea does not set up a contractual relationship between the originator and the other party; (3) because of the lack of contract, no action of any kind can be brought by the originator for breach of trust or contract; (4) ideas can be protected, provided the originator follows certain procedures governed by the law of contracts.

Another decision which emphasized the importance of drawing up a contract to protect an idea was rendered in the case of *Equitable Life Insurance Co.*, 132 N.Y. 265. In this suit it was held that, without denying there may be property rights in an idea, trade secret, or system, it is obvious that its originator must, himself, protect it from escape or disclosure. If the innovation cannot be sold or negotiated for, or used without a disclosure, it would seem proper that some contract, either expressed or implied, should guard or regulate the divulgence. Otherwise, the idea becomes the acquisition of whomever receives it.

• *Protecting Your Idea.* The law of contracts applies in all such instances, but for it to be binding, there must be a definite "meeting of the minds" (that is, agreement among the parties concerned). If you are a businessman looking for suggestions, be very careful if you advertise for them. You should state that ideas to be considered must be original and novel and the conception of the person submitting them, and that they must be submitted in explicit form. Any ambiguity could easily result in nullification of a contract because a definite proposal had not been made.

Furthermore, the fact that you as a businessman consent to examine an idea does not mean that you have to buy it or put it into use. Therefore, in your contracts or correspondence you should insert a proviso whereby you do not obligate yourself in any way by appraising the idea to be submitted. This, of course, does not free you from obligation in the event that you do make use of the idea submitted. In the *Moore v. Ford Motor Company* case, it was held that all danger of subsequent demands or obligations cannot be avoided by merely stating "no obligation whatsoever." You should, therefore, protect yourself against any obligation to utilize the plan.

Some businessmen protect themselves by setting up special methods of handling ideas. Frequently they are channeled to one individual, making it impossible for the information contained in that idea to become accessible to employees at large. By doing this, it can be proved more easily in court that the idea has not been used or permitted to escape.

At one time we had an idea that would increase magazine circulation for any publisher. The idea could not be protected by copyright and it could not be patented, so we took the course of action suggested by the government and prepared a contract as follows:

Gentlemen:

I have developed a new idea to help increase the circulation of almost any publication, record club, monthly book club; in fact, most any type of merchandise or service that is sold by mail on a subscription basis.

If you're interested in the details of my idea, I shall be glad to give you complete information if you will kindly sign the enclosed agreement form. Promptly upon receipt of the signed form, I will give you all the information I have regarding the idea.

Sincerely,

E. JOSEPH COSSMAN

EJC:pg
Encl.

* * *

AGREEMENT TO REVIEW IDEA

We, the undersigned, agree to receive in confidence full details about an idea for increasing the sale of publications, merchandise, or services that are sold on a subscription basis and delivered by mail.

It is further understood that we assume no responsibility whatever with respect to features which can be demonstrated to be already known to us. We also agree not to divulge any details of the idea submitted without permission of E. Joseph Cossman or to make use of any feature or information of which the said E. Joseph Cossman is the originator, without payment of compensation to be fixed by negotiation with the said E. Joseph Cossman or his lawful representative.

It is specifically understood that, in receiving the idea of E. Joseph Cossman, the idea is being received and will be reviewed in confidence and that, within a period of 30 days, we will report to E. Joseph Cossman the results of our findings and will advise whether or not we are interested in negotiating for the purchase of the right to use said idea.

Company ....

Street and Number ....

City .... State .... Zip ....

Official to receive disclosures:

.... Title ....

Date .... Signature ....

Accepted: ....

The idea is the copyright property of:

E. Joseph Cossman

We had the interested parties sign this agreement and then disclosed our idea to them. This signed contract gave us legal protection for recourse in the event they used the idea without our permission or without payment to us.

The acceptance of these conditions by the signing of the agreement constituted a "meeting of the minds," and once that had been accomplished, a definite contract had been established.

When the businessman agrees to review the invention and report on his decision, he also understands that he will receive complete details—something on which a definite opinion can be based. Thus, in order to make the contract binding and valid, it is up to the idea man to furnish all pertinent facts.

After the originator of the idea has submitted his material to a businessman under a definite contract, it is up to the latter to fulfill his obligations by carefully examining the material and reporting his findings to the originator within a reasonable time. In his reply to the originator, the businessman should state whether or not he is interested in the actual purchase and use of the idea.

Checklist for Handling Unpatentable Ideas

The following checklist is offered governing submission and acceptance of profitable ideas:

● *The Idea Man Can:*

(a) Establish priority to an idea.

(b) Protect his idea by complying with the law of contracts.

(c) Safely deal with others so that they may examine his idea to find out if they want to buy it.

(d) Sue for breach of contract following misappropriation of an idea submitted in confidence and under contract.

(e) Lose title to his idea if it is released to a second person under any condition other than under obligation to review in confidence.

(f) Rely on a businessman's request to disclose in confidence.

● *The Idea Man Cannot:*

(a) Broadcast the idea and still retain exclusive control.

(b) Recover damages if the idea or any of its details are submitted unsolicited.

(c) Recover damages for misappropriation of his idea unless he can prove that he is the first and true originator.

(d) Recover damages unless there is a violation of a definite "meeting of the minds" between him and the other party as to specific conditions of disclosure.

(e) Recover damages unless there has been obvious copying or use of any or all of the submitted idea.

● *Business Managers Should:*

(a) Be willing to consider ideas originating outside their business employment.

(b) Require submission of complete details under specific agreement.

(c) Report promptly their reactions and possible interest.

(d) Retain all information confidentially.

(e) Deal fairly with the originator.

● *Business Managers Should Not:*

(a) Review any material or idea not submitted under agreement.

(b) Divulge any information on an idea received in confidence.

(c) Make use of any features of an idea (even when submitted at their own request) without express permission of the originator.

Thus, an ideas man who creates something worthwhile, even though no patent or copyright protection is available, may be able to cash in on his innovation. Legal decisions aid him if he follows the procedure by which many unpatentable ideas can be safely handled. When offering intellectual property, he must be able to prove that he is the first and true originator, and he must have the assurance of a contract that his disclosure will be treated confidentially. Once an idea leaves the mind of the originator, except under specific contractual arrangement, that idea becomes public property. A business manager must deal fairly with originators of ideas who are willing to release their conceptions for consideration as to possible use. Likewise, they must protect themselves against suit for misappropriation of new ideas.

2. ANOTHER GOOD WAY TO PROTECT YOUR IDEA

Place a description or sketch (or both) in an envelope. Enclose all pertinent facts and notations regarding your idea and address the envelope to yourself. Attach a single postage stamp over the sealed flap which will, in effect, seal your envelope with a government stamp. Then take the sealed envelope to your Post Office and ask the postal clerk to cancel the stamp with a postal date stamp. Send this envelope to yourself by *registered mail.* But when your envelope arrives, do not open it, as the date-canceled stamp on the back literally "seals" your idea and establishes the actual date of the idea itself. Then, when necessity demands, you can open the sealed envelope before proper parties or authorities, thereby proving your ownership of the idea by the date stamped on the back.

3. HOW TO STOP FOREIGN COMPETITION FROM ENTERING THE UNITED STATES MARKET

If your product has a properly registered trademark, if your product has been copyrighted, or if your product has received a United

States patent, you may call on the Treasury Department of the United States to prohibit the entry of foreign-made merchandise which infringes on your rights. Such infringement by foreign manufacturers can be stopped at its inception with the assistance of officers of the United States Customs House. This governmental department will assert control over the importing of products that infringe on your rights. As owner, you must first file an application with the Treasury Department to record your copyright, trademark, or patent. This act is known as a "block entry," and if your product can fulfill the requirements demanded by the Treasury Department, it will take the proper steps to prevent foreign products similar to yours from entering this country.

At one time we manufactured a line of novelties that we had had copyrighted as "works of art." An unscrupulous American manufacturer airmailed samples of our line to Japan and had exact facsimiles made for considerably less money than we could possibly manufacture the units for in this country. We immediately applied for a block entry from the Commissioner of Customs in Washington, DC, and our competitor was not permitted to bring his merchandise into the United States because his products were a direct infringement on our copyright.

4. HOW WE USE A NOTARIZED SEAL IN OUR PROMOTIONS

Many times in merchandising you will develop a product that is almost unbelievable in its performance. How do you impress the public with the truth of this performance? We do it with a notarized seal.

For example: Our Fly Cake killed flies faster than any other insecticide on the market. Since most other insecticides claimed almost the same results, we had to offer dramatic proof of the superiority of Fly Cake. We did this by taking a sequence of four photographs of Fly Cake "in action." We then took the photographs to a notary public and swore by affidavit that the photographs were unretouched.

This use of notary seal and notarized statement proved more effective in assuring the customer of the honesty of our tests than any other method of promotion.

5. HOW TO USE A RETURN ADDRESS LABEL INSTEAD OF A RETURN ADDRESS ENVELOPE

For a change of pace, use a postage-paid, self-addressed return label instead of the familiar postage-paid return envelope. We developed this idea several years ago and found that it pulls much more effectively than the envelope. The fact that a label is unique and novel when it is used in this manner captures more attention for you.

Another reason that we have found for the return label's popularity is because many large companies wish to use their own envelopes in return mailings. The label gives them an opportunity to do so and also gives them the advantage of a postage-paid piece of mail.

6. THE "MOST READ" PAGE IN ANY NEWSPAPER

We know from experience that the position of your ad in a newspaper can mean the difference between success or failure for your product. We believe it suicidal to take "run of paper" in a newspaper; your ad will "die" before it even gets started. After making several tests and a thorough study of our newspaper results, we discovered the television page to be the best pulling page of any newspaper. Even if you must pay a premium for this page, it's worth it because of the additional reading power your ad will command. We have one test on record where our television page ad outpulled another ad in "run of paper" by more than 10 to 1!

7. HOW TO SELL TO ARMY, NAVY, AND AIR FORCE POST EXCHANGES

Some of the most lucrative markets in the United States (and overseas) are the Military Post Exchanges. The army, the navy, and the air force each have their own P.X., and these outlets are large volume buyers if you have a product that will fit in their category. We have sold thousands of sets of toy soldiers to the military exchanges, and these sales were all made through direct mail. Almost any consumer product on the market today can be sold to military post exchanges. Here are some of the more obvious advantages of selling your product to them: They buy in large volume, pay their bills promptly, and are loyal customers once you get them started.

8. SUBSCRIBE TO THE SUNDAY EDITION OF THE NEW YORK TIMES

Of all publications in the United States, the Sunday edition of the New York Times has been the most fruitful in many ways for us. The classified section of this newspaper is chock-full of business opportunities, new products, business connections, and other commercial activities that will stimulate and excite your business plans. It is not necessary to subscribe to the daily issues, since the publication has a subscription service covering the Sunday issues only. This very inexpensive subscription can be one of the best business investments you will ever make.

9. WANT A 5' × 7' WALL MAP OF THE UNITED STATES?

Yes, you can get a wall map of the U.S. printed in nine colors, measuring a full 5 feet by 7 feet. The map comes to you printed on two sheets of heavy map paper; it is not folded and is ready for mounting or hanging. To get this valuable bargain, write to the Superintendent of Documents, Government Printing Office, Washington, DC 20402, and order "Wall Map of the U.S.," catalog number 153.11:UN3/953.

10. HOW TO GET ART WORK AT PRACTICALLY NO COST

The next time you have to make up a circular, or need art work for a box, or require an illustration for a sales brochure . . . call at the used book store in your neighborhood and browse through publications dating from the last century. This may sound like an odd idea, but you'll be surprised by the new ideas for art work you'll find in these old publications. Most of these illustrations are in public domain and can be used by you in any way without charge or permission from the publisher.

• Dover Publications, 180 Varick Street, New York, NY 10014 publishes a book of old illustrations entitled Hand Book of Early American Art. This book is inexpensive and provides you with a marvelous selection of art dating from the last century. You have a choice of over 2,000 authentic illustrations that are available for your free use.

Here are some additional good sources of inexpensive art work:

• Culver Pictures, Inc., 660 First Avenue, New York, NY 10016, has over 6 million photographs, engravings, and prints of historical art work suitable for use in advertising promotions. Approval selections on any subject are sent to you within twenty-four hours for a thirty-day free examination. You can have a free folder describing Culver's services by writing to them at the above address.

• Another good source consists of silent movie stills that are furnished by Bettmann Archive, Inc., 136 East 57th Street, New York, NY 10022. The movie stills, clipped from old films, feature many situations identified with the silent movies. These pictures are best suited for humorous advertising campaigns. You can get a four-page illustrated folder on this special collection by writing to the Bettmann Archive.

• One of the prime sources of inexpensive stock photos is from our own United States Government. Virtually all the government agencies and departments in Washington take pictures of what they are doing, whether it be building roads, counting fish, or making weather reports. All of the agencies make an effort to maintain some sort of filing system to fill photo requests, and the price is amazingly low.

• In addition to government agencies, there are two other government sources in Washington you can contact. These are the Library of Congress and the National Archives. It is estimated that between them they probably have around ten million pictures on file. Here is a list of the Library of Congress's major collections and publications:

General Collections: Nonbook pictorial materials, exclusive of maps and motion pictures. Four million items. Prints and photographs documenting American history and civilization (including portraits, views, events) and artists' prints of all periods.

Special Collections: Nineteenth-century American lithographs (including Currier & Ives); Civil War photographs, drawings, prints; political cartoons and caricatures (eighteenth to twentieth centuries); documentary photographs (nineteenth century to present-day including the FSA-OWI collection); artistic photographs; early American architecture, including historic survey of American buildings and the Frances Benjamin Johnston photographs; artists' prints of many periods, countries, and techniques, including engravings, etchings, woodcuts of the old masters, the work of Joseph Pennell, Whistler, etcetera, and modern prints especially by American artists;

nineteenth-century posters (advertising, theatrical, circus) and twen-
tieth-century posters (World War I and II). Large collection of original photographic negatives.

Publications:

- *Guide to the Special Collections of Prints and Photographs in the
  Library of Congress*—compiled by Paul Vanderbilt. Available
  from the Superintendent of Documents, U.S. Government Printing
  Office, Washington, DC 20225.
- *Pictorial Americana—A Select List of Photographic Negatives.*
  Available from Chief, Photoduplication Service, Library of Con-
  gress, Washington, DC 20225.
- *Catalog of the Annual National Exhibition of Prints.* Available
  from the Prints and Photographs Division, Library of Congress.
- *Selective Checklist of Prints and Photographs Recently Cataloged
  and Made Available for Reference, Lots 4121–4801.* Available
  from the Card Division, Library of Congress.
- *Supplement to Historic American Buildings Survey Catalog.*
  Available from the National Park Service, Department of the Interior, Washington, DC 20225.

Regarding the National Archives, thousands and thousands of pictures have found their way into this government agency. For example,
during the Depression the government commissioned photographers
to record the nationwide activities of the W.P.A.—these included
pictures of art and nature projects, as well as other activities conducted by the W.P.A. In addition, the archives has over 6,000 pictures of the Civil War made by Mathew Brady. In all, it is estimated
that the archives has over three million still pictures. Since most of
them haven't been precisely cataloged, it's advised that you be quite
specific in making a request for a photograph of a particular subject.

Probably one of the best equipped departments to take care of
photo requests is the Department of Agriculture. They have over
150,000 photos on hand of farms, panoramas of forests and fields,
and other subjects dealing with agricultural backgrounds. Write to
the United States Department of Agriculture, Department of Information, Photo Library, Room 412A, Washington, DC 20250, for your
photo request.

If you don't know whom to contact for a government picture, write
the Information Director of the agency or department at the simple

address: Washington, DC 20250. This will be sufficient for your letter to get to the right destination. The Information Director will either fill the order himself or see that it is routed to the proper person. Bear in mind that in addition to the Department of Agriculture, you also have the Department of Defense, and many other outlets where you can get photographic material for reproduction purposes.

11. HOW TO SAVE MONEY ON TYPING

Wherever possible, use short typed letters and supplement them with sheets of general information covering your product or service. Here are two illustrations that demonstrate how we cut down on time and money for typed letters.

The first gives stock answers to general inquiries concerning our Ant Farm. This form merely requires a check mark to answer 90 percent of the questions usually asked by customers.

The second is a printed note we use when it's possible to get by with marginal notations as a reply to a letter.

Many thanks . . .

for your inquiry on our ANT FARM. In order to promptly reply to your inquiry, we have checked the paragraph below:

( ) *To Stock Your Ant Farm.* Each ANT FARM contains a "Stock Certificate" which is found on the Ant Farm box or on the last page of the instruction booklet, "Ant Watcher's Manual," included with each Ant Farm. Simply print your name and address on the "Stock Certificate," send it to us, and your supply of ants will be mailed immediately.

( ) *Ant Food and Feeding.* We can supply Ant Food at 50¢ per package. However, it is not entirely necessary to have special food. The "Ant Watcher's Manual" gives you a "menu" that is adequate.

( ) *Additional Supplies.* We do not make C.O.D. shipments because of the costly C.O.D. fees, etc., charged to the customer. We can supply the following, postpaid, upon receipt of remittance:

ADDITIONAL SUPPLY OF ANTS	Standard Supply	.75
	(10 to 15 ants)	
	Double Supply	1.00
	(20 to 30 ants)	
MAGNIFYING GLASS		.75
SAND	Standard Supply	.50
	Double Supply	1.00

STANDARD ANT FARM	6″ × 9″	2.98
GIANT ANT FARM	10″ × 15″	6.95

( ) *Queen Ants.* It is against Federal law to ship Queen Ants. During the warmer months you may be able to find one in your vicinity. For further information, see your "Ant Watcher's Manual."

( ) *What Kind of Ants?* You can use ants from your own vicinity. Just be sure that they are large enough so that they cannot climb through the air vents in your Ant Farm.

( ) *Cleaning and Restocking Your Ant Farm.* Remove the top and bottom parts and clean the clear plastic with a damp cloth. Be sure to use slightly dampened sand when refilling. The ants do their own "undertaking" if an ant dies. However, if for some reason you wish to remove all the ants and restock your Farm with new ants, they can be purchased as listed above.

( ) *Reading Material.* While your "Ant Watcher's Manual" gives you a list of recommended reading, we do not sell books. Most of the books listed can be obtained at your local library or bookstore.

( ) *Where Ant Farms Can Be Purchased.* Your local Department, Toy, Hobby, Pet, Drug, or Variety Store has the GENUINE COSSMAN ANT FARM in stock. If you cannot purchase the ANT FARM in your vicinity, we will be happy to make shipment direct to you, post-paid, at prices listed above.

PLEASE EXCUSE OUR INFORMALITY!

By making marginal notations on your letter, we are able to answer your inquiry by return mail.

We feel that promptness is more important than a formal reply . . . which could mean several days' delay.

Should you write to us again or wish to place an order, please return all correspondence to us.

Thank you.

E. JOSEPH COSSMAN AND COMPANY

When you must give a lot of information about your product, the best method is to use Questions and Answers. This is a simplified and interesting way of presenting "facts" that would normally require many pages of explanation.

The next illustration shows how we respond to requests for full information on our Ant Farm and Fly Cake by using the Question and Answer method.

Questions You May Ask About This Incredible Product

Q. What is FLY CAKE?

A. FLY CAKE is a completely new fly control product in solid form. It contains materials which make it attractive to flies as well as a chemical formulated to kill flies instantly. It is put into action simply by moistening the cake and placing it anywhere that flies are a problem. Released ingredients make the cake extremely attractive to flies.

Q. How does FLY CAKE kill flies?

A. FLY CAKE contains a new chemical discovery—DDVP—especially formulated to kill flies through their nervous system. A five-second exposure, even on a cool day, paralyzes the nervous system of the fly, preventing it from flying away to die somewhere.

Q. Will FLY CAKE kill other insects?

A. Definitely yes. It will kill most other crawling type insects such as roaches, ants—in fact, most any other insect with the same nervous system structure as the fly.

Q. How long will FLY CAKE last?

A. FLY CAKE will last at least a full season and will retain the same killing power down to the last "crumb."

Q. Is FLY CAKE dangerous to pets or humans?

A. Common sprays or aerosols disperse their poisons in all directions throughout living areas: FLY CAKE'S special insect-destroying chemicals are safely sealed within a solid cake— can't taint food, clothing, furniture. Pets are not attracted to FLY CAKE, and it is not harmful if touched or even tasted by humans.

Q. Does FLY CAKE require any maintenance or care?

A. Aside from keeping the cake moist, the only other care required is to occasionally brush away the dead flies from the cake so that live flies may have access to it.

Q. Will FLY CAKE kill flies that have built up a resistance to DDT?

A. Definitely yes. FLY CAKE attacks the fly through its nervous system and is a completely new departure in insecticide formulation.

Q. What are the advantages of FLY CAKE?

A. FLY CAKE can be used anywhere and is especially adaptable to those areas where you can't use fly spray. For example, in food processing plants, fly sprays are difficult to use. However, a few strategically placed FLY CAKES around the plant will give a factory fly control that it cannot enjoy in any other manner. Furthermore, the fly dies on or near the cake and not on or near the food as may be the case with fly spray. FLY CAKE is also perfect for hospitals since these institutions are reluctant to use fly spray or any other type of insecticide. We have one example in a local dairy where FLY CAKE has killed flies for 8 months and is still working well.

Here Are the Answers
to your questions about the ANT FARM

Q. WHAT IS AN "ANT FARM"?

A. The ANT FARM is a clear, unbreakable plastic, escape-proof case, measuring 6″ × 9″, containing farm buildings, a windmill, silo, trees, and barnyard, complete with soil, sandbar, and a stand. The ants work down into the soil and use the sandbar for building their hills. The FARM is so constructed that the ants are visible from every angle, both aboveground and underground.

Q. DO WE HAVE TO STOCK ANTS?

A. No. Included with every ANT FARM is a "Stock Certificate." The purchaser fills this out and mails it to us, and a supply of ants is airmailed to him direct from our desert plant.

Q. IS THE ANT FARM BACKED BY AN ADVERTISING CAMPAIGN?

A. Yes. The ANT FARM is being advertised in leading nationwide publications, such as *Redbook, House and Garden,* and *Cosmopolitan* . . . in newspapers throughout the country, including major papers such as the *New York Times, Chicago Tribune,* and *Los Angeles Times,* and on radio and TV from coast to coast.

Q. HOW WILL THE CUSTOMER KNOW HOW TO CARE FOR HIS ANTS?

A. An informative little book, *The Ant Watcher's Manual,* is included with every ANT FARM. This gives complete instructions for the care and feeding of ants, together with amusing sidelights on ant lore.

Q. HOW SOON CAN I EXPECT DELIVERIES ON ANT FARM ORDERS?

A. Immediately. We maintain a large inventory of ANT FARMS at all times and can effect "same day" delivery.

Q. HOW SOON WILL THE ANTS BE DELIVERED?

A. Under ordinary circumstances, ants are airmailed to the customer within 24 hours after we receive his "Stock Certificate."

Q. DOES AN ANT FARM SERVE A PURPOSE?

A. Yes! Aside from the fact that it is a fascinating source of entertainment, the ANT FARM is one of the most educational children's items ever offered. Educators throughout the country are enthusiastic over its educational features.

* * *

Hello there,

We are manufacturers of the Ant Farm . . . a fascinating project that actually lets you look in on the private lives of these busy little creatures.

In the past three months we have sold more than 600,000 Ant Farms, and believe it or not . . . we have 55 people in Southern California who raise ants for us . . . we buy about 200,000 ants a day from them at a penny apiece!

Why all this information to you . . . a professional photographer? Because one of these days you may be looking for a unique and attention-getting prop for one of your commercial setups, and we want you to know that an Ant Farm not only exists . . . but is capturing the imagination of the entire country.

Keep this in mind the next time you have a novel commercial setup to shoot . . . and of course you have our wholehearted permission to use the Ant Farm in any illustration you wish.

Many thanks.

Sincerely,

E. JOSEPH COSSMAN & CO.

E. Joseph Cossman

EJC:bd

12. UNBEATABLE PUBLIC RELATIONS WITH A POSTAGE STAMP

One of the smartest public relations activities you can perform in your business is to note the birthday and anniversary of your best customers and at the proper time send them an inexpensive "good wishes" card. This small investment in time and money will pay big dividends in good relations. Try it for six months and note the response you will receive in return.

13. HOW TO SAVE HUNDREDS OF DOLLARS ON BUSINESS CHRISTMAS GIFTS

Christmas gift-giving has become such a well-organized business in this country that your gifts to business contacts seldom make a strong or lasting impression on them.

We have about 2,000 good accounts and each Christmas it becomes more of a chore to find suitable gifts. A gift of any quality costs at least $5, and we found ourselves spending close to $10,000 each holiday season on gifts that brought back little comment and very few thank-you notes.

We have discontinued this practice and instead, make up a friendly note and send it to all of our accounts two weeks before Thanksgiving. The note is accompanied by a good quality pocket knife attached to a key chain . . . a practical and simple remembrance that costs us less than fifty cents each. This is a note we sent:

> The Thanksgiving Holiday got us to thinking . . .
>
> We spend eleven months saying "please" and trying to get business, but we spend so little time saying "Thank You."
>
> So this note isn't an attempt to sell you a darned thing! It's simply to say "Thank You" with a small memento of great appreciation for your valued business and interest in our products. We know you'll find it useful.
>
> May this Holiday Season be a merry one for you.
>
> Sincerely,
>
> E. JOSEPH COSSMAN AND COMPANY

The response to our Thanksgiving idea was tremendous. Where our 2,000 Christmas gifts normally brought back 150 to 200 "thank-you" notes, this small memento brought responses from over 1,500 people! We now follow this Thanksgiving practice each year.

14. HOW TO KEEP YOUR DESK CLUTTER-FREE OF CORRESPONDENCE

Make a habit of using this rule practiced by top executives. Look at each piece of correspondence, think about it, make a decision, pass it along for action, file it, or destroy it . . . but never, never handle the same piece of paper twice. Your fidelity to this one rule will keep your desk clear.

15. HOW TO DOUBLE, TRIPLE, YOUR PRODUCTIVE POWERS

Here's another simple rule that, if followed, can increase your personal production enormously. As soon as you reach your office each morning, write down the six most important things that you must do that day, then do them in that order and don't allow anything to distract you until you have accomplished all six objectives. At least 50 percent of many executives' time is wasted by interruptions, distractions, and trifling, time-consuming interviews.

By setting a goal for yourself to perform the six most important things of the day, you will soon experience a tremendous increase in the amount of work you are able to accomplish.

16. HOW TO GET YOUR COUNTER DISPLAY NEAR THE CASH REGISTER

As any good merchandiser knows, the hottest spot in any store is near the cash register. A few years ago, we had a product that needed "cash register exposure." To encourage the dealer to put our counter card display next to his cash register, we printed an illustration showing how to detect counterfeit money on the back of our display piece. This unusual idea brought us top placement for our illustrated display, and if you would like to try it for your product, write to the Treasury Department and they will send you a suitable illustration which you can have printed on the back of your display card.

17. HOW TO MAKE $1,000,000

The following list of items supposedly made a fortune for their creators:

Fountain pens	Book clubs
Zippers	Home hair waves
Roller skates	Bottle caps
Disposable diapers	Deodorants
Chipped soap	Snap fasteners
Frozen foods	Scotch tape
Dancing lessons	Teddy bears
Prepared dog foods	Chewing gum
Band-Aids	Shorthand system

Cash registers	Kinked hairpins
Cellophane	Paper clips
Kiddie cars	Rubber heels
Gelatin capsules	Ready-made bows
Sanitary napkins	Tea bags
Schools-by-mail	Corn plasters
Dixie cups	Vacuum cleaners
Good Humor bars	Alarm clocks

Ninety percent of the above items are less than thirty years old! What will the next thirty years bring?

18. A PUBLICITY APPROACH THAT'S DIFFERENT

The first year we introduced the Ant Farm to the public, we sent the following letter to the leading commercial photographers in the United States.

Dear Commercial Photographer:

There must be many times in your photographic assignments when you need an unusual prop for attention value.

Well . . . we are the manufacturer of the famous ANT FARM—as described in the enclosed circular—and we believe our product will add interest and command attention when used as a back-ground prop in some of your future photographic assignments.

If the occasion arises where you can use this unusual product, please drop us a line and we will be glad to furnish you with a "working" ANT FARM at no charge or obligation to you.

Sincerely,

E. JOSEPH COSSMAN & COMPANY
   "The Ant Farm Division"

E. Joseph Cossman, President

At least two dozen photographers requested samples of the Ant Farm, and before long we saw our product appearing as a prop in national ads throughout the country. Since we are the only company with an Ant Farm, the reader didn't need a by-line to know that it was our product in the photo. If you have a unique product, this is a good offbeat approach for some additional publicity at no charge. Give it a try!

19. HOW TO GET IMPACT IN YOUR DIRECT MAIL

For a change of pace and tremendous impact, send your customers a postcard a day for one week and then follow up the continuity with a hard-hitting sales letter. We used this approach with the Spud Gun, and the results were phenomenal. A different cartoon postcard was mailed to our jobber list each day for seven days. On the eighth day, we mailed the sales letter. The cartoons created a definite identity pattern that was followed through with the sales letter. One of the cartoon postcards, front and back sides, is shown on the opposite page.

Yes! Here's why the Cossman Spud Gun is the biggest, fastest-selling, profit-making "leader" in the nation:

1. PRE-SOLD BY NETWORK TELEVISION ON 160 STATIONS!
Hundreds of children's shows advertise the gun daily from coast to coast.

2. POINT OF SALES EXCITEMENT FREE! FREE! FREE!
Printed target balloons, colorful window streamers, Spud Gun Patrol lapel pins for sales personnel, etc. Yes . . . a complete promotional kit included free with your Spud Gun order.

3. EVERY TOWN IS SINGING THE "SPUD GUN" SONG!
Written by Felix DeCola, famous Hollywood ASCAP composer. "Hey, Ezra" and "The Spud Gun Rock" are being spun and sung by disc jockey shows throughout the country.

4. A FIVE-YEAR FACTORY GUARANTEE!
For the first time in toy history, a dollar gun is backed up with a written five-year factory guarantee . . . printed on every box!

HURRY! HURRY! HURRY! Now's the time to cash in on the hottest, newest, most exciting toy of the year . . . the Cossman Spud Gun. PLACE YOUR ORDER NOW . . . YOU'LL MAKE MONEY$ MONEY$ MONEY$

20. A LETTER THAT PULLED OVER 38 PERCENT

Usually, we are happy to pull 3 or 4 percent on our mailings, but the following letter pulled an incredible 38 percent! This is even more remarkable when you consider that the mailing went to radio and television station managers who receive a large amount of direct mail each day. The letter also contained two return cards—one torn in half and the other ready to fill out and mail back to us. Incidentally, we have used this same mailing on a dozen or more separate offers, and it has never failed to pull astonishing results.

Dear Station Manager:

You will find two return cards with this letter. One is already torn in half and ready for the wastebasket.

Here's why . . .

Human nature is a funny thing. It is easier to Z-I-P a card in two and throw it away, than it is to fill out and mail.

That's why we've enclosed the extra card already torn! That's for you to throw away on impulse.

The other card is for you to fill in and mail.

It will bring you a *tested* commercial that is bringing in orders . . . and more orders . . . from thousands of satisfied customers.

The complete offer is explained on the attached sheet. We know you'll like it!

If you want more information, call us collect . . . but mail the card NOW . . . this is REALLY the greatest!

Sincerely,

E. JOSEPH COSSMAN & COMPANY

21. TAKE ADVANTAGE OF YOUR NEWSPAPER AND MAGAZINE PUBLICITY

When your product receives a write-up in some publication, don't hide the clipping in your scrapbook. Accumulate all the publicity pieces possible, create an advertising piece from them, and use the circular prominently in your promotions.

22. MY PRIVATE LIBRARY

There is an old saying that goes: "The man who does not read books has no advantage over the man who can't read them." In my opinion, when you purchase a book you are, in effect, buying the lifetime experience of the writer.

I'm a great book collector, and over a period of years I have accumulated a basic, hard-core group of good business books. The following list contains some of my best business books, which you can find in almost every library, and also those publications that I subscribe to, which I highly recommend to anyone in the manufacturing, distributing, merchandising, promotion, or sales fields.

Name of Book	Author	Publisher
Handbook of Business Forms		Prentice-Hall, Inc.
Advertising Handbook	Roger Barton	Prentice-Hall, Inc.
How to Develop Profitable Ideas	Otto F. Reiss	Prentice-Hall, Inc.
Sales Manager's Handbook	John C. Aspley	Dartnell Corp.
Sales Promotion Handbook	John C. Aspley	Dartnell Corp.
Techniques of Creative Thinking	Robert F. Crawford	Hawthorn Books, Inc.
Printing & Promotion Handbook	Melcher & Larrick	McGraw-Hill Book Co.
Business Management Handbook	J. K. Lasser	McGraw-Hill Book Co.
Henley's Twentieth Century Formulas	Hiscox & Sloane	Norman W. Henley Publishing Co.
The Working Press of the Nation (three volumes)	Norman Seligman	National Research Bureau, Inc.
Agency List		Standard Advertising Register
Complete Secretary's Handbook	Doris & Miller	Prentice-Hall, Inc.
Standard Advertising Register		National Register Publishing Co.
Gebbie Press House Magazine Directory		The Gebbie Press
Techniques of Marketing New Products	Douglas Banning	McGraw-Hill Book Co.
Business Executives' Handbook	Stanley N. Brown	Prentice-Hall, Inc.
Writer's Market	Mathieu & Coffman	The Writer's Digest
Planning & Creating Better Direct Mail	Yeck and Maguire	McGraw-Hill Book Co.
Statistical Abstract of the United States		U.S. Department of Commerce
The Robert Collier Letter Book	Robert Collier	Prentice-Hall, Inc.
Fortunes in Formulas	Hiscox & Sloane	Alfred A. Knopf, Inc.
Reality in Advertising	Rosser Reeves	Sullivan, Stauffer, Colwell & Bayles, Inc.
Just Looking	Walter O'Meara	
Business America		U.S. Department of Commerce
Mail Order!	Eugene Schwartz	Boardroom Reports
Building a Mail Order Business	William Cohen	John Wiley & Sons
World Press Review		Stanley Foundation
How to Get Rich in Mail Order	Melvin Powers	Wilshire Book Co.

13 | How to Sell Your Products Overseas

"A stranger is a friend you haven't yet met."

Why am I devoting a full chapter to foreign trade? For two reasons:

First, because I cut my teeth on foreign trade. As you read in chapter 1, I made my start by selling 30,000 cases of laundry soap overseas. I did it with no money, no business connections, no formal education, and no experience.

I don't say that the same thing will happen to you, but if you get involved and refuse to quit, you will eventually connect!

Second, because I have seen many of my students start in foreign trade, having no more than I had, and today they are in established, financially secure businesses.

A mail order background is custom-made for foreign selling, because, short of going there in person, the best way to communicate your business desires to a party overseas is by mail. A good sales letter to an overseas buyer can bring in thousands of dollars worth of business. I know . . . I have seen it happen in my own case.

To many people, the foreign market seems remote and mysterious. But once you learn a few basic marketing tricks, it can sometimes be easier to sell 10,000 units of your product to an importer in Milan, Italy, than ten dozen to a jobber in Chicago. Quite often the same qualities that sell your product in the U.S.A. will also find a ready and willing market overseas. People are basically the same throughout the world, they have the same likes and dislikes, desires and ambitions. Usually what appeals to an American father, mother, or child will strike a responsive chord in their overseas counterpart. A case in point is our Fly Cake.

Fly Cake is a solid chemical, shaped like a small doughnut, that has the amazing ability to kill flies a few seconds after they touch the cake. Best of all, Fly Cake retains its killing power for an entire season and is effective as long as a single crumb remains. Because of these remarkable qualities, Fly Cake easily found a place in the American market. We soon began searching for other markets.

With the single exception of a flyer in export selling several years ago, we had no previous experience in this field. The first thing we did was to visit our local library and compile a list of banks located in the leading cities of the world. Reasoning that a bank would be one of the first to know the established and successful companies in its community, we wrote to various banks, describing our product and asking them to forward our material to any of their customers that might have an interest.

One big result of this promotion was that we located an organization in Australia that purchased over 200,000 Fly Cakes from us the first year. Their business was doubly welcome, since their summers come during our winters; because of this reversal of seasons, we were selling Fly Cake during the months when our sales in the United States were at low ebb. Furthermore, the orders we received from Australia were not just for one or two gross, but for 50,000 and 100,000 Fly Cakes in each order.

With an appetite whetted by this taste of success in foreign sales, we wrote to the International Trade Administration in Washington, DC (henceforth in this chapter referred to as ITA), asking for advice on how to get overseas agents. The ITA referred us to its offices in Los Angeles, and our first call there was like walking into a wonderland of overseas merchandising ideas. Here are just a few of the many aids available to you from the ITA.

LOOKING FOR AN AGENT OVERSEAS?

If you are looking for an agent overseas, you will probably have one particular country in mind. Your first step will be to locate an agent or distributor for your merchandise in that country. For this purpose, you can draw on the marvelous facilities of the ITA of the United States Department of Commerce. One of their best services for locating an agent or distributor overseas is their **Agents/Distributor Service** (A/DS).

The A/DS is used to locate foreign import agents and distributors. Essentially, the service determines an overseas firm's interest in a specific export proposal and its willingness to correspond with the U.S. requestor. U.S. Foreign Service posts abroad supply information on up to six representatives who meet your requirements. This information consists of the names and addresses of the foreign firms, names and titles of persons to contact, telephone numbers, cable addresses and Telex numbers, and brief comments about the firms or their stated interest in the proposal. The cost per application is currently $90. A/DS application forms may be obtained from Commerce Department District Offices. Trade specialists at these offices will help you prepare your applications and will provide guidance on market potential for your product. Further information can be obtained from your nearest Commerce District Office or from the Agent/Distributor Service, Room 1837, Office of Trade Information Services, International Trade Administration, U.S. Department of Commerce, Washington, DC 20230. Phone: (202) 377-2988.

WANT TO DRAW A CREDIT REPORT ON A FOREIGN COMPANY?

Perhaps you want to check on a customer who has sent you an order, or an agent or distributor you have decided to appoint. To find out the firm's financial background, apply for a World Trader's Data Report (WTDR). A WTDR is a business report prepared by the Commerce Department's U.S. Foreign Commercial Service, giving such information as the type of organization, year established, relative size, number of employees, general reputation, territory covered, language preferred, product lines handled, principal owners, financial references, and trade references. Each report also contains a general narrative account by the U.S. Commercial Service officer conducting the investigation as to the reliability of the foreign firm. Request forms and further information on this service are available from any Commerce District Office, or write: World Trader's Data Reports, Room 1837, Office of Trade Information Services, International Trade Administration, U.S. Department of Commerce, Washington, DC 20230. Phone: (202) 377-4203.

WANT A TOP AMERICAN BUSINESSMAN TO WORK FOR YOU OVERSEAS AT NO CHARGE?

The expansion of your business into overseas markets very often involves more than the finding of an agent or distributor. If your operation is successful in the United States, it is probably your unique way of doing business that has made it so. Therefore, your plans for doing business abroad may be too detailed and original to rely only on correspondence with a potential distributor or agent. Even more important, you may not be sure that your product or service is really needed in the foreign country you have in mind. At this point you may conclude that you will be forced to travel and investigate for yourself.

But there is no need for you to take out a passport and book passage for a foreign country. Chances are that a U.S. Department of Commerce Trade Mission is about to leave for the very country you wish to contact. These Trade Missions, our country's answer to the Iron Curtain nations' government level trading teams, are made up of high-caliber businessmen who volunteer their services as a patriotic gesture. Their main objective is to promote world trade for U.S. private enterprise, which, of course, includes your business.

The Trade Mission executives, well briefed on the countries they are to visit and guided by an official of the U.S. Department of Commerce, will help you investigate your product's market potential. The Trade Mission will also present your business proposal or submit your product or service licensing proposal to hundreds of businessmen with whom they will meet on their overseas tour. Or if you are looking for a source of raw material, they will try to locate an appropriate concern.

Few businesses could afford to carry these high-salaried, experienced men on their payrolls. Yet, if you check with your local field office of the Department of Commerce, you can begin arrangements to have them work for you—and it will only cost you the price of the postage to Washington, DC. This will cover the cost of sending your specific proposal, along with detailed answers to a questionnaire, to the Director of Trade Missions to the country of your choice, Bureau of International Business Operations, U.S. Department of Commerce, Washington DC. When the Trade Mission returns, you will be given a complete report that will include names and addresses of your desired overseas contacts, along with pertinent marketing information. Each year, twelve to fifteen Trade Missions visit twenty or more countries. They are usually planned to coincide with international trade fairs. At these fairs, the members of the Trade Mission ordinarily staff Trade Information Centers. Your local ITA can tell you which Trade Missions are available and what countries they will be visiting.

WANT FREE PUBLICITY FOR YOUR PRODUCTS OR SERVICES THROUGHOUT THE WORLD?

New Product Information Service (NPIS). This service provides worldwide publicity for new U.S. products available for immediate export. This exposure enables foreign firms to identify and contact U.S. exporters of specific products. This, in turn, gives the U.S. companies direct indications of market interest, and often generates substantial sales, agent contracts, and other benefits. NPIS information is disseminated through *Commercial News U.S.A.* monthly magazine and *Voice of America* radio broadcasts.

To qualify for the New Product Information Service, products must have been sold on the U.S. market for no more than two years, must be currently exported to no more than three countries on a regular basis, and must meet the other guidelines listed on the NPIS Application Form (ITA-4063P). Contact any Commerce District Office for further information and an application form.

International Market Search (IMS). This program, similar to the New Product Information Service, promotes the products and technology of a single industry. Several industries a year are selected by the Department of Commerce for promotion through this program. IMS information is also disseminated through *Commercial News USA* monthly magazine.

To qualify for IMS, products must conform to the definition of the industry being highlighted, must currently be exported to no more than fifteen countries on a regular basis, and must conform to the other requirements listed on the IMS application form (ITA-4091P). Contact any Commerce District Office for further information and an application form.

Commercial News USA (CN). Each month, short promotional descriptions of some 100–150 products, including the name and address of the exporter and black-and-white product photographs, are published in *Commercial News USA* (CN) magazine. The magazine is then distributed to 240 U.S. embassies and consulates, 50 American Chambers of Commerce abroad, and other key groups worldwide. Many of the embassies and consulates, both in developed and developing markets, publish periodical commercial newsletters that are distributed to the local business communities they serve. Through reprints in these newsletters and through other channels, the product data in CN is ultimately disseminated to more than 200,000 business and government leaders around the world.

For further information on the NPIS or IMS or on *Commercial News USA* magazine, contact the nearest Commerce District Office, or *Commercial News USA*, Room 2106, Office of Event Management and Support Services, International Trade Administration, U.S. Department of Commerce, Washington, DC 20230. Phone: (202) 377-5367.

CONNECT WITH 140,000 OVERSEAS CONTACTS WITH THE ITA'S COMPUTER FILE

Export Contact List Services. The Commerce Department collects and stores data on foreign firms in a master computer file designated as the Foreign Traders Index (FTI). Covering 143 countries, this file contains information on more than 140,000 importing firms, agents, representatives, distributors, manufacturers, service organizations, retailers, and potential end-users of American products and services. Newly identified firms are continually added to the FTI file; information on listed firms is also updated frequently. This information is available to U.S. exporters in the following forms.

1. *Export Mailing List Service (EMLS).* The EMLS consists of specific data retrievals for individual requestors wishing to obtain lists of foreign firms in selected countries by commodity classification. Retrievals are provided on gummed mailing labels or in printout form and include (as available) the name and address of each firm, name and title of the executive officer, year established, relative size, number of employees, telephone and Telex number, cable address, and product or service codes by SIC (Standard Industrial Classification) number.

2. *FTI Data Tape Service (DTS).* Through this service, information on all firms included in the FTI for all (or selected) countries is made available on magnetic tape to American companies. Users can retrieve various segments of the data in unlimited combinations through their own computer facilities. The cost is $5,000 (prepaid). Users may also purchase segments of the file on tape. Customized retrievals can be based on product, country, or other data. The cost includes a $400 basic fee plus, should the list exceed one thousand names, 12¢ for each additional name. Estimates of the total tape cost can be made at the time the tape is ordered. Tapes containing all the information for a particular country can be purchased for $300 per country.

MAKE A COMMERCIAL "MARRIAGE" WITH AN OVERSEAS CONTACT

Trade Opportunities Program (TOP). This program offers export opportunities, originating from either private or government sources overseas, which are transmitted to the TOP computer in Washington, DC, by U.S. Foreign Service posts around the world. As subscribers to TOP, U.S. business firms indicate the products and services they wish to export to particular countries of interest, and the types of opportunities desired (direct sales, overseas representation, or foreign government tenders). The TOP computer matches product interest of foreign buyers with those indicated by the U.S. subscribers. When a match occurs, a "trade opportunity notice" is mailed to the subscriber. Foreign trade opportunity notices include: descriptions of the products and services needed, their end-users, and the quantities required; information about the foreign buyer; transaction requirements and preferences; trade and credit references; bid deadline dates; and other pertinent information. Notice subscriptions are available in units of 50, 100, and 250.

As an alternative, U.S. companies may subscribe to the *TOP Bulletin* or the TOP Datatape Service. Published weekly, the *TOP Bulletin* is a compilation of all export leads received and processed by TOP. The cost to subscribers is $100 a year. The Datatape Service provides the same information on computer tape on a weekly or biweekly basis. Subscription and other information on the TOP services can be obtained from Commerce District Offices or by writing: Trade Opportunities Program, Room 1324, Office of Trade Information Services, International Trade Administration, U.S. Department of Commerce, Washington, DC 20230. Phone: (202) 377-2988.

PLUG INTO THE GOVERNMENT'S WORLDWIDE COMPUTER SYSTEM

Automated Information and Transfer System (AITS). This system enables an exporter to find commercial information quickly and conveniently by using the AITS network of Wang VS minicomputers, terminals, and word processors in ITA offices in the U.S. and abroad.

The main information file in AITS consists of the name, address, product lines, trade and marketing interests, size, and other information on individual firms listed in each local office of the Department of Commerce. These are "client" companies which use various ITA services, are targeted for export promotion efforts, are very active in trade, or represent good prospects for the purchase of U.S. goods. The file is not an exhaustive list of exporters or importers in the area. Also, current ITA trade information programs, such as TOP, FTI, and WTDR's (discussed earlier in this chapter), are operated using the AITS computer system.

In addition to storing and transferring different types of trade information, AITS provides the capability to electronically match up selected buyers and sellers through various services offered by ITA.

For further information, contact the Office of Trade Information Services, Room 3011, International Trade Administration, U.S. Department of Commerce, Washington, DC 20230. Phone: (202) 377-4561.

WANT A COMPLETE COURSE IN FOREIGN TRADE?

Buy a copy of *A Basic Guide to Exporting* from the ITA. This wonderful book gives more complete information on foreign merchandising than any commercial course costing many times more. This book is written primarily for people without previous experience in foreign trade and costs just a few dollars.

WANT TO BE WINED AND DINED BY BUSINESS PEOPLE ALL OVER THE WORLD?

Using most of these merchandising tools, we began a concentrated overseas direct mail campaign on Fly Cake, and before long we were selling our product in countries I hadn't heard of since taking geography in high school. Finally, it came to the point where our overseas business required my visiting Europe. Again I was amazed at the services available. I told the ITA of my expected tour, and they suggested I write them a letter giving a precise and exact itinerary of my trip. What cities would I visit? When would I arrive? What hotels would I be staying at? How long would I be there? What was the objective of my trip? In my letter, I answered the last question by telling them that I was not only anxious to find additional markets for our Fly Cake and other products, but I would also like to meet with overseas businessmen who were interested in exchanging ideas or who might have a product for me to take back to the States. The ITA published my letter in each of the cities on my itinerary. They also advised their foreign offices of my plans. And what did I receive as a result of their efforts?

When I landed in London, I was met at the airport by one of the largest manufacturers of plastic products in England. In Paris, I was met by the president of a company operating a large chain of appliance stores in France. Through him, I was greeted in Milan by the biggest manufacturer of electric fans in Italy. In Tel Aviv, I was met by two men who were developing a new chemical business in Israel. In Nuremberg, the owner of one of the biggest toy companies in Germany met me at the airport. In Copenhagen, I was received by a gentleman who ran a tremendous business selling used injection molds and dies.

In each case I was treated like visiting royalty. I was chauffeured around Europe in Rolls Royces and Mercedes Benzes; I was wined and dined in the homes of these businessmen; I was taken on tours of factories and plants; I was invited to trade shows; I was escorted through department stores and markets and bazaars until I thought I had seen every product made in Europe. In each city I met total strangers on my arrival and left good friends on my departure. These were the people I would never have met without the help of the ITA.

And what happened to our Fly Cake? In Switzerland, I negotiated a contract with one of the largest chemical companies in Europe. They took our product for the entire world with the exception of the United States and Canada, which we kept for ourselves.

The one big thing I learned from my European trip was a fact so simple and so obvious that many of us tend to overlook it in our daily business activities. It is simply that you do not have to be a big man to do big business. The same opportunities are available to everyone, regardless of their station in the business world. When I was in grade school, my teacher made a remark I have never forgotten; she said that all people in the United States are born equal to the point of exertion. This certainly proved true for my European trip. I discussed business on equal terms with men who employed thousands of people, and in all cases I was treated with courtesy, respect, and interest. I want to bring this point home to the reader: Many of us go through life thinking that big business is a mysterious realm inhabited by people unlike us. It is a pleasant surprise to discover that we are all very much alike.

Again I must say a great portion of the success of my business trip to Europe was due to the fine assistance given me by the ITA, a branch of the United States Department of Commerce. The bureau maintains 120 United States Foreign Service Posts in 66 countries throughout the world, and information gathered by this wonderful organization is available to you for the asking. Here is a list of ITA field office locations in the United States. If none are in your city, you can write directly to the United States Department of Commerce, International Trade Administration, Washington, DC 20230, for all the questions you may have on foreign trade.

INTERNATIONAL TRADE ADMINISTRATION DISTRICT OFFICES

Albuquerque, 87102, 505 Marquette Ave. N.W., Rm 1015. (505) 766-2386.

Anchorage, 99513, P.O. Box 32, 701 C St. (907) 271-5041.

Atlanta, 30309, Suite 600, 1365 Peachtree St., NE. (404) 881-7000.

Baltimore, 21202, 415 U.S. Customhouse, Gay and Lombard Sts. (301) 962-3560.

Birmingham, 35205, Suite 200–01, 908 S. 20th St. (205) 254-1331.

Boston, 02116, 10th Floor, 441 Stuart St. (617) 223-2312.

Buffalo, 14202, 1312 Federal Bldg., 111 W. Huron St. (716) 846-4191.

Charleston, W. Va., 25301, 3000 New Federal Office Bldg., 500 Quarrier St. (304) 343-6181, Ext. 375.

Cheyenne, 82001, 8007 O'Mahoney Federal Center, 2120 Capitol Ave. (307) 772-2151, Ext. 2151.

Chicago, 60603, Room 1406, Mid-Continental Plaza Bldg., 55 E. Monroe St. (312) 353-4450.

Cincinnati, 45202, 10504 Fed. Bldg., 550 Main St. (513) 684-2944.

Cleveland, 44114, Room 600, 666 Euclid Ave. (216) 522-4750.

Columbia, S.C., 29201, Strom Thurmond Federal Bldg., 1835 Assembly St. (803) 765-5345.

Dallas, 75242, Room 7A5, 1100 Commerce St. (214) 767-0542.

Denver, 80202, Room 119, U.S. Customhouse, 721 19th St. (303) 837-3246.

Des Moines, 50309, 817 Federal Bldg., 210 Walnut St. (515) 284-4222.

Detroit, 48226, 445 Federal Bldg., 231 W. Lafayette. (313) 226-3650.

Greensboro, N.C., 27402, 203 Federal Bldg., W. Market St., P.O. Box 1950. (919) 378-5345.

Hartford, 06103, Room 610-B, Federal Bldg., 450 Main St. (203) 722-3530.

Honolulu, 96850, Federal Bldg., 300 Ala Moana Blvd., P.O. Box 50026. (808) 546-8694.

Houston, 77002, 2625 Federal Bldg., 515 Rusk St. (713) 226-4231.

Indianapolis, 46204, 357 U.S. Courthouse & Federal Office Bldg., 46 E. Ohio St. (317) 269-6214.

Jackson, Miss., 39213, Suite

3230, 300 Woodrow Wilson Blvd. (601) 960-4388.

Kansas City, 64106, Rm. 1840, 601 E. 12th St. (816) 374-3142.

Little Rock, 72201, Rm. 635, 320 W. Capitol Ave. (501) 378-5794.

Los Angeles, 90049, Rm. 800, 11777 San Vincente Blvd. (213) 209-6712.

Louisville, 40202, Rm. 636B, U.S. Post Office and Courthouse Bldg. (502) 582-5066.

Miami, 33130, Rm. 821, City National Bank Bldg., 25 W. Flagler St. (305) 350-5267.

Milwaukee, 53202, 605 Federal Bldg., 517 E. Wisconsin Ave. (414) 291-3473.

Minneapolis, 55401, 218 Federal Bldg., 110 S. 4th St. (612) 725-2133.

Nashville, 37239, Suite 1427, 1 Commerce Pl. (615) 251-5161.

New Orleans, 70130, 432 International Trade Mart, 2 Canal St. (504) 589-6546.

New York, 10278, 37th Floor, Federal Office Bldg., 26 Federal Plaza, Foley Sq. (212) 264-0634.

Oklahoma City, 73105, 4024 Lincoln Blvd. (405) 231-5302.

Omaha, 68102, Empire State Bldg., 1st Floor, 300 S. 19th St. (402) 221-3664.

Philadelphia, 19106, 9448 Federal Bldg., 600 Arch St. (215) 597-2866.

Phoenix, 85073, 2950 Valley Bank Center, 201 N. Central Ave. (602) 261-3285.

Pittsburgh, 15222, 2002 Federal Bldg., 1000 Liberty Ave. (412) 644-2850.

Portland, Ore., 97204, Room 618, 1220 S.W. 3rd Ave. (503) 221-3001.

Reno, Nev., 89502, 1755 East Plum Lane, Rm. 152. (702) 784-5203.

Richmond, 23240, 8010 Federal Bldg., 400 N. 8th St. (804) 771-2246.

St. Louis, 63105, 120 S. Central Ave. (314) 425-3302.

Salt Lake City, 84101, Rm. 340, U.S. Post Office and Courthouse Bldg., 350 S. Main St. (801) 524-5116.

San Francisco, 94102, Rm. 15205 Federal Bldg., Box 36013, 450 Golden Gate Ave. (415) 556-5860.

San Juan, P.R., 00918, Room 659 Federal Bldg., Chardon Ave. (809) 753-4555, Ext. 555.

Savannah, 31401, 27 East Bay St., P.O. Box 9746. (912) 944-4204.

Seattle, 98109, 706 Lake Union Bldg., 1700 Westlake Ave. North. (206) 442-5616.

Trenton, 08608, 240 West State St., 8th Fl. (609) 989-2100.

14 | How to Sell a Service

"Success is often just an idea away . . ."

Many readers write to me and ask, "Is it possible to promote a service with the formulas you set forth in your books? All of the examples given are for products! Have you ever tried these techniques in marketing an intangible service rather than a tangible product?" My answer is **Yes!** The formulas and techniques set forth in this book can be used with great success in marketing a service. Let me tell you a story.

I semi-retired from the business world at the age of fifty, bought a home in Palm Springs, California, and began leading the life of a gentleman of leisure. This luxurious inactivity continued for all of three months. Then I became so bored that my minutes seemed like hours, and my hours seemed like days. About this time, I got a phone call from a television personality who had a very popular talk show in Los Angeles. He asked if I would appear as a guest on his show. At first I was going to refuse because this man had a reputation of tearing into his guests and ripping them apart. He was one of the most controversial television personalities in Los Angeles, and his popularity hinged on the fact that he brought guests on his show and then did everything possible to expose them, ridicule them, or make them look foolish. However, since I was retired from the business world, I thought I had nothing to lose by accepting his invitation—anyway, after three months of inactivity, sitting around my swimming pool was my alternative for that day.

I appeared on his show the following week and was surprised at the courtesies he extended to me. We talked about my books, my business background, my hobbies, my products; he constantly encouraged me with great kindness and consideration. I was absolutely amazed at this treatment and did not know why I was getting it until after the program. But during the show he said, "If you have this skill for making money, why don't you hold a seminar and pass it on to other people?" I replied, "The thought never entered my head, and I do not know if there is a market for seminars." His answer was, "Why not ask the TV audience and see what they say?" Well, he did ask the TV audience if they would be interested in attending a seminar based on my business background, and I received over 15,000 letters . . . all saying **"Yes!"** I held my first seminar at the Biltmore Hotel in Los Angeles. I rented a room that held 300 people, and over 1,000 people showed up. There was such a crowd that the police and fire department were called in, which ended the seminar for that evening. However, I realized I had touched a nerve in this country when I saw the tremendous interest exhibited for this kind of information. I began holding seminars across the country.

To get back to the TV personality who started it all, at the end of the show, he whispered to me, "Wait in my office; I want to talk to you." I waited in his office and then learned why he had treated me so well during the show. As he entered the room, he pointed a finger at me and said, "Joe, I have a product I want to promote." I asked him, "What is your product?" He replied, "I want to start bronzing baby shoes and sell them by mail order." I asked, "How much money do you make a year now?" He replied, "With my radio and TV programs, my residuals, my other commissions, I end up with about $300,000 a year." I asked him, "With all the money you are making, why do you want to go into the Bronzed Baby Shoe business?" His reply to that question was something I have heard many, many times since. He said, "Because I want to own something!" Here was a man making over $300,000 at a job; yet, he felt unfulfilled because he did not own anything.

In any event, over 30,000 people have attended my seminars to date, and every one of them was solicited and sold through the techniques you have in this book. I am telling you this story to emphasize that a service can be sold with my techniques as well as a product—for what can be more intangible than a seminar?

I also want to impress something else on you. Money-making is a skill that can be learned. No one is born with it; it is acquired in one of two ways:

1. Through the school of hard knocks and practical experience.
2. Or by studying under someone who has already had the experience. As you read this book, you are standing on my shoulders and benefiting from my mistakes and successes.

And how do I know that money-making is a skill you can learn? Well, let me tell you another story.

I was recently offered the opportunity to take a Master's degree program in business with a leading university in California. This was quite a prize for me, for I had never attended college. I had been surprised to learn that I could exchange my life experiences for college credits, and I had enough business experiences to skip over the Bachelor's degree program and go directly into a Master's degree program.

To graduate from my Master's degree program, it became necessary to present a thesis. Since I wanted this project to have practical as well as educational advantages, I selected for my thesis, "The Study of Successful and Unsuccessful Graduates of the E. Joseph Cossman Entrepreneur's Program."

In order to complete this thesis, it was necessary to acquire a representative sampling of my graduates and test them in a manner that might indicate a difference between them. Although Cossman Graduates were in almost every state of the Union, it was decided to limit the sampling to those graduates residing in southern California, so that better control could be exercised in the study.

One thousand Cossman graduates were invited to a reunion in Hollywood, California. Each attendee was given a confidential questionnaire to fill out. This was a special questionnaire to determine which Cossman graduates were successful and which were unsuccessful. This method was chosen as the most practical way to rate each Cossman graduate and put him or her in the appropriate group.

Before I put the thesis together, I thought, "Well, possibly success can be attributed to the age of a person, maybe the environment, perhaps what the father did, maybe religion, perhaps education, possibly race." I even went so far as to get the exact moment of birth and the time and place where they were born. I turned this information over to an astrologer thinking that possibly there might be something in astrology to determine why one person is successful and another is not. We accumulated two years of study in this thesis, and I was shocked and surprised to see the results of that two-year study. I learned that your age has nothing to do with success, your religion has nothing to do with success, your education has nothing to do with success, your environment has nothing to do with success—because I had successful graduates from all levels of life, all economic levels, all environmental levels. The only thing that stood out strong and clear in every case was that the successful graduate did not quit. And in every case, without fail, the unsuccessful graduate did not do the work of the course. I cannot give you anymore conclusive proof and evidence of success than this two-year study. These successful people absolutely did not quit; they hung on! Sure they had disappointments! They had dead ends! Sure they had losses, but they always bounced back. In fact, the average successful graduate reported that he was able to increase his income by 40 percent or more after taking the course. This proved conclusively that money-making is a skill you can learn.

Unfortunately, you cannot learn this skill in school! Today if you do not graduate from a college or university as a doctor, a lawyer, an accountant, or some other profession, you are programmed to become a corporate employee. Now there is nothing wrong with a job, providing you are aware of the other options you have in this country. Many people go through their entire lives thinking they must work for others when they have the abilities and skills to work for themselves. What do they lack? Direction! So if you are in this category and have a strong desire to be your own boss, clear off your kitchen table now and start an enterprise you can control, not one that controls you!

Here is the letter I used to sell the first seminar. Please note that it does not differ much from similar letters that I have used to sell products, even though the seminar is strictly a service.

COSSMAN INTERNATIONAL INC.

POST OFFICE BOX 4480 — PALM SPRINGS, CALIFORNIA 92263 — PHONE (619)327-0550

ANY ONE OF THESE LITTLE-KNOWN SECRETS
COULD MAKE YOU BETWEEN $1,000 AND $10,000
IN THE NEXT 30 DAYS!

Learn over 300 of them in one of the most thrilling days of your entire life! Here's how:

Dear Friend:

    This is your personal invitation to a "Seminar for Future Millionaires"! It is given by America's most successful small businessman ... E. Joseph Cossman, who, today at the age of 49, has retired with over $1,000,000!

        And the most important fact of all ... Joe Cossman made this $1,000,000 by starting in business with a kitchen table for his desk, a few hundred dollars and an idea!

    You'll learn how he did it, and how you can do it, too, when you attend his Seminar on Saturday, September 27th at the Hollywood Palladium, 6215 Sunset Boulevard, Hollywood, California.

    If you are on salary, working for a living, and want to be your own boss ... if you want to make additional income in your spare time ... if you have a product, or an idea for a product, and want to know how to market it ... if you are in your own business and want to increase your sales ... then this one day seminar can be the most profitable ... as well as exciting ... you have ever spent in your life.

    Here are only a few of the hundreds of money-making secrets E. Joseph Cossman gives you in this unique GROW YOUR OWN MONEY TREE Seminar. You'll learn how to:

$ Protect a hot new idea, so you can show it to every big company in the world, <u>and they haven't got the slightest chance to steal it</u>!

$ <u>Test a new product five ways,</u> before you invest a cent in it!

$ Exhibit at a trade show, even if you don't want to pay a penny for the space, the travel or the personnel to get there!

$ Get the United States Government to display your product in 100 foreign lands, FREE!

$ Hire a $100,000-a-year executive as consultant for your company, for nothing!

$ Put on a top-notch national sales organization in one evening!

$ Sell the Super Product! It costs 40¢, sells for as much as $10, needs no tools or dies ... and anyone can make it!

$ Get orders for thousands of dollars of a NEW product, before you bring it out or even spend one penny to make it!

$ Be wined and dined in top executives' homes all over the world by making a simple phone call.

$ Receive a free list of hundreds of brand-new products every month, that you can tie up for a song.

$ Run a "Disguised Ad" for your product in one hundred top magazines, for as little as 50¢ each!

$ Get FREE art work from now on for your ads.

ACT NOW! RESERVE YOUR PLACE TODAY!

Remember ... To make money you need no special training, higher education or unusual abilities. All you need are the proven, practical money-making techniques and formulas you will learn at this Seminar.

Since the E. Joseph Cossman Seminar will be limited to a certain number of people and no more, please do the following to assure yourself of a reservation:

1. Fill out the enclosed APPLICATION FOR ENROLLMENT. Also fill out the CONFIDENTIAL QUESTIONNAIRE.

2. Detach and mail with your check in the enclosed self addressed, postage paid envelope.

Do it NOW ... and start yourself on the road to financial independence.

Sincerely,

James Douglas

James Douglas
for COSSMAN SEMINARS

I would like to give you another example of how a service can be sold using the techniques in this book. This example comes from one of my students, Duane Shinn of Medford, Oregon. Mr. Shinn was a struggling music teacher, earning less than $75 a week. You will have to admit that selling music is selling a service. What did he do with this skill? He converted his service into a product. Here is the letter that he sent me that tells you, in his own words, how he was able to use the Cossman Techniques to make a new life for himself.

Mr. E. Joseph Cossman
COSSMAN INTERNATIONAL INC.
P.O. Box 4480
Palm Springs, Calif. 92262

Dear Joe:

It doesn't seem possible that it has only been ten years since I attended your seminar in Los Angeles at the Biltmore Hotel. So much has happened since then, I hardly know where to start. I had traveled all night on the Greyhound Bus from Sacramento to Los Angeles, and I went straight from the bus depot to the Biltmore Hotel, feeling very much out of place in my slept-in windbreaker. But when I heard you speak of the possibilities in marketing, I began to get excited, and that excitement has lasted for 10 years! You showed me how to create a product from my own skills, produce that product, package it, get publicity for it, and market it. As you know, I was a struggling music teacher at the time, earning less than $75. per week. Since music was my primary skill, I began to think of ways of creating a product based on music. I thought back to an instructional manuscript I had written a year previously to help some of my music students learn to read music quickly. It was titled "How To Read Music...In One Evening". That was to become my first product.

In your seminar you had told how simple it was to protect a printed product through a copyright, so I promptly had the book copyrighted. Each new product that I have created since then has also been copyrighted -- 36, as of this date -- and I've never had any problems with people stealing my ideas because of this simple copyright proceedure.

I remember that you showed me how to use Prestype for headline copy, and I rented an IBM typewriter to set the text of the book. I used one of the clip art sources you suggested for the cover illustration, and did the entire layout myself, even though I had never attempted anything like that before. Since then I have purchased an IBM Executive typewriter and hundreds of dollars worth of clip art and headline type, but I still personally design and layout and paste-up every book, chart, or course that we publish, as well as all the sales letters, circulars, etc. The amount of sound information you provided on the subject of "preparing your own copy" is incredible, and I have used it and benefited from it for 10 years

Publishers of music courses, books, charts, games, cassettes, and other musical aids

2

now. The other day I received a letter from a purchasing agent of a large
firm who wrote "You have a very clever advertising man working for you
there. Your mailings are facinating." The truth was, of course, that I design
and layout all our material personally, based on the Cossman formula.

The first thing I did after publishing "How To Read Music...In One Evening"
was to put out a news release on it, as you had instructed. I remember you
made a big point about sending out the release to all magazines, regardless of
subject matter, instead of just to logical prospects. I didn't really understand
the logic behind your reasoning at the time, but I went ahead and followed
your advice, since I was convinced you knew what you were doing. It was a good
thing that I did, as I received news releases in House Beautiful, Pennsylvania
Farmer, Mississippi Educational Advance, and many other "unlikely" magazines.
In fact, Popular Mechanics published the news release in a tiny one-inch
paragraph with no photo, and it alone brought in almost $2000. in orders at no
cost to me. Since then, each time we come out with a new product, it is
standard proceedure to put out a general news release. It not only brings in
retail orders, but I have gotten many dealers this way, and have located new
musical products to sell in addition to my own.

As valuable as all the other parts of the seminar were to me, the real
"meat" lay in your marketing principles. I learned more in one day about
marketing a product than many businessmen learn in a lifetime. That sounds
like an overstatement, but I know it to be a fact, and I know many of your
other students could attest to its truthfulness. Let me share with you just a
couple of the marketing methods I use to promote my musical products, which
were learned at your seminar:

1. We sell through mail order houses. At the seminar, you handed out
a list of 12 large mail order firms, and told how to go about selling to
these firms. My first order was for 144 books from Miles Kimball.
Then I picked up Sunset House, Holst Inc., Greenland Studios, Johnson
Smith, Two Brothers, Clymers of Bucks County, Walter Drake, Hanover
House, Foster & Gallagher, Spencer Gifts, and others. Most orders
range around 300 to 500 units, but orders for 4000 to 7500 are not all
that unusual. I have sold hundreds of thousands of books through this
marketing channel alone.

2. We sell through drop-ship dealers. You showed how to get dealers
to sell your products on a drop-ship basis, and I now have about 200
dealers all over the U.S. and Canada selling for me under a drop-ship
arrangement. They secure the order, and I ship to their customer under
their label.

3

3. We sell through direct mail. You demonstrated at the seminar how
to create a circular, write a sales letter, and all the other elements
which go into a successful direct mail package. We earn about $40,000.
per year from direct mail alone, and we haven't scratched the surface
yet.

We also sell to schools, libraries, stores, overseas, and other ways. Since
this letter is much too long already, I'll let you read about the other methods
in my new binder-course titled "How To Publish Your Own Book, Song, Course,
Or Other Printed Product, And Make It Go!"

I might mention, too, that all this was accomplished without hiring a
single employee -- just my wife and I and our four kids. Of course we use
lots of free-lance help such as housewives that address and stuff envelopes
for us, but no in-house employees. That makes us free to come and go as we
please, so we're able to travel a lot as a family. I credit this also to your
ingenious management methods.

Like I tell my friends, "Joe Cossman can teach you more about marketing
in one day than you can learn in college in four years."

Cordially,

Duane Shinn
SHINN MUSIC AIDS

15 | Using a Billboard to Sell Yourself and Your Business

"Humor is to selling what oil is to machinery."

You've heard the story about the mean old man who died and at whose funeral the preacher could elicit no kind word from those attending the service. After several vain pleas by the minister for a fitting remembrance, a tall, lanky individual in the back row slowly rose to his feet, looked around at the audience, and drawled, "Well, if nobody wants to say anything about the deceased, I'd like to say a few words about Texas!"

That's how I feel about the subject of billboards. Although it had nothing directly to do with the mail order business, our billboard has proved one of the most dynamic promotion tools we've used.

The billboard stood outside our office building and was a two-sided, changeable sign that could be seen from both directions. Since we changed the sayings each week, it became a landmark in Hollywood and hardly a week went by in which we didn't receive a half dozen or so letters commenting on the sign. However, the billboard's most profitable function was heralding visits of VIP's. The standard message put on the board when a VIP arrived in Hollywood was, "Hollywood welcomes John Jones of the John Jones Manufacturing Company of New York City." Mr. Jones drives into Hollywood and sees this message emblazoned on our billboard. Being human, he is flattered. It puts him into a pleasant mood and has him walking into our office purring like a kitten. To complete the red-carpet treatment, usually we had a picture taken of the VIP standing in front of the board. This photograph invariably rested in a place of honor in the VIP's office and thereby helped in advertising and making our company known to others doing business with the VIP. We can trace back many excellent business connections which began as a result of this indirect exposure.

I once flew from Hollywood to New York for the sole purpose of spending an hour with a mail order VIP named Dave Geller. It was Mr. Geller's busy season, apparently, for I cooled my heels in his reception room for two hours while he was "in conference." I finally gave up in disgust and flew back to Hollywood. A few days later Mr. Geller phoned me from New York to advise that he was flying to Hollywood for the sole purpose of apologizing to me for the New York incident. As he taxied into our parking lot, he was confronted with our billboard. It read: "Thanks, Dave Geller, for coming all the way from New York to spend ten minutes with us." The relationship that developed as a result of this unusual welcome was so satisfactory that we have made it standard practice to give all our out-of-town visitors billboard welcome.

Local wiseacres say they could gauge my love life, diet, and business prospects by the quotations placed on our billboard. They claim that when I was happy the signs had an optimistic slant; when I was glum, the signs went downbeat. I do recall that once, when business suffered a rare and unexpected slump, I became quite morose. Although I wasn't aware of it, the billboard copy reflected my state of mind. Conversely, when a deal I had been worried about suddenly broke affirmatively, the sayings I had placed on the board took an upward slant and reflected a happier frame of mind. I wasn't aware of these changes until I received an anonymous postcard which read:

Gentlemen:

Congratulations! Felicitations! And tally-ho! Things are actually looking up. Your little sayings on your billboard have been indicating a definitive positive attitude for the past few weeks or so which makes me wonder if there has not been a complete change of management in your company? Whatever has happened, we are all for it. Stick with it! These encouraging comments come from one who, up until the past few weeks, has been continually and incessantly antagonized, irritated, annoyed, rebuked, and rebuffed by your sign. Thanks for the new lease on life!

... A Billboard Fan

I had no idea how popular the billboard had become until one Monday morning I put up this comment:

"If you tilted the country sideways, all the loose ends would fall into Los Angeles."

On Tuesday, our office was flooded with thirty telephone calls, two Special Delivery letters, one telegram, and three people calling on us in person. The public reaction to the saying was so critical we changed the sign immediately. Since then, we try to stay away from sayings that tend to offend anyone's sense of civic pride.

If you are just starting your mail order business and do not have facilities for a full-fledged billboard, a sign hung from a front window will serve much the same purpose.

Or, if erection of a billboard or sign is impractical or impossible, you may adapt the principle for use in mail order advertising and promotion. Through your local civic and business organizations, you can discover when visiting businessmen will be in your town. Find out their hotel or business address while in the locale and have a "Welcome to our town" greeting awaiting them upon arrival.

For general purposes, clever sayings can be featured on the billboard and in your mail order materials.

We have assembled some first-rate legends for the billboard, and here are some of the best.

"The older a man gets, the farther he had to walk to school as a boy."

"Never hit a man when he's down. He may get up!"

"The difficulty in life is choice."

"The trouble with election jokes is that sometimes one gets elected."

"Middle age is when your broad mind and narrow waist begin to change places."

"Don't grumble because roses have thorns. Just be thankful thorns have roses."

"What you have become is the price you paid to get what you used to want."

"It is better to be small and shine than to be great and cast a shadow."

"Suspicion is a mental picture seen through an imaginary keyhole."

"Many a man is saved from being a thief by finding everything locked up."

"The most flammable kind of wood is the chip on the shoulder."

"Try to keep an open hand. If you go through life with a clenched fist, nobody can put anything into it."

"Middle age is when you feel on Saturday night the way you used to feel on Monday morning."

"Never raise a finger to a cranky child—particularly if he has teeth."

"Everybody is intelligent only on different subjects."

"No man is a failure who is enjoying life."

"If you must cry over spilled milk, condense it."

"The way to love anything is to realize it might be lost."

"To stay youthful, stay useful."

"It is better to tighten your belt than to lose your pants."

"Happiness is a perfume you cannot pour on others without getting a few drops on yourself."

"These days, when Grandma sits at the spinning wheel, chances are she's in Las Vegas."

"The greatest power is often simple patience."

"Worry never robs tomorrow of its sorrow; it only saps today of its strength."

"The time to relax is when you don't have the time for it."

"A candle loses nothing by lighting another candle."

"Effort means nothing without results."

"Whether something is cheap or expensive depends on if you're buying or selling."

"Most of the money a businessman calls profit is merely money that has not been wasted."

"An advance diagnosis is worth a lot of post-mortems."

"Love may be blind but marriage is an optometrist."

"The only man who ever got all his work done by Friday was Robinson Crusoe."

"Some men make difficulties; difficulties make some men."

"It's only eighteen inches between a pat on the back and a kick in the pants."

"You can always tell luck from ability by its duration."

"Square meals often make round people."

"A good way to forget your troubles is to wear tight shoes."

"Sending them up in rockets sure seems like an expensive way to get rid of mice."

"Don't pray when it rains if you don't pray when the sun shines."

"The greatest remedy for anger is delay."

"What this country needs is a vending machine that honors credit cards."

"It is easy to save face. Just keep the lower half of it tightly shut."

"A little explained, a little endured, a little forgiven, and a quarrel is cured."

"Secret of success: Think big, work hard, have a dream."

"One good turn usually gets the whole blanket."

"Success is getting what you want; happiness is wanting what you get."

"Middle age is when you stop having emotions and start having symptoms."

"The best place to find a helping hand is at the end of your arm."

"Parents are people who bear infants, bore teenagers, and board newlyweds."

"After a man makes his mark in the world, a lot of people come around with erasers."

"If you want to leave your footprints in the sands of time, wear your work shoes."

"The cost of a thing is the amount of life you must exchange for it."

"To be without some of the things you want is an indispensable part of happiness."

"Having fun is like insurance. The older you get, the more it costs."

"Drive-in banks were established so most of the cars today could see their real owners."

"Los Angeles is washed by the Pacific Ocean on the West and cleaned by Las Vegas on the East."

"Have patience; in time the grass becomes milk."

"May you always have the strength to enjoy your weaknesses."

"Worry often gives a small thing a big shadow."

"Instead of loving your enemies, treat your friends a little better."

"Anatomy is something that everyone has, but it looks better on a girl."

"Don't criticize your wife's judgment; look whom she married."

"God gave us a memory so we can have roses in December."

"Happiness is nothing more than good health and a short memory."

"A nice thing about old age—you can whistle while you brush your teeth."

"Success is won by taking the risk of failure."

"A halo has to slip only a few inches to become a noose."

"Even if you are on the right track, you'll get run over just sitting there."

"Obstacles are things a person sees when he takes his eyes off the goal."

"Your opinion of the world is chiefly your opinion of yourself."

"The surest test of a square deal is when both parties are dissatisfied."

"Make other people like themselves a little better and they'll like you a lot more."

"A man is always as young as he feels but seldom as important."

"Anger is only one letter short of danger."

"The best way to remember your wife's birthday is to forget it once."

"Work hard—the job you save may be your own."

"Man is dust. A woman cries on his shoulder and then he is mud."

"Here's a verse that isn't funny. Too much month at the end of the money."

"Stopping at third base adds no more to the score than striking out."

"Women, like children, need to be loved most when they deserve it least."

"Psychiatry is the only business where the customer is always wrong."

"Women's intuition is nothing more than man's transparency."

"Your calendar shows the passing of time. Your face shows what you are doing with it."

"There is no better exercise for the heart than reaching down and lifting somebody up."

"Heaven may forgive your sins, but your nervous system won't."

"Many things which seem simple at twenty are impossible at sixty, and vice versa."

"Diplomacy is the art of saying "Nice doggie" until you can find a rock."

"Since the discovery of elastic, women take up one third less space."

"A man never knows what he can do until he tries to undo what he has done."

"Do something every day to make other people happy; even if it's to let 'em alone."

"The most enduring thing in a woman's life is what she builds in a man's heart."

"Love is to human behavior what warmth is to wax."

"Only men with no imagination love beautiful women."

"Don't retire; retread."

"A love song is a caress set to music."

"To keep friends, always give your candied opinion."

"Some people are lonely because they build walls instead of bridges."

"A person all wrapped up in himself generally makes a pretty small package."

"The three essentials of happiness are: something to do, someone to love, and something to hope for."

"Anyone who angers you, conquers you."

"When temptation knocks, imagination usually answers."

"Forgive us for not changing the sign lately. We're too busy selling Ant Farms."

"Luck is what happens when preparation meets opportunity."

"If you want to test your memory, try to remember what you were worrying about one year ago today."

"There are two well-known finishes for automobiles: lacquer and liquor."

"The best bridge between despair and hope is a good night's sleep."

"It's amazing how much you can accomplish when you don't care who gets the credit."

"Contentment is the smother of invention."

"Boredom is an emptiness filled with insistence."

"Love is a friendship set to music."

"Pleasant memories must be arranged for in advance."

"Home is where you can scratch any place it itches."

"The best things in life are free. It's the worst things that are so expensive."

"You have to do your own growing regardless of how tall your grandfather was."

"Personality is to a man what perfume is to a flower."

"The trouble with opportunity is that it always looks bigger going than coming."

"Beautiful young people are accidents of nature. Beautiful old people are works of art."

"No problem can exist without a solution."

"A genius is a stupid kid with very happy grandparents."

"Money often costs too much."

"A girl with cotton stockings never sees a mouse."

"A friend is a gold link in the chain of life."

"The penalty of success is to be bored by the people who used to snub you."

"The only way some people will get ahead in this world is to have it sculptured."

"Flattery never hurts a man unless he inhales."

"You've reached middle age when your wife tells you to pull in your stomach and you already have."

"When you're right, no one remembers; when you're wrong; no one forgets."

"There are three kinds of people: those who make things happen, those who watch things happening, and those who don't know what's happening.

I like that last legend. Make certain you get into and stay in that first group of imaginative doers, and you'll experience both fun and growth in your own mail order activity.

16 | Your Best Friend—The United States Government!

"The world can be your oyster with government help."

A harassed farmer sat down one day and penned a letter:

"Dear Government: Will you please tell me how to get rid of dandelions? I've tried everthing."

Eventually he got his answer:

"Dear Sir: We don't know of anything that will get rid of dandelions, but here's a great recipe for dandelion wine."

While Abraham Lincoln was still a village postmaster, citizens were turning to Uncle Sam with their problems. Then, as now, Uncle was ready to help out if he could, and if he could not, he could always suggest dandelion wine. When the mail got too heavy for the friendly postmaster, form letters were substituted. Finally the present practice evolved of issuing publications on every subject an American citizen might be interested in.

Housewife, mariner, trout fisherman, or astronaut; chess player, rock hound, farmer, or mortician: whatever your interest, your Uncle

Sam has valuable help and information for you. Much of it is yours for the asking. The rest is offered well under cost.

If this surprises you, if you haven't seen any of this help around, believe me, it's your fault, not his. Uncle Sam conducts the biggest printing plant in the world—the Government Printing Office (GPO)—and from it he pours out floods of valuable material to assist you in every possible phase of your business life.

And right here I want to introduce you to a man who can become the greatest business contact you will ever make. He is the man to see about the hundreds of government publications I'm going to tell you about, as well as hundreds of thousands of other publications put out by the GPO. Whenever you are in doubt about how to get any of the books, magazines, leaflets, and booklets from any department of the government, you can write to: Superintendent of Documents, U.S. Government Printing Office, Washington, DC 20402.

The Superintendent of Documents has been the official sales agent for United States Government Books since 1895. An arm of the United States Government Printing Office, the Superintendent's organization now handles over 2 million orders per year and administers over 500 subscriptions on a continual basis. The entire sales program is self-sustaining, operating on funds derived from the sale of publications. There are more than 16,000 titles available from the Superintendent of Documents.

To give you an idea of some of these 16,000 titles, send them a letter asking for "U.S. Government Books—Catalog #P-3." This free catalog will give you a description of about a thousand of the most popular publications covering the following subjects: Agriculture, Business & Industry, Careers, Children & Families, Consumer Aids, Diet & Nutrition, Education, Energy, Environment & Weather, Gardening & Landscaping, Government, Health & Physical Fitness, History, Hobbies, Housing, International Topics, Law & Law Enforcement, Military, Miscellaneous, National Topics, Recent Releases, Science & Technology, Senior Citizens, Space Exploration, Transportation, Vacation & Travel.

I have listed below just a few of the thousand subjects and books that you will find in the catalog; the ones I have selected are taken from the Business and Industry section. Here they are:

Doing Business with the Federal Government. Helps firms determine where in the government to market their products and how to bid on contracts. Also tells how to learn about the government surplus property sales and where businesses can get advice from trained counselors.

U.S Government Purchasing and Sales Directory. Contains an alphabetical listing of the products and services bought by both military and civilian departments with specific information on the offices that purchase them.

Selling to the U.S. Government. Tells how to secure government business and details ways the Small Business Administration can help.

Managing the Small Service Firm for Growth and Profit. A self-assessment guide for the owner-manager.

A Basic Guide to Exporting. A step-by-step guide to establishing profitable international trade. Tells how to get assistance in reaching this goal.

European Trade Fairs: A Guide for Exporters. How to choose a market in Europe, how to identify the right fairs, and how to make fairs as productive as possible.

Export Marketing for Smaller Firms. Presents guidelines to help the small business owner decide whether exporting is appropriate.

How to Build an Export Business. A step-by-step guide for small businesses.

Franchise Index/Profile. Presents an index of basic information needed for a valid determination of the returns of a given franchise.

Ideas into Dollars: A Resource Guide for Investors and Innovative Small Businesses. Information on the government and private organizations, programs, and publications that aid invention and innovation.

Buying and Selling a Small Business. Tells how to evaluate the business, negotiate the transaction, and conduct the transfer.

Handbook for Small Business: A Survey of Small Business Programs of the Federal Government. Information on programs and services offered to small businesses by 25 federal agencies.

Handbook of Small Business Finance. Sets forth the principles of financial management, explains ratio analysis, and reviews ways of financing growth and obtaining working capital.

Managing for Profits. Discusses production and marketing, purchasing and collections, financial management, taxation, insurance, and more.

Financial Recordkeeping for Small Stores. For the owner-manager without a full-time bookkeeper.

Cost Accounting for Small Manufacturers. Accounting for labor costs, overhead, cost estimates, data processing, planning and control, cost and benefit analysis, and more.

Purchasing Management and Inventory Control for Small Business. Explains how to evaluate existing purchasing policies and improve on them.

Decision Points in Developing New Products. Provides a path through new product development, from the idea stage to marketing strategy.

Credit and Collections for Small Stores. Helps you tell whether it is practical to offer credit to your customers.

Starting and Managing a Small Service Business. Helps sort out personal capabilities and weaknesses, evaluate ideas, and set priorities before taking the big step.

The United States Government Printing Office also operates twenty-six bookstores all around the country where you can browse through the shelves and buy the books that interest you. Naturally these stores cannot stock all of the more than 16,000 titles, but they do carry the ones you are most likely to be looking for. And they will be happy to special-order any government book currently offered for sale. All of the book stores accept Visa, Mastercard, and Superintendent of Documents Deposit Account Orders. A listing of these twenty-six stores can be found at the end of this chapter.

YOUR FRIEND, THE DEPARTMENT OF COMMERCE

Many departments and agencies of the government help the businessman, but the Department of Commerce (as you can tell from its name) is by far your best source of help in the business field. About half of the publications I'll be bringing to your attention in this chapter come from that department. If one of the department's field offices is near you (see the end of chapter 13 for their locations), go in and get acquainted. I think your eyes will be opened.

Many of the publications you will want will be available in the Field Office, so you can save time by asking there before you write to the Superintendent in Washington.

Also, certain libraries are designated as depositories for government publications. The Superintendent sends them all, or almost all, of the government publications as they come out. The list of the more than four hundred libraries is too long to give here, but if you ask for the United States Department of Commerce Publications, Annual Supplement (prices vary), you will find the depository libraries listed. If one is in your city, you will be able to use it to save time and expense by borrowing or consulting the library's files.

Another name you are going to come across in these pages is the Small Business Administration. The SBA is the first independent agency of the federal government ever established in peacetime solely to advise and assist the nation's small businesss concerns. This agency also has regional and branch offices throughout the country; a listing of them is at the end of this chapter.

To get copies of the different publications that the SBA supplies, contact the U.S. Small Business Administration, P.O. Box 15434, Fort Worth, TX 76119, or you can call toll free 800-433-7212. (for Texas only, call 800-792-8901). Call or write to them today and have them send you a copy of their 115-A list of Free Publications and a copy of their 115-B list of For Sale Publications.

Here is a list of some of the many free publications you can order from the SBA:

The ABC's of Borrowing
What Is the Best Selling Price?
Pricing for Small Manufacturers
Cash Flow in a Small Plant
Credit and Collections
Keeping Records in Small Business
Problems in Managing a Family-Owned Business
Finding a New Product for Your Company
Planning and Goal Setting for Small Business
Can You Make Money with Your Idea or Invention?
Can You Lease or Buy Equipment?

Can You Use a Minicomputer?
Check List for Going into Business
Factors in Considering a Shopping Center Location
Computers for Small Business-Service Bureau or Time Sharing
Exhibiting at Trade Shows
Developing New Accounts
Public Relations for Small Business
Introduction to Patents
Outwitting Bad-Check Passers
Introduction to Patents
Handicrafts
Home Businesses
Selling by Mail Order
Statistics and Maps for National Market Analysis
National Directory for Use in Marketing
Basic Library Reference Sources
National Mailing-List Houses
New Product Development
Ideas into Dollars

I can personally tell how one of these books saved a friend of mine thousands of dollars. We were having lunch together one day, and he casually mentioned that he and his father were going to buy a motel the following day. I asked him what he knew about the motel business, and he replied, "Nothing at all, and neither does my father, but the place we're buying is a real gold mine! You should see the business they do each day!"

He went on to tell me that they had examined the owner's books, and he was ready to put his life savings and the life savings of his father into this new venture.

I persuaded him to go down to the offices of the Small Business Administration in Los Angeles and buy a copy of the book *Starting and Managing a Small Motel*. He promised to buy the book and read it before he completed his negotiations on the purchase of the motel. Two days later he came into my office full of gratitude. He told me that this simple book was responsible for saving him and his father their life savings. The book pointed out many facets of motel operation that he never suspected existed. It also told him what to look for when buying an established motel, and it was this particular information that opened his eyes to the poor investment he was ready to make.

When you consider that you have at your disposal, through the Small Business Administration, the talents and brains of some of the best business heads in the country, it is really a crime to start any business endeavor without first taking the advice and help available to you. You are paying for these services with your taxes. Take advantage of them!

Another great government business tool for you to use is the *Consumer Information Catalog*. This catalog lists booklets from almost thirty agencies of the federal government. And more than half of them are free. You will find booklets on fixing your car, on saving money on food, health care, energy, and other household expenses, on slimming down and trimming up, and on many other interesting topics.

The catalog is published four times a year by the Consumer Information Center. The Center was established by presidential order in 1970 to encourage federal agencies to share useful consumer information and to increase public awareness of this information. Consumers have suggested many of the topics for publication listed in this catalog. You can get a free catalog and get on the mailing list at no charge by sending your name and address to: Consumer Information Center, Pueblo, CO 81009. Please be sure to write the word "FREE" on the outside of the envelope and tell them that you want to receive the new issue of the *Consumer Information Catalog*.

If you take off your merchandising blinders and look at these publications with fresh eyes, you will discover many profitable products that can be developed from this information. A few years ago, for example, I was looking through the *Consumer Information Catalog* and found a booklet for 50¢ called "How to Grow Dwarf Fruit Trees." This booklet explained the Japanese technique called *Bonsai* that has been cultivated for thousands of years in Japan. This technique shows you how to grow miniature fruit trees that bear edible apples, pears, oranges, plums, and so forth—yet the trees do not grow over twelve inches high.

Now before I bought this book for 50¢, I was under the impression that to grow a dwarf tree you had to use a special kind of seed. I was surprised to learn that you used a regular seed—the trick was in the way you pruned the roots. Based on the techniques that were explained in this book, we assembled the tools, equipment, and instruction necessary to grow a dwarf tree and came out with a DWARF TREE KIT for $5.00. The kit permitted you to grow nine different dwarf fruit trees and showed you the step-by-step procedures to follow to keep your trees miniature. The first year that we came out with this kit, we sold 100,000 of them across the United States. And I got all the research, knowledge, and information from the 50¢ government book. So as you look at the *Consumer Information Catalog's* different listings and different books, consider how they relate to the general public and how they can be developed into a product or service that you could market.

YOUR FRIEND, THE GENERAL SERVICES ADMINISTRATION

While we have talked about the Small Business Administration, the Department of Commerce, the government bookstores, and the *Consumer Information Catalog*, let's not ignore another outlet which can be of great value to you. I am referring to the General Service Administration, which, as the name indicates, is a kind of catchall business and supply agency for the other government agencies. The GSA buys, stores, distributes, and maintains government property supplies. It also handles all the transportation, paper work, and record work for the other agencies.

For example, the Small Business Administration may find it easier and cheaper to get its paper clips, wastebaskets, janitor supplies, etcetera, from the GSA than to go out and contract for such things on its own. Since hundreds of government agencies do the same, this makes the GSA a gigantic and very convenient market for you, as well as for the manufacturer or distributor of paper clips, wastebaskets, or janitor supplies. Instead of knocking on the doors of a hundred departments, you can sell a hundred times more to one buyer— the GSA.

Don't be backward about putting in your order. The GSA, like the SBA, wants to do business with the smaller supplier. You will be received just as cordially as General Motors when you have something to sell. The GSA maintains twelve regional offices throughout the country in addition to the Washington headquarters; so you don't have to travel far to do your business face to face. These offices will inform you of the locations of contracting offices and will advise you as to how to get bidders' mailing lists. They will tell you where and how to get government specifications so that you'll know your product or service will meet the standards. They'll show you how to keep up to the minute on current bidding opportunities. They'll even give you valuable tips on how to introduce new products to government supply systems, and how to promote demand and sales of your present products. In short, they'll knock themselves out to tell you what steps to take, what forms to use, and who to contact when you want to do business with the government. And all this will be done by trained people whose knowledge is at your disposal at no charge or fee.

Like the Small Business Administration, the General Services Administration puts out heaps of printed material specially tailored to the small businessman looking for a government contract. Some recent books available for the asking are:

Leasing Space to the Government
Doing Business with the Federal Government
Guide to Specifications and Standards of the Federal Government
Buying Government Surplus Personal Property
Partners in Progress (Minority Business Program)
Federal Buying Directory
Government Business Opportunities
Contract Opportunities for Maintenance and Repair of Equipment

The booklet, Leasing Space to the Government, for example, will tell you that the GSA acts as the government's rental agent not only on building and warehouse space, but in other areas as well. For instance, the GSA is open for bids on auto-repair contracts and car rentals at the seventy-five or more motor pools it runs.

SELLING TO THE MILITARY

A booklet published by the Department of Defense, Selling to the Military, is your guide and source book on selling to the United States Army, Navy, Marine Corps, Air Force, and the Joint Agencies. As you know, the biggest slice of Uncle Sam's budget dollar goes for defense spending, and most of that slice is funneled right back into the business world. Iron and steel, dynamos and transistors, airplanes and ships, are contracted out to private firms to design, build, and ship. Even where the government handles the work itself, salaries and wages are paid to soldiers and sailors, civil-service engineers and steam fitters, planners and draftsmen. What happens to all that money? Why, they spend it to buy the things you sell to the

Military Exchange Service, of course! So whether your business is apples or zithers, get in there and cash in on the military dollar.

The Department of Defense wants to do business with all competent firms; it wants competition to be as wide as possible. Small firms and firms in labor surplus areas are especially invited to offer their products to supply defense needs.

That word *needs* is the key here. As in any successful business, you must learn your customer's needs. Then you must find out his buying policies and follow leads to search out selling opportunities. One of the best ways to find the needs of the government is through the *Commerce Business Daily.*

This is a newspaper published every day, Monday through Friday, that keeps you posted on the very latest information you will need in order to sell to both the military and civilian sides of the government. All proposed contract awards of over $10,000 are listed, as well as awarded contracts above $25,000. The listing of firms which have received good-sized contracts is your direct lead for subcontracting opportunities. Most of these firms will want to farm out jobs for parts, subassemblies, services, and supplies to another firm, and it might as well be yours. To get the *Commerce Business Daily* order form, write to: Superintendent of Documents, U.S. Government Printing Office, Washington, DC 20401.

You will find it one of the best investments you ever made.

The military arm of the government uses supplies not only in great quantity but also in bewildering variety. Glancing through the book, *Selling to the Military,* you expect to see calls for ammunition and generators, explosives and jet planes. But golf clubs? Ant farms? Women's panties? Toy soldiers? Caviar? Insecticides? Absolutely! The Post Exchanges and the Quartermaster Corps need just about everything under the sun. The book lists the principal interests of the Military Exchange Service (the Post Exchange or "PX"), which include candy and confections; beverages; tobacco and smoking accessories; toiletries and drugs; stationery and supplies; clothing; jewelry; toys; housewares; sports and recreational equipment and supplies; automotive accessories; food.

Sometime ago, we manufactured plastic toy soldiers to retail at $1.00 for a box of one hundred pieces. Naturally, we saw our primary market as toy stores throughout the country. But imagine our surprise when sales to PX's soon began to outstrip our sales to toy stores! And not only did the PX's move thousands and thousands of sets for us, but we had no credit losses, for, in effect, we were selling to the United States government.

So the next time you think of selling a product to the government, don't necessarily think in terms of guided missiles or electronic equipment running into millions of dollars; instead, think of those little toy soldiers that we sold by the thousands—that should give you a broader view on marketing your products to Uncle Sam. So jump right in and get your share of the billions of dollars being spent to make our country strong. If you miss out on this fertile source of business, you are not only hurting yourself but passing up a wonderful chance of help your country.

Here are the addresses of the military exchanges. *For Overseas Navy Exchanges,* write to: Commanding Officer U.S. Naval Resale Systems Office, 3rd Avenue and 29th Street, Brooklyn, NY 11232.

For Overseas Marine Corps Exchanges, write to: Marine Corps, Exchange Service Headquarters, U.S. Marine Corps, Washington, DC 20380.

For Overseas Army and Air Corps Exchanges, write to: Army and Air Force Exchange Service Headquarters, (AAFES) Dallas, TX 75222.

YOUR FRIEND, THE NATIONAL TECHNICAL INFORMATION SERVICE

When Aladdin first set foot inside the treasure cave, he didn't stop to make a catalog of the goodies that it contained. He didn't classify the pearls for size and luster, the gold for fineness, the diamonds for carat weight. He didn't have to because he realized that he had stepped into something the like of which the world had never seen, which was all his for the taking.

Well, I felt a lot like Aladdin when I discovered the National Technical Information Service (NTIS). Here is a central, permanent source of the specialized business, economic, scientific, and social information originated by most of the federal agencies. All of this information is permanently available.

The NTIS is an agency of the United States Department of Commerce and is a central source for the public sale of United States government sponsored research, development, and engineering reports as well as foreign technical reports and other analyses prepared by national and local government agencies, their contractors, or grantees. It is one of the world's leading processors of specialized information.

The NTIS Information Collection exceeds a million titles. More than 300,000 of them contain foreign technology or marketing information. All are permanently available for sale, either directly from the 80,000 titles and shelf stock, or from the microfiche master copies of documents in less demand. Over 70,000 new reports of completed research are added to the NTIS data base annually. In the same period, NTIS supplies its customers with more than 6 million documents and microforms, shipping about 23,500 information products *each day.*

What does all this have to do with you? Well, the next time you have a technical manufacturing or personnel problem, before you run out and hire expensive help, send a letter to the NTIS and see if they don't have an answer already nestled in their computer files. For free literature describing NTIS's amazing collection of services and information, write to NTIS, 5285 Port Royal Road, Springfield, VA 22161.

U.S. GOVERNMENT BOOKSTORES

ALABAMA
Roebuck Shopping City
9220-B Parkway East
Birmingham, AL 35206
(205) 254-1056
9:00 AM–5:00 PM

CALIFORNIA
ARCO Plaza, C-Level
505 South Flower Street
Los Angeles, CA 90071
(213) 688-5841
8:30 AM–4:30 PM

Room 1023, Federal Building
450 Golden Gate Avenue
San Francisco, CA 94102
(415) 556-0643
8:00 AM–4:00 PM

COLORADO
Room 117, Federal Building
1961 Stout Street
Denver, CO 80294
(303) 837-3964
8:00 AM–4:00 PM

World Savings Building
720 North Main Street
Pueblo, CO 81003
(303) 544-3142
9:00 AM–5:00 PM

DISTRICT OF COLUMBIA
U.S. Government Printing Office
710 North Capitol Street
Washington, DC 20402
(202) 275-2091
8:00 AM–4:00 PM

Commerce Department
Room 1604, 1st Floor
14th & E Streets, NW
Washington, DC 20230
(202) 377-3527
8:00 AM–4:00 PM

Dept. of Health and Human Services
Room 1528, North Building
330 Independence Avenue, SW
Washington, DC 20201
(202) 472-7478
8:00 AM–4:00 PM

State Department
Room 2817 North Lobby
21st and C Streets, NW
Washington, DC 20520
(202) 632-1437
9:00 AM–5:00 PM

All stores with the exception of Houston are open Mon–Fri (Houston, Mon–Sat).

US Information Agency
1776 Pennsylvania Avenue, NW
Washington, DC 20547
(202) 724-9928
9:00 AM–5:00 PM

Pentagon
Room 2E172
Main Concourse, South End
Washington, DC 20310
(703) 557-1821
8:00 AM–4:00 PM

FLORIDA
Room 158, Federal Building
400 W. Bay Street
P.O. Box 35089
Jacksonville, FL 32202
(904) 791-3801
8:00 AM–4:00 PM

GEORGIA
Room 100, Federal Building
275 Peachtree Street, NE
Atlanta, GA 30303
(404) 221-6947
8:00 AM–4:00 PM

ILLINOIS
Room 1365, Federal Building
219 S. Dearborn Street
Chicago, IL 60604
(312) 353-5133
8:00 AM–4:00 PM

MASSACHUSETTS
Room G25, Federal Building
Sudbury Street
Boston, MA 02203
(617) 223-6071
8:00 AM–4:00 PM

MICHIGAN
Suite 160, Federal Building
477 Michigan Avenue
Detroit, MI 48226
(313) 226-7816
8:00 AM–4:00 PM

MISSOURI
Room 144, Federal Building
601 East 12th Street
Kansas City, MO 64106
(816) 374-2160
8:00 AM–4:00 PM

NEW YORK
Room 110
26 Federal Plaza
New York, NY 10278
(212) 264-3825
8:00 AM–4:00 PM

OHIO
1st Floor, Federal Building
1240 E. 9th Street
Cleveland, OH 44199
(216) 522-4922
9:00 AM–5:00 PM

Room 207, Federal Building
200 N. High Street
Columbus, OH 43215
(614) 469-6956
9:00 AM–5:00 PM

PENNSYLVANIA
Room 1214, Federal Building
600 Arch Street
Philadelphia, PA 19106
(215) 597-0677
8:00 AM–4:00 PM

Room 118, Federal Building
1000 Liberty Avenue
Pittsburgh, PA 15222
(412) 644-2721
9:00 AM–5:00 PM

TEXAS
Room 1C50, Federal Building
1100 Commerce Street
Dallas, TX 75242
(214) 767-0076
7:45 AM–4:15 PM

45 College Center
9319 Gulf Freeway
Houston, TX 77017
(713) 229-3515
10:00 AM–6:00 PM

WASHINGTON
Room 194, Federal Building
915 Second Avenue
Seattle, WA 98174
(206) 442-4270
8:00 AM–4:00 PM

WISCONSIN
Room 190, Federal Building
517 E. Wisconsin Avenue
Milwaukee, WI 53202
(414) 291-1304
8:00 AM–4:00 PM

RETAIL SALES OUTLET
8660 Cherry Lane
Laurel, MD 20810
(301) 953-7974
7:45 AM–3:45 PM

FEDERAL INFORMATION CENTERS

If you have questions about any program or agency in the Federal Government, you may want to call the Federal Information Center (FIC) nearest you. FIC staffs are prepared to help consumers find needed information or locate the right agency—usually federal but sometimes state or local—for help with problems. Each city listed below has an FIC or a tieline—a toll-free local number connecting to an FIC elsewhere.

ALABAMA
Birmingham	(205) 322-8591
Mobile	(205) 438-1421

ALASKA
Anchorage	(907) 271-3650

ARIZONA
Phoenix	(602) 261-3313
Tucson	(602) 622-1511

ARKANSAS
Little Rock	(501) 378-6177

CALIFORNIA
Los Angeles	(213) 688-3800
Sacramento	(916) 440-3344
San Diego	(714) 293-6030
San Francisco	(415) 556-6600
San Jose	(408) 275-7422
Santa Ana	(714) 836-2386

COLORADO
Colorado Springs	(303) 471-9491
Denver	(303) 234-7181
Pueblo	(303) 544-9523

CONNECTICUT
Hartford	(203) 527-2617
New Haven	(203) 624-4720

FLORIDA
St. Petersburg	(813) 893-3495
Tampa	(813) 229-7911
Other locations	**(800) 282-8556**

GEORGIA
Atlanta	(404) 221-6891

HAWAII
Honolulu	(808) 546-8620

ILLINOIS
Chicago	(312) 353-4242

INDIANA
Gary/Hammond	(219) 883-4110
Indianapolis	(317) 269-7373

IOWA
Des Moines	(515) 284-4448
Other locations	**(800) 532-1556**

KANSAS
Topeka	(913) 295-2866
Other locations	**(800) 432-2934**

KENTUCKY
Louisville	(502) 582-6261

LOUISIANA
New Orleans	(504) 589-6696

MARYLAND
Baltimore	(301) 962-4980

MASSACHUSETTS
Boston	(617) 223-7121

MICHIGAN
Detroit	(313) 226-7016
Grand Rapids	(616) 451-2628

MINNESOTA
Minneapolis	(612) 349-5333

MISSOURI
Kansas City	(816) 374-2466
St. Louis	(314) 425-4106
Other locations within area code 314	**(800) 392-7711**
Other locations within area codes 816 and 417	**(800) 892-5808**

NEBRASKA
Omaha	(402) 221-3353
Other locations	**(800) 642-8383**

NEW JERSEY
Newark	(201) 645-3600
Paterson/Passaic	(201) 523-0717
Trenton	(609) 396-4400

NEW MEXICO
Albuquerque	(505) 766-3091
Santa Fe	(505) 983-7743

NEW YORK
Albany	(518) 463-4421
Buffalo	(716) 846-4010
New York	(212) 264-4464
Rochester	(716) 546-5075
Syracuse	(315) 476-8545

NORTH CAROLINA
Charlotte	(704) 376-3600

OHIO
Akron	(216) 375-5638
Cincinnati	(513) 684-2801
Cleveland	(216) 522-4040
Columbus	(614) 221-1014
Dayton	(513) 223-7377
Toledo	(419) 241-3223

OKLAHOMA
Oklahoma City	(405) 231-4868
Tulsa	(918) 584-4193

OREGON
Portland	(503) 221-2222

PENNSYLVANIA
Allentown/Bethlehem	
	(215) 821-7785
Philadelphia	(215) 597-7042
Pittsburgh	(412) 644-3456
Scranton	(717) 346-7081

RHODE ISLAND
Providence	(401) 331-5565

TENNESSEE
Chattanooga	(615) 265-8231
Memphis	(901) 521-3285
Nashville	(615) 242-5056

TEXAS
Austin	(512) 472-5494
Dallas	(214) 767-8585
Fort Worth	(817) 334-3624
Houston	(713) 229-2552
San Antonio	(512) 224-4471

UTAH
Ogden	(801) 399-1347
Salt Lake City	(801) 524-5353

VIRGINIA
Newport News	(804) 244-0480
Norfolk	(804) 441-3101
Richmond	(804) 643-4928
Roanoke	(703) 982-8591

WASHINGTON
Seattle	(206) 442-0570
Tacoma	(206) 383-5230

WISCONSIN
Milwaukee	(414) 271-2273

SMALL BUSINESS ADMINISTRATION FIELD OFFICES

Address	City, State, Zip Code
150 Causeway St., 10th Floor	Boston, MA 02114
302 High St., 4th Floor	Holyoke, MA 01040
Federal Building, 40 Western Ave., Rm. 512	Augusta, Maine 04430
55 Pleasant St., Rm. 213	Concord, NH 03301
1 Financial Plaza	Hartford, CT 06103
Federal Building, 87 State St., Rm. 210	Montpelier, VT 05602
57 Eddy St., Rm. 710	Providence, RI 02903
26 Federal Plaza, 31st Floor	New York, NY 10007
U.S. Courthouse and Federal Office Bldg.	Hato Rey, Puerto Rico 00919
970 Broad St., Rm. 1635	Newark, NJ 07109
Federal Bldg., 100 So. Clinton St.	Syracuse, NY 13202
111 West Huron St., Rm. 1112, Federal Bldg.	Buffalo, NY 14202
180 State St., Rm. 412	Elmira, NY 14901
99 Washington Ave., Twin Tower Bldg., Rm. 922	Albany, NY 12210
Federal Bldg., Rm. 601, 100 State St.	Rochester, NY 14604
425 Broad Hollow Rd., Rm. 205	Melville, NY 11746
U.S. Federal Office Bldg., Veterans Dr.	St. Thomas, Virgin Islands 00801
1800 E. Davis St.	Camden, NY 08104
1 Decker Square E. Lobby	Philadelphia, Bala Cynwyd, PA 19004
1500 North 2nd St.	Harrisburg, PA 17108
Penn Place, 20 N. Pennsylvania Ave.	Wilkes-Barre, PA 18702
844 King St., Federal Bldg., Rm. 5207	Wilmington, DE 19801
Oxford Building, Rm. 630, 8600 LaSalle Rd.	Baltimore, Towson, MD 21204
109 N. 3rd St., Rm. 301, Lowndes Bldg.	Clarksburg, WV 26301
Charleston National Plaza, Suite 628	Charleston, WV 25301
Federal Bldg., 1000 Liberty Ave., Rm. 1401	Pittsburgh, PA 15222
Federal Bldg., 400 N. 8th St., Rm. 3015	Richmond, VA 32340
1030 15th St., NW., Suite 250	Washington, DC 20417
1720 Peachtree St., NW., 6th Floor	Atlanta, GA 30309
908 So. 20th St., Rm. 202	Birmingham, AL 35205
230 So. Tryon St., Suite 700	Charlotte, NC 28202
215 So. Evans St.	Greenville, NC 27834
1801 Assembly St., Rm. 117	Columbia, SC 29201
Petroleum Bldg., Suite 690, 200 E. Pascagoula St.	Jackson, MS 39201
111 Fred Haise Blvd., Gulf National Life Insurance Bldg., 2nd Floor	Biloxi, MS 39530
Federal Bldg., 400 W. Bay St., Rm. 261	Jacksonville, FL 32202
Federal Bldg., 600 Federal Place, Rm. 188	Louisville, KY 40202
2222 Ponce de Leon Blvd., 5th Floor	Miami, Coral Gables, FL 33184
700 Twiggs St., Rm. 607	Tampa, FL 33602
404 James Robertson Pkwy., Suite 1012	Nashville, TN 37219
502 So. Gay St., Rm. 307, Fidelity Bankers Bldg.	Knoxville, TN 37902
Federal Bldg., 167 N. Main St., Rm. 211	Memphis, TN 38103
Federal Bldg., 219 So. Dearborn St., Rm. 437	Chicago, IL 60604
1 North Old State Capital Plaza	Springfield, IL 62701
1240 E. 9th St., Rm. 317	Cleveland, OH 44199
Federal Bldg., U.S. Courthouse, 85 Marion Blvd.	Columbus, OH 43215
Federal Bldg., 550 Main St.	Cincinnati, OH 45202
477 Michigan Ave., McNamara Bldg.	Detroit, MI 48226
550 West Kaye Ave.	Marquette, MI 49855
575 No. Pennsylvania St., Federal Bldg.	Indianapolis, IN 46204

122 West Washington Ave., Rm. 713	Madison, WI 53703
517 E. Wisconsin Ave., Rm. 246, Federal Bldg.	Milwaukee, WI 53202
500 So. Barstow St., Rm. 16, Federal Bldg.	Eau Claire, WI 54701
12 So. 6th St., Plymouth Bldg.	Minneapolis, MN 55402
1100 Commerce St., Rm. 300	Dallas, TX 75202
5000 Marble Ave., NE., Patio Plaza Bldg.	Albuquerque, NM 87110
1 Allen Center, Suite 705, 500 Dallas St.	Houston, TX 77002
611 Gaines St., Suite 900	Little Rock, AK 72201
1205 Texas Ave.	Lubbock, TX 79408
4100 Rio Bravo St.	El Paso, TX 79901
222 East Van Buren, Suite 500	Lower Rio Grande Valley, Harlingen, TX 78550
3105 Leopard St.	Corpus Christi, TX 78408
100 So. Washington St., Federal Bldg.	Marshall, TX 75670
1001 Howard Ave., Plaza Tower, 17th Floor	New Orleans, LA 70113
200 NW 5th St., Suite 670	Oklahoma City, OK 73102
727 E. Durango	San Antonio, TX 78206
U.S. Post Office and Courthouse Federal Bldg., 500 Fennin St.	Shreveport, LA 71163
1150 Grand Ave.	Kansas City, MO 64106
New Federal Bldg., 210 Walnut St., Rm. 749	Des Moines, IA 50309
19th and Farman Streets	Omaha, NE 68102
1 Mercantile Tower	St. Louis, MO 63101
110 E. Waterman St.	Wichita, KA 67202
721 19th St., Rm. 426A	Denver, CO 80202
Federal Bldg., Rm. 5001, 100 E. B St.	Casper, WY 82601
Federal Bldg., 563 2nd Ave., Rm. 218	Fargo, ND 58102
618 Helena Ave.	Helena, MT 59601
Federal Bldg., 125 So. State St., Rm. 2237	Salt Lake City, UT 84111
National Bank Bldg., 8th and Maine Ave., Rm. 402	Sioux Falls, SD 57102
515 9th St., Federal Bldg.	Rapid City, SD 57701
211 Main St.	San Francisco, CA 94102
301 E. Stewart	Las Vegas, NV 89101
1129 No. St.	Fresno, CA 93721
1149 Bethel St., Rm. 402	Honolulu, HI 96813
Pacific Daily News Bldg., Rm. 507	Agana, Guam 96910
350 So. Figueroa St., 6th Floor	Los Angeles, CA 90014
112 No. Central Ave.	Phoenix, AZ 85004
880 Front St., Federal Bldg.	San Diego, CA 92101
2800 Cottage Way	Sacramento, CA 95825
50 So. Virginia St., Rm. 308	Reno, NV 89501
915 2nd Ave., Federal Bldg.	Seattle, WA 98104
1016 West 6th Ave., Suite 200	Anchorage, AK 99501
Legal Center	Fairbanks, AK 99701
501½ 2nd Ave.	Boise, ID 83701
1005 Main St.	Portland, OR 97205
1220 Southwest 3rd Ave., Courthouse Bldg., Rm. 651	Spokane, WA 99210

GENERAL SERVICES ADMINISTRATION BUSINESS SERVICE CENTERS

	Areas Covered
GSA Center Business Service Center, GSA 7th and D Streets, SW. Room 1050 Washington, DC 20407	Washington DC, and nearby Maryland and Virginia.
Business Service Center, GSA John W. McCormack Post Office and Courthouse Boston, MA 02109	Connecticut, Maine, Vermont, New Hampshire, Massachusetts, and Rhode Island.
Business Service Center, GSA 26 Federal Plaza New York, NY 10007	New Jersey, New York, Puerto Rico, and Virgin Islands.
Business Service Center, GSA 600 Arch Street Philadelphia, PA 19106	Pennsylvania, Delaware, Virginia, West Virginia, and Maryland.
Business Service Center, GSA Richard B. Russell Federal Building, U.S. Courthouse 75 Spring Street, S.W. Atlanta, GA 30303	Alabama, Florida, Georgia, Kentucky, Mississippi, North Carolina, South Carolina, and Tennessee.
Business Service Center, GSA 230 South Dearborn Street Chicago, IL 60604	Illinois, Indiana, Ohio, Michigan, Minnesota, and Wisconsin.
Business Service Center, GSA 1500 East Bannister Road Kansas City, MO 64131	Iowa, Kansas, Missouri, and Nebraska.
Business Service Center, GSA 819 Taylor Street Fort Worth, TX 76102	Arkansas, Louisiana, Texas, New Mexico, and Oklahoma.
Gulf Coast Business Service Center, GSA FOB Courthouse, 515 Rusk Street Houston, TX 77002	Gulf Coast from Brownsville, TX, to New Orleans, LA.
Business Service Center, GSA Building 41, Denver Federal Center Denver, CO 80225	Colorado, North Dakota, Utah, South Dakota, Montana, and Wyoming.
Business Service Center, GSA 525 Market Street San Francisco, CA 94105	Northern California, Hawaii, and all of Nevada, except Clark County.
Business Service Center, GSA 300 North Los Angeles Street Los Angeles, CA 90012	Los Angeles, Southern California, Clark County, and Arizona.
Business Service Center, GSA 440 Federal Building 915 Second Avenue Seattle, WA 98174	Alaska, Idaho, Oregon, and Washington.

17

Think Yourself Rich with These Little-Known Secrets

"With money in your pocket, you are wise, you are handsome, and you can sing well, too!"

How would you like to learn company secrets for 50¢ . . . get free artwork for your ads . . . have Uncle Sam do your research . . . use government publications to sell your products . . . find royalty-earning inventions for your company . . . sell your talents to others?

A few years ago I produced a newsletter called *Think Yourself Rich*. It was very successful and we had over 25,000 subscribers in the first six months. I would like to share with you some of the interesting items discussed in the newsletter. Some of the items are for people already in their own business and other items are for those just starting in business. But whether you're a beginner or a veteran in the business world, I'm sure you will find many good "Idea Starters" you can use.

A NEW WAY TO GET GOOD ARTWORK

If you are in the market for artwork for advertising or for packaging, give the assignment to the art class of a local school. The instructors are usually anxious to have new ideas as projects for their classes, and most often will give you full attention. The result: You will end up with many good ideas to select from. Suggestion: Offer a prize to the winner. All in all, the whole thing won't cost you more than a fraction of what you would pay a professional artist and you will have exactly what you need. This is also a good idea if you are looking for a good photograph of your product: Just contact a local photography school and let the students go to work on your product.

COMPANY SECRETS FOR ONLY 50¢

The other evening, my wife and I decided to have fried chicken for dinner and I went out to a local carryout store called Colonel Sanders Southern Fried Chicken. They make the most delicious fried chicken I have ever eaten. While waiting for my order, I noticed a sign that read, "This chicken is prepared by a patented process," and it gave the patent number of the process. I was so curious about how they made such good food that I wrote to the Commissioner of Patents, U.S. Patent Office, Washington, DC 20231, and asked for a copy of the patent. I enclosed 50¢ to cover costs, and a few days later received a copy of the actual patent. I do not intend to go into the fried chicken business; I did it purely out of curiosity. The reason I am telling you this story is to let you know that you can do just what I did. For 50¢, you can actually get full detailed information, completely illustrated, on anything in the United States that is patented.

SOURCES FOR NEW PRODUCT IDEAS

One of the best sources for new product ideas is the local printer. Since anyone with a new product or service must first have a brochure or circular printed, it is obvious that the printer is one of the first to know about any new items to hit the market, and in many cases he can put you in touch with his customer. Another good source for new product ideas is your college university, as most of them have research departments. Some of the best-selling consumer items in the United States today were born in a college laboratory; all it takes is a phone call from you to find out what they are working on in your area.

LET THE U.S. GOVERNMENT DO YOUR RESEARCH

In the computer world, memories must be planned in advance. Such memories are planned on a commercial scale by the United

States commercial specialists who provide hundreds of reports of all kinds on the prospects for individual products in various countries. If your business is interested in agriculture, forestry, fisheries, mining, construction, manufacturing or manufactured products, service industries, apparel and related products, furniture, chemicals, rubber and miscellaneous plastic products, aircraft or medical instruments and apparatus, contact the Clearinghouse for Federal Scientific and Technical Information, U.S. Department of Commerce, Springfield, VA 22151, and get on their mailing list. You can get comprehensive reports covering any of these categories.

DO YOU KNOW ALL YOUR CUSTOMERS?

What is the potential market for your product; what is the most number of units you could possibly sell if you sold everyone? My company makes a fishing lure, for example, and it is easy for me to find out how many fishermen there are in this country. Since every fisherman must have a fishing license, I can find out how many fishermen there are in each state and concentrate my sales efforts in the states with the greatest potential. The same holds true for automobiles, marriages, births, and so forth. You can even find out which states have the most insects and when they are in greatest abundance.

YOU CAN SAVE MONEY WITH TEMPORARY HELP

You can save a lot of money by using temporary help. In the mail order business, as well as in many other enterprises, there is frequently a need for many people to work frantically for a few hours or days, after which the demand drops to zero. In many cases, a business will hire people who have very little to do most of the time just so they will have the required staff when the rush is on. These employees can be replaced by temporary help. There are a number of nationwide companies offering temporary help in all fields, and you can find them in the Yellow Pages. In addition to enabling you to trim your staff while still meeting periodic demands, using temporary help will also save money on accounting. You receive one bill a month from the temporary-help agency; they have the expensive task of calculating deductions and making out the individual checks.

SELLING ON CREDIT WILL INCREASE YOUR PROFITS

No matter what your business, you should be thinking about selling goods or services on credit. The latest survey has shown that 76 percent of all business in the U.S. is conducted on credit—and it is highly profitable for the businessman. There are two courses you can take. You can subscribe to an existing credit plan like Mastercard or BankAmericard and pay a percentage for the privilege, or you can start your own plan and issue your own cards. If you deal with a lot of strangers, it would be best to have the protection of a large credit-extending firm. If you are a small-town merchant, however, you might consider issuing your own credit cards to existing customers and potential new customers. A local printer will handle the whole job, from design to finished plastic card. You can offer various plans to make it easy for your customers to pay the big bills they are going to run up with you: Offer them thirty-day, ninety-day, TEN PAY (one-tenth down, one-tenth per month until paid off), or Deferred Budget (another way of saying, by installment). Go over this with your accountant and you will see the profit in the various charges that go with these plans.

HERE IS A UNIQUE WAY OF ADDRESSING DIRECT MAIL

One very sharp direct mail expert discovered a unique way of addressing direct mail . . . and it works! First, go to a computer paper supply house. Ask them to show you samples of paper that go into the computer. Select the one that you want to use. Take some paper samples to an artist and have him design a brochure, letter, leaflet, folder, or whatever you need. Have him pinpoint the exact location of the address. This is important! Now take the finished design to a computer facility and ask the manager to place the address exactly where the artist has located it. He will then run the paper through the machine and print the mailing list of your choice directly on the paper. Note that this is being done before the paper is printed. The advantage here is obvious: You will not have to use labels or type the addresses after the piece is printed, since it will be addressed before it even goes to the printer. Have the computer people "trim and burst" the pages. Now you have a stack of blank paper all addressed and ready for printing. Take the paper to the printer and tell him to set up his press so that he will not spoil any of the pre-addressed sheets. He can do this by running scrap paper through the machine before he makes the print run on your stock. Now when he prints the paper (including the bulk rate postage indicia, if you wish), it will be ready for mailing.

If you use first-class mail, you merely have to run the folders through the postage meter and drop them in the mail. It works like a charm, and can be most helpful in some instances.

HOW TO GET INTO THE BILLION-DOLLAR MARKETS

1. *Spend time with young people.* That is where the money is today. A recent survey shows that teenagers have more cash to spend than their parents. Try to learn what new sport, hobby, or skill interests these kids. The number of teenagers grows by about two million each year.

2. *Develop two or three serious hobbies.* You may find your big market in a spare-time interest. Leisure is growing throughout the world. More people have more free time than ever before. For instance, boating is a wonderful hobby on which American enthusiasts spend nearly $3 billion per year. There are many other hobbies in the billion-dollar class—golf, skiing, tennis, etcetera.

3. *Read a good daily paper every day.* Learn what is going on. Spot trends as they develop. The first mention of the European discothèque was in a popular daily newspaper. Alert American businessmen sensed a need for similar dance places. Some opened places of their own while others went into business supplying the needed equipment. Everyone prospered.

4. *Subscribe to—and read—two popular magazines.* Time and *Newsweek* are useful and will keep you up to date. And since many of today's billion-dollar markets are for mechanical, electrical, and related items, read *Popular Mechanics, Popular Science,* or *Science and Mechanics.* Each will help keep you posted on new and interesting items.

5. *Listen to what people say.* If more than one person tells you about a new summer recreation area in your vicinity, check it out. You may be able to buy land or

open a concession that will be highly profitable. So
listen and learn.

6. *Observe—see—what goes on around you.* Do not walk
around in a daze. Look at people. Notice the clothes
they wear, what they are carrying. Get in touch with
daily life around you. Then you will be better
equipped to jump in on a new trend early in its
popularity.

USE GOVERNMENT PUBLICATIONS TO SELL YOUR PRODUCT

There are many inexpensive or free books and booklets published
by the United States government that can be used as a premium to
sell your product.

Example: The United States government publishes a booklet
called *Hearing Loss—Hope Through Research.* This booklet tells
what causes hearing loss and explains the different kinds of hearing
loss. It tells you how to select a hearing aid, if and when you should
consider ear surgery, and what you can expect from surgery. It also
tells you where you can go to get additional help on your hearing
problem. A large manufacturer of hearing aids put display ads in
newspapers and magazines, offering the book free. Not only did it
give the manufacturers an excellent mailing list of people who had
hearing problems, but the ad and offer built a tremendous amount of
good will for the company.

Example: A publisher sells *An Encyclopedia Dictionary of Business Law.* It cost $39.50 and can be ordered for a ten-day free exami-
nation. However, to encourage you to place your order, the publisher
also offers you a free copy of the official *Guide to Record Retention
Requirements.* This ninety-two-page guide covers the record retention requirements of no less than seventy-four federal agencies, telling you what records must be kept, who must keep them, and how
long they must be kept. The guide sells for $1.00 from the Superin-
tendent of Documents in Washington, DC 20402. The publisher
clearly sees great value in using this $1.00 guide as a free premium,
since the first two pages of a four-page letter tell you how valuable it
is, and only the second two pages of the four-page letter talk about
their $39.50 publication.

Check with your local Department of Commerce or other federal
agencies to see what inexpensive publications you can purchase that

are pertinent to your product or business. Then follow the examples of these two large advertisers and offer the publication at no charge as a premium for your product or service.

GET ROYALTY-FREE PATENTS FROM THE GOVERNMENT!
SELL GOVERNMENT INVENTIONS!

The United States government has hundreds and hundreds of patents that are offered to the public on a royalty-free, non-exclusive basis. A friend of mine picked up one of these patents having a toy application and made a fortune. United States government owned patents that are released for license by the public on a royalty-free, non-exclusive basis are announced in the *Official Gazette*, a weekly publication of the United States Patent Office. The *Official Gazette* is sold by the Superintendent of Documents, U.S. Government Printing Office, Washington, DC. However, most large libraries get the *Official Gazette* each week, and you can study it there.

The abstracts described in the *Official Gazette* will give you an idea of the essentials of an invention. If you are interested in one of the inventions after studying the abstract, you can get a copy of the specifications of the patent by sending 50¢ to the Commissioner of Patents, Washington, DC. If you want to use the patent, you can apply for a free license to the government agency administering the patent.

WHO ARE YOUR OVERSEAS CUSTOMERS? WHO IS
BUYING WHAT FROM THE U.S.A.?

Which overseas markets have been good customers for products like yours? The answer to that question can help you select those that show best future potential. An excellent place to start your investigation is the U.S. statistics on exports—the Census Bureau's FT–410 series—which shows exports, by commodity, to country of destination.

From these monthly reports, you can learn which of some 169 countries have bought any of more than 3,000 U.S. products. By checking U.S. exports of your products for three or four years, you can determine which countries have been the largest and most consistent markets. In some instances, the FT–410 statistics will also give you an indication of the average price for your product in a given market.

SAMPLES HELP SELL IF ADDED TO SALES LETTER

You do not have to be a saddlemaker to take advantage of what a friend of mine—who is a saddlemaker—did to drum up business. Instead of throwing away his scraps of leather, he cut them into small squares and sent them along with a sales letter to potential customers. There was good response from both old and new customers. Many people brought in the sample and asked if they could have something made up—chaps, jackets, etcetera. Turn this tip into profit for your business. Add a sample of your product to your next letter of solicitation. If you are in lumber, send along a thin sheet of some exotic wood; if you are a tailor, try deckle-edged scraps from the last suit you made. Let your materials speak for your product.

HIRE A CONSULTANT TO HELP SOLVE YOUR BUSINESS PROBLEMS

Take a tip from the Number One businessman in the U.S.—the President. When he has to make a decision about running the government, he calls in an expert and benefits from the man's specialized knowledge. You should do the same. Let's say, for example, that you own a clothing store and you must move to a new location. Are you going to take just any vacant store where the rent is within your means? That could be disastrous. You need the advice of an expert in marketing and real estate. A major savings and loan association, for example, called in a consultant *after* they had sent out a mailing to 8,000 prospects from which they did not receive a single reply. The first thing the direct-mail expert suggested was that they should have sent out 800 copies of the mailing as a test to check the response. If they had called the consultant in earlier, it would have cost them about $400.00 to find out that the mailing was no good, plus the consultant's fee of $100.00. Instead it cost them $4,000.00. If you are the sole owner of a business, you cannot possibly know everything about everything. A small amount of money invested in a professional consultant will save you a large amount of money in the long run. You can find the appropriate consultant listed in the Yellow Pages, or try the local Chamber of Commerce. You might also contact friends in the same field and find out who they use.

STARTING A SHOPPER NEWSPAPER

A newspaper that runs free classified ads has been very successful

in certain localities and is worth a try, especially if you know something about printing and graphic arts. If not, go to your local printer;
he will give you a quick course in exchange for your business. Examine the local newspaper's classified ads. Write each individual
who advertises something for sale and offer them a FREE ad in your
paper. They pay nothing in advance for the ad, only a commission to
you when they sell the item. You publish the ads and distribute the
paper by mail or by private carrier to homes in the area. It is obvious
that a lot of money can be made this way, since millions of dollars
worth of items are sold each month in large and medium-sized communities between private parties. To ensure the honesty of your
advertisers, you send them an agreement form that states: "If the
item is sold through the medium of this free ad paper, I agree to pay
10% to the publisher." For example, if the person sells a car for
$1,000 you get 10 percent, or $100. The people running the ads get a
good deal because they might spend considerably more than 10 percent trying to sell the $1,000 car. To make sure you know when the
sale is made, you place a continually running ad in the paper stating
that the buyers will receive 500 or 1,000 blue-chip stamps for sending in the report of the transaction. That keeps everyone honest and
happy. It is a lot of work and you will be busy as a two-headed cat in
a dairy, but you will make lots of money and have an interesting
occupation, either part- or full-time.

SELLING YOUR PRODUCT TO THE U.S. GOVERNMENT

Want to know who is the world's largest buyer? That's easy . . . the
U.S. government wins hands down. Each year the U.S. government
purchases vast quantities of goods and services ranging from peanuts
to rocket engines. So do not forget to include Uncle Sam in your
customer list. Probably the best way to learn how to sell to the
government is to get a copy of: *The U.S. Government Purchasing and
Sales Directory*. This tells you how to offer your products or services, and which agencies buy what. It even has a section on what
the government sells to private individuals through surplus sales.
For more information on obtaining this directory, write Superintendent of Documents, GPO, Washington, DC 20402.

THE PERSON ANY COMPANY CAN REALLY USE

Several years ago, I met a man who had a business card that revealed him to be a vice president of one of the largest direct mail firms on the West Coast. As we talked, I learned an amazing thing. He had arrived in this country from Germany with lots of enthusiasm and energy—and little money. Rather than try for a salaried job, he went to the direct mail firm and told them he would work for them on a *commission-only* basis. He told them that he wanted to work for them because he understood they were on the way up in the burgeoning field of sales by mail. All he wanted from them was a business card proclaiming him a "Vice-President."

The company was impressed by his impeccable appearance and his obvious ambition. Any firm would be happy to have a well-groomed salesman for free. Thus, they agreed to the card and his commission-only terms. The rest of the story is pure Horatio Alger. He went out into the big town and sold direct mail to every big client he could find. Soon his monthly income from commissions was in four figures, and he was smoking $5 cigars and driving a Lincoln Continental. Later, he expanded his area to include foreign manufacturers selling in this country.

From this little story, you can draw many conclusions. First, use your imagination. Second, emphasize *what you can do for a client*, not what he has to give for your services. Lastly, think big. It is still the rule that it is easier to make $1,000 than it is to make $100.

18 | New Techniques in Mail Order and What Is to Come

"Yesterday is a canceled check. Tomorrow is a promissory note. Today is the only cash you have—so spend it wisely."

I started my business in 1947. At that time there was very little activity in the mail order field. In fact, the *Los Angeles Times* ran no mail order ads. I remember the day their advertising manager called me to discuss the formation of a Shopper's Mart which would be exclusively used for mail order offers.

Mail order grew by leaps and bounds in those days because it answered a definite need. Right after the war, merchandise was in very short supply, so it was easy to run any kind of an ad on any kind of a product and be all but sure that you would make a profit. The country was hungry for new merchandise.

In those days your ad usually had an order coupon in it, requesting the buyer to send cash, check, or money order. Not too long after, credit cards came on the scene, so a new line was added to the coupon, giving the buyer the option of sending in his credit card number to pay for the merchandise. Not long after that, the 800 number appeared on the scene. This eliminated, in many cases, the expensive coupon. Today, many ads run only the 800 number and do not waste dollar space by printing a coupon.

Now you can buy hundreds of products by mail, merely by calling a toll-free 800 number and giving the operator your credit card information, your name and address, and what product or service you are buying. The 800 number not only started a revolution in the mail order field, but is used extensively in other fields throughout the country. It is estimated that over one billion toll-free phone calls are made every year, and none of these calls costs the callers a single cent.

Celebrity Publishing Inc., P.O. Box 98, Suffern, NY 10901, publishes three national directories of toll-free phone numbers. One covers the travel and vacation field, the second covers the "shop at home" toll-free numbers, and the third covers most business and service outlets in the United States, from airlines to financial services to hotels and motels to United States government agencies and their different departments. Of course you can get any 800 number in the United States by dialing Information at 1-800-555-1212.

If you would like to have your own 800 number to put in your mail order ads, your outgoing direct mail pieces, and so forth, you can rent one from one of the following services. Call them for information on prices, availability, etcetera.

Ring Response: 800-338-3338
Dial America: 800-356-5656
National Communications Center: 800-824-7888

"PIGGYBACK" MAILINGS

What with the high cost of postage today, there had to be new methods developed whereby people could deliver their messages to thousands of other people at lower costs, so "piggyback" mailing came into being. What is "piggyback" mailing? Let's take a company that processes film by mail. They mail half a million pieces of mail every month, and you can rent space in their envelopes for maybe a penny or two apiece. Department stores mail out thousands of invoices each month, and you can rent space in their invoice envelopes as well. Oil companies mail out thousands of letters each month; credit card companies do the same, and so on.

This is a well-organized activity, and if you contact a mailing list broker and ask for information on inserts and co-op mailings, you will be put in touch with hundreds of companies throughout the United States who offer this service for your product. These are companies that cater to men, women, outdoor sportsmen, children, professionals, etcetera. You can put your message in a one-thousand, ten-thousand, fifty-thousand, or even a half-million mailing and it will go direct to the type of individual you want to reach. Remember, you will be riding on the other man's postage and addressed envelope, requiring very little money on your part. Two of the many mailing-list brokers that offer this service are:

Walter Carl Inc., 135 Bedford Road Armonk, NY 10504
Leon Henry Inc., 455 Central Avenue, Scarsdale, NY 10583

The material you insert in the "piggyback" mailing is called a package insert. Here are some questions and answers on this unusual service:

A NEW MARKETING TECHNIQUE—THE PACKAGE INSERT

1. What is a package insert?
   - A package insert can be any piece of printed material giving a complete sales presentation that is included in mail order shipments of merchandise. Package inserts usually are circulars, brochures, folders, wallet-flap envelopes, miniature catalogs, double postcards, or film mailers.
   - Some firms enclose a sales letter, circular, and a reply form in an envelope printed with a special sales message to get maximum attention.
2. What are the advantages of using package inserts?
   - A package insert can be designed to tell a complete sales story with liberal space for copy, illustrations, and order form.
   - The cost of producing a package insert and the charge for inserting it is less than the cost of postage alone would be; hence, it is a very inexpensive form of promotion.
   - As your package insert will be included in merchandise shipments going to known mail order buyers, they will reach preferred prospects—people who buy by mail.
   - Your package insert enclosed in the merchandise shipments to a firm's customers carries an implied endorsement of your products or services, which helps to stimulate response.

- When a customer opens the parcel in which your package insert is included, you are reaching the prospect under the most favorable conditions. People usually read anything included in the package. This is the first step in landing the order.
- Scores of firms now offer package insert services. Hence, you can reach millions of mail order buyers who are not generally available through the usual channels of distribution.

3. How do you design an effective package insert?
   - Select standard formats. Some firms limit the size of package inserts; check before you put your insert into production.
   - Check the weight of a dummy of the format you select, since some firms accept inserts only if they do not increase the postage on shipments.
   - By including a coupon, reply card, or envelope as part of the package insert, you have a device that stimulates action. If it is an envelope, it encourages remittances. Also, it saves the customer the trouble of finding and addressing an envelope.
   - Assign a key to each firm enclosing your inserts. That way you will be able to keep an accurate record of which firm's mailing got results. This will help you determine future commitments.
   - Prepare the layout to meet printing requirements—litho, letterpress, or flexo.
   - Select type faces that are readable and have good display value.

4. How do you select the firms most suitable for mailing your insert?
   - Contact your list broker for a list of firms that mail package inserts.
   - For maximum results, there must be a definite relationship between the product or service you offer and the known characteristics or purchases made by the prospect.
   - Determine whether the firms sends out enough volume to give you appropriate exposure.
   - Find out if the firm does a national business or if it is confined to a given area.

- Be sure the demographics of the buyers fit your product.
- Choose a firm that has a good image.
- Check whether the firm offers geographic selection . . . product selection.
- Most firms will accept a minimum quantity for a test. It is always wise to test your package and the firm's list before ordering a large quantity of inserts.

5. How do you write copy that appeals and gets action?
   - Try to arrange for a copy tie-in recommendation with the mailer, or, if the insert is enclosed in an envelope, put a message about your insert on the envelope.
   - Fully describe your product or service. Remember, the more you tell, the more you sell! But above all, sell the **benefits!**
   - Make liberal use of illustrations if they add to the sales appeal.
   - Testimonials sell! What one of your customers says about your merchandise or service is more convincing than any sales copy you can write. The reason? It comes from a disinterested person. Hence, it is believable.
   - Write copy that is tailor-made for the customers you plan to contact.
   - Determine what offer will pull best. Cash? Billed? On approval? Credit card? Short-term offer? Specialty item at a bargain price? Emotional appeal?
   - Emphasize your guarantee of satisfaction or money refunded.
   - Avoid misunderstandings: Spell out the terms of the offer clearly.
   - Plan the order form so that there is ample space for the customer's name and address. Make it easy to order.
   - In other words, good direct mail copy principles apply.

6. What are the financial arrangements?
   - Ask the firm what the customary charge per thousand insertions is. Ask whether there is an extra charge for geographical selection or picking certain products only?
   - Inquire whether one pays upon completion of mailing. Does the mailer provide proof of mailing?

- Ask whether there are exchange arrangements with noncompetitors.
- Find out if "P.I." deals (per inquiry or order) are available.

7. How do you schedule a package insert campaign?
   - Get an okay from the mailer for your insert before you proceed. Decide which are the best months for mailing your package insert.
   - Find out how many inserts the mailer can enclose monthly.
   - Arrange for a "start mailing date," and plan your production schedule accordingly. Be sure you have enough lead time.
   - Be aware that as shipments containing your package inserts are mailed daily, it may take several months to enclose all of your inserts. Hence, the response will be slower than a solo mailing dropped at one time.

8. How do you estimate costs and profits?
   - Prepare a cost analysis sheet covering the cost of filling the order; administrative overhead; handling returns, refunds, or cancellations; cost of producing the insert; and charge for inserting. This will tell you the number of orders per thousand you need to break even.

9. Who can use package inserts?
   - Mailers of package inserts will not accept competitive offers. However, there are scores of mailers who offer their services to firms selling related but noncompetitive products or services.

10. What are some good examples of propositions that are logical for package inserts?
    - Subscription offers of specialized magazines in shipments of related merchandise. For example, *Bow and Arrow* magazine in shipments of archery supplies.
    - Books on specialized subjects. For example, a book on flower arrangements going to buyers of flower seeds, nursery stock, etcetera.
    - Offers of investment services included in stock brokers' correspondence or mailings.
    - A request-for-more-information card about a correspondence course on invisible weaving would be a logical offer to send to women ordering needlework supplies.

Printed with permission of Virgil D. Angerman, Sales Promotion Manager, Boise Cascade Envelope Company.

THINGS TO COME IN MAIL ORDER INNOVATIONS

ENIAC, a highly advanced computer that was built at the University of Pennsylvania's More School of Engineering in 1948 contained more than 17,000 vacuum tubes and 1,500 relays. Today almost any modern calculator that costs $100 could beat ENIAC hands down. There are over 4 million personal computers in the U.S., and it is estimated that this figure will double or triple within the next few years.

What does this have to do with you? Whether you like it or not, you are in the middle of an information explosion brought on by the computer. My advice is that if you do not have a computer, go out and buy an inexpensive model and start playing with it, so that you can at least become familiar with computer language.

Let me give you one advantage a computer can offer in direct mail. One service offered by the United States Postal Service is called E-COM (Electronic Computer Originated Mail). Let's say that you have a list of names and addresses in your computer. The list can be of any category: your personal customer list, your inquiry list, or your direct mail list. Using the telephone, call the post office via a modem connected to your personal computer. This permits your personal computer to transmit to the post office your entire address list *plus* a form letter you have composed that you want to be mailed to every name on that list.

What does the post office do at this point? They take your computerized name-and-address list, merge it with the letter that you have written, and print both of them on bond paper. The post office then folds the letter, puts it into an addressed envelope and mails the entire package first class with a guaranteed two-day delivery anywhere in the United States.

What does this entire service cost you? You pay only 26¢ for the first page and 5¢ for the second page! And since this price includes the paper, the envelope, the addressing, the labor for preparing the mailing, and the first-class postage, E-COM is quite a service.

For example, let's say that you have a new product that you would like to announce to all of your customers. With E-COM service, all you do is submit the message and mailing lists directly to the destination-serving post offices nearest you via telecommunication lines. Once your messages have been relayed to the appropriate destination-serving post offices they are delivered to your customers. All in two days or less anywhere in the continental United States.

Since the only requirement is that you must have 200 mailing pieces per serving post office, why not use E-COM Service soon? You get fast, reliable, low-cost delivery. And your messages get special attention since they are delivered in highly visible, blue envelopes.

Consult the list of post offices in the United States which offer E-COM to find the one nearest you. Also on this list is the telephone number of the local E-COM sales representative.

As you can see by this one example, the computer is creating a revolution in the direct mail field. If you want to be kept abreast of these new developments, you should subscribe to some of the computer magazines that are on the market today. The one I like best is *Personal Computing*, P. O. Box 2941, Boulder, CO 80321. Two other excellent publications are *Byte*, published by McGraw Hill, and *Creative Computing*, published by Ziff-Davis. These three magazines, plus several others, can usually be found in any computer store in your neighborhood.

Looking at the tremendous size of the computer industry and its influence on our daily life reminds me of the story of a farmer who came to visit his brother in Los Angeles. Since the farmer lived in mid-America, he had never seen an ocean before. So as a special treat, the brother drove him down to the shores of the Pacific and asked him, "What do you think of that?" His brother replied, "I never saw anything like it in my life. I had no idea that it was so big!" His brother replied, "You bet it's big . . . and don't forget, you're only seeing the top of it." And that is how it is with the computer business. Today, although it seems very big, you are only seeing the top of it.

WHERE TO FIND E-COM

Office of E-COM
Operations
USPS Headquarters,
Rm 6636
Washington, DC
20260-7140
(202) 245-5780

Atlanta, GA
3900 Crown Road
Atlanta, GA 30304
(404) 763-7161

Boston, MA
75 Dorchester
Avenue
Boston, MA 02109
(617) 223-2558

Charlotte, NC
2901 S. Interstate 85
Charlotte, NC 28228
(704) 393-4463

Chicago, IL
433 W. Van Buren
Street
Chicago, IL 60607
(312) 886-3130

Cincinnati, OH
Liberty Street &
Dalton Street
Cincinnati, OH 45234
(513) 684-5018

Dallas, TX
401 Dallas/Ft. Worth
TP
Dallas, TX 75212
(214) 767-6655

Denver, CO
1501 Wynkoon
Denver, CO 80202
(303) 837-2814

Detroit, MI
1401 W. Fort Street
Detroit, MI 48233
(313) 226-7880

Kansas City, MO
315 W. Pershing
Road
Kansas City, MO
64108
(816) 374-9145

Los Angeles, CA
900 North Alameda
Los Angeles, CA
90052
(213) 688-2355

Milwaukee, WI
345 W. St. Paul
Milwaukee, WI 53203
(414) 291-1415

Minneapolis, MN
100 First Street South
Minneapolis, MN
55401
(612) 349-5828

Nashville, TN
901 Broadway
Street
Nashville, TN 37202
(615) 251-7106

New Orleans, LA
701 Loyola Avenue
New Orleans, LA
70113
(504) 589-2211

New York, NY
341 Ninth Avenue
New York, NY 10001
(212) 971-5394

Orlando, FL
10401 South Florida
Road
Orlando, FL 32812
(305) 855-6130 Ext.
286

Philadelphia, PA
30th & Market
Street
Philadelphia, PA
19014
(215) 596-0444

Phoenix, AZ
1441 East Buckeye
Drive
Phoenix, AZ 85026
(602) 261-3272

Pittsburgh, PA
Seventh Avenue &
Grant Street
Pittsburgh, PA 15219
(412) 644-6461

Richmond, VA
1801 Brook Road
Richmond, VA 23232
(804) 771-2892

St. Louis, MO
1720 Market Street
St. Louis, MO 63155
(314) 425-5882

San Antonio, TX
10410 Perrin Beitel
San Antonio, TX
78233
(512) 229-5987

San Francisco, CA
99 Mission Street
San Franciso, CA
94119
(415) 550-5238

Seattle, WA
3rd South & Lander
Seattle, WA 98134
(206) 442-2400

Washington, DC
N. Capital &
Massachusetts Ave.
Washington, DC
20013
(202) 523-2229

Well, that's it! The tip of the tip of the iceberg. But if you follow the methods and techniques set forth in this book, you will find not only a life of security, but a life of excitement and challenges. I'd like to close this book with the following:

Take a hundred pound of iron—on today's market it is worth about $20. Turn the hundred pound of iron into horseshoes, and suddenly it is worth $200. Turn the same hundred pound of iron into sewing machine needles, and suddenly it is worth $2,000. Turn the same hundred pound of iron into fine watch springs, and suddenly it is worth over $500,000!

We all start with a hundred pound of iron . . . what we do with it determines our value in life, and I hope everyone reading this book turns into a fine watch spring.